ENTERPRISE
ZONES

OTHER RECENT VOLUMES IN THE
SAGE FOCUS EDITIONS

ENTERPRISE ZONES

New Directions in Economic Development

Roy E. Green
editor

SAGE PUBLICATIONS
The International Professional Publishers
Newbury Park   London   New Delhi

For information address:

SAGE Publications, Inc.
2455 Teller Road
Newbury Park, California 91320

SAGE Publications Ltd.
6 Bonhill Street
London EC2A 4PU
United Kingdom

SAGE Publications India Pvt. Ltd.
M-32 Market
Greater Kailash I
New Delhi 110 048 India

Printed in the United States of America

Library of Congress Cataloging-in-Publication Data

Main entry under title:

Enterprise zones : new directions in economic development / edited by
  Roy E. Green.
    p.   cm. — (Sage focus editions ; 126)
  Includes bibliographical references and index.
  ISBN 0-8039-3690-7. — ISBN 0-8039-3691-5 (pbk.)
  1. Enterprise zones—United States.   I. Green, Roy E.
HC110.D5E58   1990
  382.7'1'0973—dc20   90-20104
                                                              CIP

FIRST PRINTING, 1991

Sage Production Editor: Astrid Virding

This volume is dedicated to the ongoing story of the
"Volga Deutsche," who as emigrés have contributed their energies
and enterprise to two new homelands: Russia and the United States.

Contents

Acknowledgments

Special thanks go to Dr. Michael Brintnall, Staff Associate with the American Political Science Association in Washington, DC., who has been my close collaborator in studying state administered enterprise zone programs—and who would have been co-editor of this volume had not administrative responsibilities precluded him from doing so. Nevertheless, Dr. Brintnall found the time to read all of the essays and analyses included in this volume, and to add his valuable insights to the collection's concluding chapter.

Preface

It has been more than a decade since the notion of a government sponsored enterprise zone program burst upon the American political scene as a novel approach for stimulating economic and job development. Advocates promoted the concept of enterprise zones as a new strategy for offering targeted tax incentives and regulatory relief to entice businesses, and thus new jobs, back into distressed neighborhood areas. Arguing that small businesses were the most efficient means for creating "net" new jobs and for fostering economic growth within the impoverished areas of our communities, most of the enterprise zone programs at the state level, and those that have been proposed over this decade in federal legislation, have tried to emphasize small business development as key to bringing about this desired recovery through commercial development.

Almost as soon as legislation was drafted in the Congress—and the earliest state programs unveiled—critical analyses began to focus upon the various political, economic, and cross-national dimensions associated with the concept's introduction in the United States. One early assessment of enterprise zone programs concluded in a 1982 report that:

> The presentation of enterprise zones revolves, not around a specification of economic process, but around a constellation of words. "Enterprise," "innovation," "technology," "independent," "small business," "venture," "risk." These are the terms assembled to characterize the proposals. As a group, such words clearly have very definite political overtones, but what is important for the moment is that they are not woven into a detailed argument about economic mechanisms. For most of the time it is assumed that the things referred to somehow "go together." The main function of the words is to conjure up an image.

1

From the outset, many promoters of the enterprise zone concept offered that it was but one experimental approach to tackling the seemingly entrenched and complex problems posed by local economic and social distress. Although effective federal legislation has yet to be enacted—nor has the potential vehicle of administrative fiat been attempted—to test the merits of a national program, the concept continues to stimulate interest and debate because it seems to promise a new context (some might say a new catalytic metaphor) for viewing and addressing these vexing problems. For still others, it appears to offer a new evaluative framework for testing alternative sets of areal rejuvenation techniques.

What is important about the current resurgence in attention—and different from that given to it in the early 1980s—is that we have the experience of 37 American state programs and several foreign laboratories to draw upon to guide deliberations about possible federal roles. The steadily increasing number of American states willing to develop enterprise zone programs on their own seems to have taken the policy debate one step beyond some of the early reservations about its political saliency, adaptability, and the catastrophic risks that were thought to be associated with its use. Earlier concerns were raised because of the concept's unique lineage and linkage with Pacific Rim countries in Asia after World War II, and the much different unitary system of authority exercised at the local level by the national government in Great Britain.

Enterprise Zones: New Directions in Economic Development, is composed of four parts: (I) Urban Development and the Concept and Design of Enterprise Zones, (II) The Practice of Enterprise Zones, (III) Placing the American Enterprise Zone Experiences Within the Context of Its International Antecedents, and (IV) The Future of Enterprise Zones in the United States. The first part, Urban Development and the Concept and Design of Enterprise Zones, is composed of five chapters that provide an analytical overview and a historical context to the economic, political, and programmatic policy streams from which the American experience with enterprise zones emerged. The second part, The Practice of Enterprise Zones, is composed of two sections. The first section includes three of the most recent case studies of state enterprise zone programs. These programs were selected because of the breadth of variation in their features and histories. The second section presents two of the most sophisticated attempts at comparative analysis of state enterprise zone programs available to us at this time.

The third part of the volume, Placing the American Enterprise Zone Experience Within the Context of Its International Antecedents, offers chapters that summarize three nondomestic sets of governmental arrangements—all of which have been referred to by various advocates and analysts as sources of continuing influence on the path of enterprise zone experience in the United States. The final part, The Future of Enterprise Zones in the United States, presents two concluding essays that review the methodological and policy issues raised by the collection's separate analyses—but they also range to other studies, methods, and issues beyond the covers of this volume. These chapters provide assessments about what—and how—lessons can be derived from this decade of experimentation and study of enterprise zones.

The collection of research and thinking represented by the articles in this volume present most of the latest available empirical analyses focusing on the status and impacts of state enterprise zone programs in the United States. But there is a scope of interest implicit within this volume that goes beyond a mere recapitulation of contemporary findings, to an examination of the issues that are tied to the emergent era of third-party, government sponsored, multiple organization, service delivery mechanisms (i.e., the functioning of the governmental, private, and target beneficiary program components). In this context, our compilation represents a type of meta evaluation, which incorporates the wide array of perspectives offered, such as those offered by our contributing authorities who are by training: economists, political scientists, sociologists, geographers, business administrationists, lawyers, urban planners, and public administrationists. Professionally, and occupationally, the viewpoints represented in this collection include those of: elected public officials, academicians, the economic and government policy development network, and the research arms of federal, state, and local government.

Finally, and perhaps as important as any of the attributes possessed by this volume, it is worth noting that many of this collection's contributors have been influential in the actual policy importation, exportation, adaptation, and critical assessment of the enterprise zone mechanism and experience within and outside of the United States. In the aggregate, these essays offer an authoritative reference point for future research and policy discussions on the concept of enterprise zone programs; but they also offer a valuable perspective on the broader issues in urban economic development.

—Roy E. Green
Volume Editor

PART ONE

Urban Development and the Concept and Design of Enterprise Zones

1

Comparing Enterprise Zones to Other Economic Development Techniques

SUSAN B. HANSEN

This chapter will provide a historical and comparative perspective on enterprise zones. As we shall see, state and local government involvement in the economy is hardly novel, but the rationale for such involvement has varied greatly across time and across jurisdictions. The choice of specific policy tools has also changed over time. Enterprise zones have much in common with several recent approaches to economic development, yet they are unique in one major respect: Policies to encourage economic development are limited to particular geographic areas. This salient feature has little precedent in American political economy, but has profound implications for trends in investment and job creation.

Historical Overview of State/Local Economic Development Policy

Plant closings and unemployment in basic industries have become painfully frequent occurrences in many regions of the United States. Although *deindustrialization* has recently emerged as a political and economic issue,[1] it is by no means a new phenomenon. The economic base of the United States has changed considerably throughout its history. Population growth, technological innovation, new forms of

7

economic organization, and expanding wealth have accompanied the shift from a colonial society based largely on agriculture to a leading industrial nation. Most states have thus witnessed a succession of declines in particular industries as subsistence agriculture, logging, trapping, mining, and river transport were replaced by commercial agriculture, large-scale manufacturing, interstate highways, and airlines. Even in industrial regions, the manufacturing base by 1970 was very different from that of 1920 or 1880.

Compared to technological advances or the activities of private capital, public policy efforts have contributed relatively little to such changes. Nevertheless, some state and national policies have had significant impacts on the direction or location of economic change.[2] Before 1789, colonial governments granted charters (essentially monopoly rights) to companies, and used tariffs to protect their own industries and agricultural products. Colonies also built toll roads, supported shipping, and improved rivers and harbors. The U.S. Constitution ended internal tariffs, but state representatives in Congress could (and did) lobby actively for national tariffs to protect "infant industries" from overseas competition. State governments granted water, property, and mineral rights to favored companies. The steel industry in Pennsylvania could not have grown as it did without state laws permitting incorporation, access to the rivers, and strategic location of railroads.[3] The nation's banking and credit system was largely a state policy area before 1913, and state laws permitting the establishment of cartels, beginning with New Jersey in 1872, facilitated the growth of large-scale, integrated oligopolies in some industries.

Since early in the nineteenth century, the states have been involved in infrastructure and human capital investment. State and local monies funded toll road, canals, and many railroads. These investments were not always wisely made; scandals, high indebtedness, and bankruptcy often resulted, and many more canals were built than were necessary. Neoclassical economists tend to discount the contribution of governments to national and regional economic growth, because government taxing and spending throughout the nineteenth century were modest (less than 5% of GNP except during wartime) compared with much larger inputs from capital, the growing labor force, and technological advance. However, the *institutional economics* approach tends to give much greater credence to government's role in creating the conditions that encouraged private entrepreneurial activity. North et al. argue that the social rate of return on investment in state-funded education, agricultural research, and public health can be demonstrated to have exceeded their initial direct costs.[4] These are all examples of public goods that would not have been provided by private market forces.

Free public education (at least through grade school) was widely available in the North even before the Civil War, and greatly assisted the progress of industrialization. The Morrill Act of 1862 set up land-grant colleges; states made use of these to finance research on agriculture, mining, and engineering, which contributed significantly to advances in productivity. In fact, Lester Thurow uses the successful precedent of agricultural research and dissemination to argue for a national industrial policy for the 1980s.[5] Others have documented the *commonwealth tradition,* which since the early nineteenth century has sought to protect both businesses and consumers from the ravages of unbridled economic competition by means of licensing and regulation.[6]

Any economic history of the United States will describe dramatic changes in the mix of industries, their scale, and their location. Local craftsmen and small factories serving local markets were replaced by large-scale, increasingly mechanized industry serving broader markets. The center of population moved steadily westward; farming grew in scale and became mechanized; modes of transportation changed from rivers and toll roads to canals and railroads. In human terms, each of these changes meant the displacement of workers and communities tied to an older technology or resource base.

In the American tradition, the cost of these transitions has been borne almost entirely by individuals. Songs, novels, and plays dramatize the impact of economic change upon individuals caught up in the Gold Rush, the opening of the West, the abandonment of the worn-out farms of New England for the prairies, massive immigration from Europe and the Far East, and the mechanization of agriculture in the South. Francis Parkman's *Oregon Trail,* Laura Ingalls Wilder's *Little House on the Prairie* series, John Steinbeck's *Grapes of Wrath,* and Margaret Mitchell's *Gone with the Wind* all show characters dealing with massive economic changes with little help from government. In fact, treatment of Mormons, Native Americans, Chinese railroad workers, and the Confederate states during Reconstruction shows that in some cases it was deliberate government policy to make economic readjustment even more difficult for certain groups.

In a few instances, minimal government assistance was provided to encourage economic growth in a particular direction, or to assist individuals. The Freedman's Bureau provided some economic assistance to both whites and blacks during the early years of Reconstruction.[7] The Homestead Act provided cheap land to settlers willing to till it. Western lands were also offered to Union Army veterans. Federal land grants to railroads helped the railroads attract business and immigrants along their routes. County agricultural agents provided considerable technical assistance to farmers. But with a few exceptions such as these, the American legacy of economic individualism has meant that the *creative destruction* (in Schumpeter's terms) of previous methods of production was necessary to free up resources for new investments, regardless of the human cost involved.[8] In a vast land rich in resources, this strategy attracted few critics. A "young man" could "go west," but those who could not or would not relocate had to accept diminished living standards. Few mourned the ghost towns of Western mining regions or the played-out farms of the Northeast.

As a consequence of the Depression, however, "people's faith in the market system as basically fair and reasonably efficient waned. It was replaced with an ideology that held that major government intervention was essential to a healthy and just society."[9] A few federal regional programs emerged to challenge the prevailing capitalist ethos. Even by Depression standards, the South lagged behind the rest of the country, and TVA was developed under Franklin Roosevelt to improve the economic base of the rural South and Appalachia by means of flood control and cheap electrical power. Other large-scale water projects (the Grand Coulee and Hoover Dams, irrigation in the arid West) date from this period as well. The phenomenal growth of Southern California would not have been possible without the large-scale state and federal investments needed to bring water to the Los Angeles basin.[10]

In the 1960s, Kennedy's and Johnson's War on Poverty led to regional policies aimed at rural areas (Appalachia, the Mississippi delta) and central cities. In spite of general postwar prosperity, rising living standards, and high productivity growth in most parts of the economy, these regions lagged behind. The term *structural unemployment* was coined to describe those out of work because of lack of skills, prejudice, resource depletion, or impaired mobility in a period of low cyclical unemployment. Solutions to structural unemployment included community development grants, job creation efforts, job training, and public works projects. An Area Redevelopment Administration (ARA) was set up in 1962 within the Department of Commerce to provide direct assistance (grants or loans) to firms if they established plants in particular areas. This evolved by 1965 into the Economic Development

Administration (EDA), established to "enhance employment opportunities in specific areas by making aid available that might encourage the expansion of private enterprise."[11] EDA ended up spending most of its budget on public works (sewerage and water systems), but its early conceptualization as the ARA included elements of the later enterprise zone idea.

Critics took note of the adverse impacts of previous federal policies on central cities: Urban renewal had displaced homes and businesses, and highway construction had produced suburban growth at the expense of downtowns.[12] By the 1970s several attempts had been made to revitalize downtown business centers, with notable successes including Boston's Fanueil Hall, Baltimore's Harborfront, and Pittsburgh's Renaissance I and II. These projects made extensive use of federal funds— Urban Development Action Grants (UDAGs), Community Development Block Grants (CDBGs)—but were designed and managed by state and local governments, with active participation by private interests. Conditions in ghetto regions on the fringes of downtowns worsened, however. Infrastructure deteriorated and homelessness increased as federal funds were cut back under Reagan; unemployment remained high. Few businesses could be induced to locate in the ghettos, despite vacant land and surplus labor, due to fear of crime, redlining by banks, and a poorly educated workforce. By the 1980s there was little political support, either in state capitals or in Washington, for policies to deal with such urban problems, and declining federal support for mass transit often meant that inner-city residents had few means of commuting to jobs elsewhere.

State and Local Economic Policies

State and local governments have been engaged in economic development policies for many years. In the 1920s, Sinclair Lewis satirized local "boosterism" in *Main Street* and *Babbitt*. Beginning even before the Depression, Mississippi's "Balance Agriculture with Industry" efforts provided low-interest loans, site preparation, and worker training programs to business; other Southern states soon emulated these examples.[13] These Northern states, faced with the migration south of industries such as shoes and textiles, followed suit in the 1940s and 1950s. In 1960, Gilmore described hundreds of state programs designed to attract businesses from other states.[14] Most of these were tax breaks of various kinds, but industrial development bonds (IDBs) played a major role as well. Labor policy was viewed as a significant cost to business; low-wage and right-to-work states touted these advantages, although the more unionized industrial states endeavored to keep the costs of workmen's compensation and unemployment benefits as low as possible.[15] And all states advertised heavily in business publications.

Were such policies effective? Most studies find quite limited impact, for several reasons.[16] First, taxes are only a small proportion of total business costs, and are seldom the most significant factor in business location decisions. Second, tax breaks, advertising, and industrial development bonds are used by so many states that they tend to cancel out. In fact, some studies have found that *higher* taxes are associated with economic growth, especially if the taxes are used for education or other "quality of life" services.[17]

Third, state officials began to question the relative costs and benefits of tax giveaways and other subsidies. A turning point came with "The Rabbit That Ate Pennsylvania," the costly effort to lure a German Volkswagen auto plant.[18] Pennsylvania "won" a bidding war among the states by agreeing to an incentive package worth between $70 and $80 million (for 3,000 jobs, this works out to between $23,000 and $26,000 per job). As Osborne notes, however, this package of concessions depleted the state's principal loan fund, the Pennsylvania Industrial Development authority, for several years.[19] An expensive highway link was constructed, and tax concessions to the surrounding communities were only partially offset by sales tax revenues and increased real estate values. In a year in which it produced over 80,000 Rabbits, VW's total property taxes were less than the value of one vehicle.[20]

The VW plant was a modern production facility, with considerable quality control equipment. But the Rabbit did not do as well as expected in the American market after gasoline prices dropped in the 1980s. The New Stanton plant was plagued by labor unrest and by 1983 was operating only one shift. Finally, in July 1988, it closed its doors completely, idling nearly 3,000 workers. The number of employees never reached expectations and the plant operated on reduced shifts during the last years of its existence. Governor Richard Thornburgh's economic policies for Pennsylvania used the VW example to argue against state subsidies and in favor of entrepreneurial development and the fostering of technological change, based on a mixture of public and private sources.[21]

In the 1970s and 1980s, loss of export markets and manufacturing jobs heralded an era of deindustrialization, of long-term structural changes in the economy far more extensive than periodic cyclical downturns in employment. Manufacturing jobs were lost in large numbers, as had happened in the past, but it became increasingly difficult to replace them with jobs offering comparable wages and benefits. Communities, states, and whole regions (particularly the Great Lakes and Plains areas) lost population, declined in income, and experienced a variety of social pathologies as a result.[22] At the national level, various theories and measures of this phenomenon were debated. Declining productivity, soaring labor costs, high levels of government taxing and spending, American managerial practices, and international competition were all blamed.[23]

Nevertheless, many economists disputed the basic thesis of deindustrialization. Although the rate of growth in manufacturing had slowed dramatically, the absolute number of jobs declined little if at all between 1970 and 1982. Despite dire predictions, the American economy improved considerably after the 1982 recession. Some manufacturing sectors experienced modest growth, and the Big Three auto companies and USX (U.S. Steel) were profitable once again. Even if individuals or regions experienced short-term difficulties in adjustment, classical economic thought does not view this as a problem requiring government intervention. From this perspective, the decline in manufacturing industries in the Frost Belt contributed to growth in other areas, both in the Sun Belt and in newer industries in the Northeast and Midwest. In the United States as a whole, new jobs were being created at a far higher rate than in Western Europe.[24]

Nevertheless such national trends were not always reflected in particular states, regions such as Appalachia, or central cities. The Northeast, Midwest, and Plains states faced absolute declines in manufacturing unemployment and loss of population. Even within prosperous states, particular cities or regions (Bridgeport in Connecticut, Oakland in California) still had unacceptably high unemployment levels four or five years after recovery from the 1981-1982 recession. Future prospects for industries such as coal, steel, and automobiles were not optimistic—nor were problems confined to manufacturing. Many of the farm states had record bankruptcies as export markets and federal subsidies declined; U.S. agricultural exports fell from $44 billion in 1981 to $26 billion in 1986, and the drought of 1988 hurt as well. Mining states faced worldwide gluts in commodities like copper and oil; the collapse of prices (and of OPEC) led to unemployment and drastically reduced revenues in states such as Texas, Louisiana, and Alaska.

By the 1980s, states were already beginning to question their earlier smokestack-chasing efforts. Since little help was forthcoming from Washington, the states began experimenting with new policies to deal with unemployment. New evidence suggested that growth in jobs came, not from relocating plants, but from expansion of existence plants and the founding of new small companies within a state or region.[25] Accordingly, state and local policies were developed to foster such entrepreneurship through assistance to small business, venture capital programs, and the development of business incubators and industrial parks. In addition, long-range forecasts for the national and international economy pointed to technological advances as a source of competitive advantage. Therefore, policies to encourage research and technology transfer (the manufacturing and marketing of new ideas) have attracted increasing state and local attention. Eisinger terms such policies *demand-side,* in contrast with earlier *supply-side* efforts involving tax breaks, advertising, and low-interest loans granted indiscriminately to all types of businesses.[26]

These newer policies differ in several ways from previous economic development efforts. First of all, the targeting of economic activities has become more explicit. Sometimes specific industries or sectors are singled out for some type of state support, or depressed regions may be eligible for particular types of aid. High technology industries are a favored target, but in many states the revitalization of such traditional activities as farming, food processing, or forestry products has been stressed.[27] In other cases certain activities are to be encouraged: innovations in management or technology, small business, the marketing and production of new inventions. Under previous economic development programs, state aid was far less differentiated; tax subsidies, industrial development bonds, and small business encouragement were made available to many types of firms in all parts of the state.

Second, cost and financing: Tax subsidies involved generalized benefits provided at little direct cost to taxpayers, whereas high technology and entrepreneurial policies have necessitated more direct expenditures allocated to more clearly defined winners and losers. In some states, aid is made available only to sectors or activities targeted according to articulated economic criteria. In other states, some type of competitive review process evaluates proposals for development.[28] Thanks to Proposition 13 and other financial limitations, relatively little has been spent on industrial policies from state general funds. Instead, bond monies, private-sector matching, or state pension funds have been tapped; many state venture-capital programs exemplify innovations in public-sector financing.[29] However, spending in many other areas (education, infra-structure, welfare) has increasingly been justified because of its potential contribution to state economic development.

Third, state and local governments have been actively engaged in economic planning and forecasting. Whereas traditional policies relied more on market cues, many recent efforts represent concerted public-sector efforts to improve on the market allocation of capital and labor— to anticipate, speed up, or stretch out the process of adjustment to national and international trends. Many states rely on federal departments of Labor or Commerce in forecasting, but several of the larger states have developed their own capabilities for econometric analysis of regional trends. State planners and bureaucrats, in cooperation with politicians and representatives of major interest groups, are making conscious efforts to influence the future direction of state economies.[30]

States and localities have long been constrained by what Lindblom termed "the market as prison": if governmental requirements are too restrictive, investment or expansion in a particular area will be discouraged.[31] Nevertheless, a fourth change in economic policy is the greater willingness of public officials to challenge managerial prerogatives. Only four states have formally adopted plant-closing legislation, but many others have considered it. Several states (led by Minnesota) have taken action to discourage hostile takeovers of state corporations. Legal steps have also been initiated to try to recover the public's investment in firms that close or relocate.[32] Many of the newer loans and grant programs impose more strings (cooperation with universities, technology emphasis, location, job creation, careful screening by public-private boards) than did most tax subsidies and industrial development bonds[33] and states have begun more vigorous enforcement of environmental legislation.

These new policy directions have involved political change as well: a greater degree of policy coordination by decision-making bodies, and increased insulation of policy from the political pressures and ideological cleavages characteristic of parties and legislatures. Previous economic development activities were largely piecemeal efforts scattered across a number of state departments, and in some instances working at cross-purposes. Policy coordination is still more of a goal than a reality, but most states have made considerable efforts to rationalize their economic policy process. In part because of the fragmented policy structure, traditional economic development activities responded more directly to political pressures, especially lobbying by business groups. Increasingly, major affected interests (business and labor, but also universities and local communities) are involved in nonpartisan, nonideological *public-private* forums, which share at least some characteristics of European meso-corporatism.[34]

In practice, of course, one can question whether the "new" activist policies are much different from prevailing forms of state economic activities. Certainly the older forms persist, as illustrated by the unseemly scramble for General Motors's Saturn plant in 1986 and Pennsylvania's $23 million package to attract Sony to its shuttered Volkswagen plant in 1990. Neither market forces nor political pressures have disappeared from the state policy process, despite some grandiose claims to the contrary. Attempts at policy planning and coordination have been frustrated, as well, by the structural and institutional barriers so familiar to students of American politics; cooperation across different levels of government, or among states, is largely nonexistent. Yet scholars have noted a general increase in state governing capacity; state governments two or three decades ago were deficient in professional expertise, executive leadership, and financial capacity.[35] Such governments could not have attempted many of the ambitious industrial policies recently undertaken.

What of the Unemployed?

In the early 1980s, growing state involvement in the economy was justified as a means to reduce unemployment. The 1981-1982 recession had produced levels of unemployment not seen since the Depression, and led many states to make economic development a priority. In the early 1970s governors had paid little attention to unemployment or economic policy in their State of the State addresses, but by 1981 these issues ranked with education and tax increases at the top of the list of gubernatorial priorities.[36] In Pennsylvania, the Ben Franklin Partnership's early publications proclaimed "Our job is to create jobs." Governor James Blanchard of Michigan campaigned in 1982 on a platform of "Jobs, jobs, and jobs." The states also petitioned Washington to extend unemployment benefits to more workers over a longer period of time, but except for a temporary extension and a small amount of public works spending (both in the context of the 1982 midterm elections), little federal aid was forthcoming, due both to the federal deficit and to the core philosophy of the Reagan administration.

The new state demand-side industrial policies, however, stressed adaptation to international market trends. An emphasis on high technology and increased productivity was not likely to produce many new jobs in the short run, and direct job creation by traditional methods (countercyclical spending, public works programs) was not an option for the states, for several reasons. First of all, state revenues were severely impacted by the 1981-1982 recession; all states except Vermont are legally required to balance their general-fund budgets, and there was little money for new programs. Second, spending on welfare, health, or social services had come under attack as detrimental to state economic growth. And third, previous employment policies (notably CETA) had come under severe criticism (some justified, some largely on ideological grounds) for inefficiency, corruption, and high costs relative to the benefits derived.[38]

By choice, necessity, or both, most states tended toward a trickle-down strategy: Encourage investment, entrepreneurship, and technological development, and jobs will follow eventually. In Michigan, the *Path to Prosperity* study that guided that state's economic efforts explicitly relegated social problems such as unemployment to a "second blackboard," to be considered after the state solved its financial problems and the auto industry recovered (Michigan's first enterprise zone was not established until 1986). In Pennsylvania, Republican Governor Thornburgh rejected attempts by House Democrats to pursue the Saturn plant, assist distressed communities, or provide assistance to the steel industry (although he moderated his positions somewhat during the 1986 gubernatorial primary, when his economic record came under strong criticisms in Western Pennsylvania). In Massachusetts, the state's very low unemployment (at least before recent budget problems developed) encouraged the development of employment and training programs to move people off welfare.

Scholars and critics on the Left have been increasingly critical of state economic development policy for its pro-business orientation. As Ambrosius found, state adoption of economic assistance policies showed a positive relationship to mobilization by business interests.[39] Silver, in her thoughtful analysis of the defeat of Rhode Island's Greenhouse Compact, noted both labor's opposition to most economic development policies and its weakness in pushing for its own agenda.[40] Labor union membership in the United States, as a percentage of the total work force, has declined to only about half of its level in the 1950s. Business strategy and international competition have forced labor to accept concessions and have blunted its organizing efforts;[41] thus there has been little organized political opposition to state pro-business policies. Balance, instead, has derived from the increasing professionalization of legislatures.[42]

States and localities have participated actively in the federal Job Training Partnership Act and Trade Adjustment Assistance programs, but they have provided some job-creation incentives to business on their own initiative. Loans and grants to business have been predicated on job-creation potential—although there is serious question as to the realism of job-creation claims by business as well as by state programs.[43] As of 1988, 17 states offered tax credits for job creation.[44] Some state spending on infrastructure has helped to create jobs, but financial constraints and cutbacks in federal funding for highways, water projects, and mass transit have limited this option. California's Targeted Jobs Tax Credit gives tax subsidies only to businesses that hire welfare recipients or the long-term unemployed. Several states require that minority-owned businesses be guaranteed a certain percentage of state-financed loans or contracts. In Pennsylvania, displaced steelworkers are granted free tuition at retraining programs in community colleges.

Compared to several European countries, the United States does little to foster mobility of the labor force. Each state has its own Employment Service, which advertises openings and provides (usually minimal) counseling. Clark is highly critical of the scope and quality of these services and their limited geographic focus; he argues for a national, computerized job search endeavor, on the Canadian model, which would greatly facilitate labor mobility.[45] Information, however, is not the only cost impeding mobility: Job-hunting trips, new housing, and moving costs are all so expensive that many low-paid workers cannot afford to search outside their immediate environment. Sweden not only assists displaced workers in finding new jobs, but provides assistance with housing and moving costs.[46] In the United States, such relocation allowances have been available only to a few workers covered by the Trade Adjustment Act. Regional economists argue on strong economic grounds for increasing labor mobility on a par with capital mobility,[47] but U.S. public policy has preferred to bring jobs to people within their community (the enterprise zone approach) rather than to move people to jobs.

What About Poor Communities?

Despite partial recovery from the 1980 and 1982 recessions, the variation of unemployment and incomes across standard metropolitan statistical areas (SMSA) within states has remained high.[48] A number of states have addressed such inequalities through their economic development policies. Distressed regions and communities have been identified, using a variety of indicators: unemployment, age of housing stock, population loss. It is often easier administratively to target geographic units rather than people, even though in practice even poor regions contain relatively well-off individuals, while wealthier locations may have a number of poor residents.[49] In theory, enterprise zones will help the unemployed, although in practice employers locating in the zones may hire people who live elsewhere.

Any state and federal aid to distressed communities has obvious implications for local efforts to deal with the consequences of de-industrialization. If a small town or city is dependent on one or two large plants and these close down, the local government may face serious financial problems. Retail sales and services are affected, property values plummet, infrastructure crumbles, and schools suffer. The erosion of the tax base leads to drastic reduction in services and (in a few cases) bankruptcy for local or county governments, even if local taxes are increased to the legal or political limit. Under such conditions, it becomes exceedingly difficult to attract any new industry or to retain existing business; poor people become hostage to poor communities.

Several states have responded to such distressed communities with programs including assistance with planning, aid in applying for federal grants, tax relief, maintenance of basic services, marketing assistance, and low-interest loans. These policies may be pursued independently or may form part of an enterprise zone program. In Pennsylvania, interest rates on state loans to business are lower the higher the unemployment in a given county. Also in Pennsylvania, provisions have been enacted for temporary state managerial and financial assistance for distressed communities and for local school districts facing bankruptcy. Attempts have been made at more drastic reforms—local government reorganization, revised tax laws—to help communities maintain services and attract new industry, but these have been difficult to implement because of local government resistance to any loss of autonomy and to any new taxes.

In economic terms, investment in declining regions may serve as one means to speed up the cyclical process of regional growth and decline. Even declining regions often contain growing industries, and their low wages and reduced property values may constitute an asset to attract capital from regions where high wages are paid to established, unionized industries with entrenched managerial practices. Casson, using data from British industries in the 1930s, found that despite the Depression, a number of sectors and regions were growing. These eventually became the source of recovery (although he questions whether governments can in practice locate or assist such growth).[50]

In economic terms as well, efforts to aid distressed communities often make sense as a means to capitalize on existing social investment. Established communities often represent years of social capital accumulation: schools, roads, sewer and utility systems, cultural amenities such as churches, libraries, recreational facilities, and museums.[51] Constructing such facilities in new *greenfield* sites would be enormously expensive at today's prices, and residents of fast-growing communities often face rapidly rising taxes as growth outpaces existing infrastructure.[52]

State efforts to aid distressed communities have been confounded by several factors. First, targeting by need often conflicts with targeting on the basis of growth potential. Advanced technology industries in which the United States enjoys a comparative advantage are unlikely to employ the long-term unemployed: educationally and socially disadvantaged minorities, functional illiterates, the handicapped, high school dropouts, or many of the older people laid off from manufacturing industries.[53] The existing infrastructure may be in need of expensive repairs as well.

Second, the states with the greatest needs often lack resources, and larger states spread their resources too thinly. Mississippi, Idaho, or West Virginia are simply too poor to channel many resources to poor people or poor communities within their boundaries. Thus in this analysis, wealthier states proved more likely to establish enterprise zones, and to make the needs of minorities and the chronically unemployed a priority.[54] New York, with its strong tax base and elastic revenue structure, thus has been able to do more than most states. Aid to New York City or Buffalo, however, must be counterbalanced by assistance formulas that benefit other upstate counties as well, and the total aid package has helped push New York's taxes well above the national and regional averages.[55]

Third, regional economists are often critical of policies emphasizing *place* prosperity rather than *people* prosperity. Once some poor regions have been in decline for many years, recovery becomes successively less likely if infrastructure has deteriorated and the most productive sectors of the work force have emigrated, leaving an increasingly large dependent population to be supported on a dwindling tax base.[56] It becomes progressively more difficult to attract either industry or labor in such circumstances, and former mining and steel producing regions face a legacy of environmental problems as well. Areas such as much of Appalachia, Michigan's Upper Peninsula, rural Arkansas, and northern Idaho thus face the prospect of permanent decline, as do many central cities with large black populations. Hoover and Giarratani argue that "the best way to help disadvantaged people living in a particular region may be to encourage them to move on . . . attacking human hardship and lack of opportunity solely through place prosperity might be like using a shotgun to kill flies."[57] Resources committed to some declining regions could be more productively invested elsewhere.

Finally, governments are limited in the offsetting subsidies they can use to persuade businesses to locate in a particular area. Firms and their employers value clean air, good schools, pleasant surroundings, and low crime rates—amenities not often available in inner cities or depressed mining regions. Businesses also value the availability of business services and skilled labor, often preferring to locate near companies doing similar work (agglomeration effects). Pennsylvania's Governor Casey was widely criticized in 1987 when an Eastman Kodak subsidiary chose to locate in wealthy Chester County (with $14 million in state subsidies), but even a larger state subsidy might not have been sufficient to attract the plant to the depressed Mon Valley steel region or inner-city Philadelphia.

Economists are by no means in agreement as to which declining regions should be, in effect, written off and which should be aided. But economics aside, there are compelling political reasons for the geographical targeting of state and local economic development efforts. As we have seen, the long-standing American tradition is that people should move (at their own expense) to areas of greater economic opportunity, and many do. But those who choose to remain will defend their communities and occupations, and will seek political allies in support of their claims. Representatives of declining regions (Pennsylvania's Mon Valley, Minnesota's Mesabi Range, older central cities) have argued in state legislatures for a larger share of the economic pie. Black urban areas now have state representatives with seniority and well-developed political skills,[58] and groups with a vested property interest in declining regions—banks, retail sales, real estate, small business—will engage in political activities to protect their investments.

Territorial representation is a political fact of life, and few declining regions will willingly accept economic losses, regardless of the economic logic. Members of the labor force most prone to unemployment are also the least mobile; politicians, churches, and civic groups argue on fairness grounds that assistance to such persons in their place of residence is merited. One likely result, however, is that economic development efforts will be so diluted among competing claimants that costs will rise disproportionately and no one will benefit.[59] A second result is that programs to assist labor mobility have received little political support.

Conclusions

This chapter has described the evolution of economic development policy since its mercantilist origins in the American colonies. Efforts to encourage growth, attract investment, and create jobs are hardly new to the American scene, but recent state and local efforts have concentrated less on smokestack-chasing and more on fostering the conditions to encourage new businesses to develop. Enterprise zones share with other recent policies an emphasis on targeting of resources, reliance on tax incentives, job creation as the major justification, small business assistance, and the involvement of the private sector. Investment in human and physical capital has been a focus of economic development policy in many localities, and some enterprise zones have adopted this strategy as well. Exactly how that is to be accomplished varies greatly across states: Subsequent chapters in this book will document the differences among states and across programs in the use of private-sector initiatives, tax breaks, direct public investment, and degree of state and local government intervention in program management. The specific geographic area ranges from inner-city neighborhoods, to depressed rural areas, to small towns or cities devastated by loss of key industries.

Enterprise zones are unique in their attempts at geographic targeting and their repudiation of the notion that growth elsewhere will redound to the advantage of depressed regions. In practice, this has meant focusing of state and local resources in areas not favorably regarded by market forces. Although some positive effects of other state economic policies have been identified, gains in new business creation, exports, and productivity do not readily translate into a net increase in jobs. Subnational governments have found it easier to encourage the mobility of capital than of labor. It remains to be seen whether enterprise zones will succeed where other state and local policies have not: by creating jobs and investment in disadvantaged or declining regions.

Notes

1. Bluestone, B.. & Harrison, B. (1982). *The deindustrialization of America.* New York: Basic Books.

2. This viewpoint is stressed in Hughes, J.R.T. (1977). *The governmental habit.* New York: Basic Books, and North, D. C. et al. (1983). *Growth and welfare in the American past.* Englewood Cliffs, NJ: Prentice-Hall.

3. Achs, Z. J. (1984). *The changing structure of the U.S. economy: Lessons from the steel industry.* New York: Praeger. Hansen, S. B. (1987). State governments and industrial policy in the United States. In J. J. Hesse (Ed.), *Regions, structural change and industrial policies in international perspective* (pp. 89-122). Frankfurt, FRG: Nomos Verlag.

4. North et al., *Growth and welfare,* pp. 92-100.

5. Thurow, L. (1988). *The zero-sum solution.* New York: Simon and Schuster.

6. Handlin, D., & Handlin, M. (1969). *Commonwealth: A study of the role of government in the American economy.* Cambridge, MA: Harvard University Press.

7. Franklin, J. H. (1961). *Reconstruction after the civil war.* Chicago: University of Chicago Press.

8. Schumpeter, J. (1942). *Capitalism, socialism, and democracy.* New York: Harper and Row.

9. North et al., *Growth and welfare,* p. 156.

10. Henton, D. C., & Waldhorn, S. A. (1988). California. In R. Scott Fosler (Ed.), *The new economic role of the American states* (pp. 203-250). New York: Oxford University Press.

11. Hoover, E. M., & Giarratani, F. (1984). *An introduction to regional economics* (3rd ed.). New York: Knopf, p. 390.

12. Mollenkopf, J. (1983). *The contested city.* Princeton, NJ: Princeton University Press.

13. Wood, P. (1986). *Southern capitalism.* Durham, NC: Duke University Press.

14. Gilmore, D. R. (1960). *Developing the little economies.* New York: Committee for Economic Development.

15. Estimates of the impact of labor costs and right-to-work laws differ. Bartik argues that right-to-work laws assisted in the growth of the Sunbelt, while Hirsch and Addison and Hansen find little or no impact for the periods they analyze. Bartik, T. J. (1985). Business location decisions in the U.S.: Estimates of the effects of unionization, taxes, and other characteristics of states. *Journal of Business and Economic Statistics, 3,* 14-22; Hirsch, B. T., & Addison, J. T. (1986). *The economic analysis of unions: New approaches and evidence.* Boston: Allen and Unwin; Hansen, S. B. (in press). *The political economy of state industrial policy.* Pittsburgh: University of Pittsburgh Press, chapter 8.

16. The empirical evidence is ably summarized in Eisinger, P. K. (1988). *The rise of the entrepreneurial state.* Madison: University of Wisconsin Press.

17. Helms, L. J. (1985). The effect of state and local taxes on economic growth: A time series-cross section approach. *The Review of Economics and Statistics, 67,* 574-582; Plaut, T. R., & Pluta, J. E. (1983). Business climate, taxes and expenditures, and state industrial growth in the U.S. *Southern Economic Journal, 50,* 99-119.

18. Chernow, R. (1978, October). The Rabbit that ate Pennsylvania. *Mother Jones, 2,* 54-58.

19. Osborne, D. (1988). *Laboratories of democracy.* Boston, MA: Harvard Business School Press.

20. Allan, W. (1986, February 16) Disassembled dreams: Market realities cast pall over VW car plant. *Pittsburgh Press,* pp. D15-16.

21. For further discussion of the Volkswagen decision and subsequent changes in Pennsylvania's policies for economic development, see Hansen, S. B. (in press). Economic development policy in Pennsylvania. In E. Katz (Ed.), *The government and politics of Pennsylvania.* University of Nebraska Press.

22. Bluestone & Harrison, *Deindustrialization of America.*

23. Johnson, C. (Ed.). (1984). *The industrial policy debate.* San Francisco: ICS Press.

24. Critics of the deindustrialization hypothesis are represented by Lawrence, R. Z. (1984). *Can American compete?* Washington, DC: Brookings Institution. On job creation in the United States, see Schwartz, J. (1986). *America's hidden success* (2nd ed.). New York: W. W. Norton.

25. Birch, D. L. (1979). *The job generation process.* Cambridge: MIT Program on Neighborhood and Regional Change.

26. Eisinger, *Rise of the entrepreneurial state.*

27. Clarke, M. (1986). *Revitalizing state economies.* Report prepared for the National Governors Association, Washington, DC.

28. The Ben Franklin Partnership in Pennsylvania uses public-private boards to review proposals jointly developed by businesses and universities.

29. U.S. Small Business Administration. (1985, June). *State activities in capital formation: Venture capital, working capital, and public pension fund investments.* Washington, DC: U.S. Government Printing Office.

30. For a detailed comparison of strategic planning efforts in several states, see Eisinger, *Rise of the entrepreneurial state.*

31. Lindblom, C. (1982). The market as prison. *Journal of Politics, 44,* 324-336.

32. Eisinger, *Rise of the entrepreneurial state,* pp. 307-330.

33. Congress since 1984 has greatly restricted the tax advantages of industrial development bonds, and has generally limited them to public rather than private purposes. In

earlier years, IDBs were used widely for retail establishments such as restaurants and massage parlors.

34. Hansen, S. B. (1989). Industrial policy and corporatism in the American states. *Governance, 2*(2), 172-197.

35. This argument has been made by Bowman, A. O'M., & Kearney, R. C. (1986). *The resurgence of the states.* Englewood Cliffs, NJ: Prentice-Hall. See also Van Horn, C. (Ed.). (1989). *The state of the states.* Washington, DC: Congressional Quarterly Press.

36. Herzik, E. B. (1983). Governors and issues: A typology of concerns. *State Government, 56,* 58-64.

37. Bureau of Labor Statistics forecasts show the greatest *rate* of increase in high technology fields, but the greatest *numbers* of jobs in future decades will be in retail sales and secretarial and janitorial services. An analysis of time-series data from 1970 to 1987 found that indicators of state economic growth (new businesses created, increase in exports, productivity) all showed *negative* relationships with employment levels for 1, 3, and 5 year lags (although more positive relationships may emerge in the long run). Hansen, *Political economy,* chapter 9.

38. Baumer, D. C., & Van Horn, C. E. (1985). *The politics of unemployment.* Washington, DC: Congressional Quarterly Press.

39. Ambrosius, M. M. (1989). The role of occupational interests in state economic development policy-making. *Western Political Quarterly, 42,* 53-69.

40. Silver, H. (1987). Is industrial policy possible in the United States? The defeat of Rhode Island's Greenhouse Compact. *Politics and Society, 15*(3), 333-368.

41. Bluestone, B., & Harrison, B. (1988). *The great U-Turn: Corporate restructuring and the polarization of America.* New York: Basic Books.

42. Brace, P. (1988, September). *Legislatures and economic performance.* Paper presented at the Annual Meeting of the American Political Science Association, Washington, DC.

43. Thompson, L. (1983). New jobs versus net jobs: Measuring the results of an economic development program. *Policy Studies Journal, 12* (2), 365-375.

44. National Association of State Development Agencies. (1986). *Directory of incentives for business investment and development in the United States* (2nd ed.). Washington, DC: Urban Institute Press.

45. Clark, G. L. (1983). *Interregional migration, national policy, and social justice.* Totowa, NJ: Rowman and Allanheld.

46. Kuttner, R. (1984). *The economic illusion: False choices between prosperity and social justice.* New York: Houghton Mifflin.

47. Hoover & Giarratani, *Introduction to regional economics.*

48. As of 1987, California, Texas, and Kentucky had the largest variation in unemployment rates across SMSAs. States with greater internal variation in unemployment rates were those most likely to adopt enterprise zones. Hansen, *Political economy,* chapter 6.

49. Lurie, I. (1987, December). *Dimensions of distress: The need for state targeting.* Paper presented at Targeting by the States: A Research Conference, Rockefeller Institute, Albany, NY.

50. Casson, M. (1983). *The economics of unemployment.* Oxford: Martin Robertson.

51. Ironically, loss of population helped Pittsburgh to a national ranking as "most liveable city" in a Rand McNally survey. Although the city had lost more than a quarter of its population in the preceding two decades, Rand McNally's measures were on a per

capita basis, thus highlighting Pittsburgh's past efforts to serve the needs of a considerably larger population.

52. Sawyers, L., & Tabb, W. K. (Eds.). (1984). *Sunbelt/snowbelt*. New York: Oxford University Press. On recent state efforts, see U.S. Advisory Commission on Intergovernmental Relations. (1985). *The states and distressed communities*. Washington, DC: U.S. Government Printing Office.

53. Long, N. (1987, August). Labor intensive and capital intensive urban economic development. *Economic Development Quarterly, 1,* 196-202.

54. Hansen, *Political economy,* chapter 4.

55. Mauro, F., & Yago, G. (1989). State government targeting of economic development in New York. *Publius, 19,* 63-82.

56. Cameron, G. (1970). *Regional economic development: The federal role*. Washington, DC: Resources for the Future.

57. Hoover & Giarratani, *Introduction to regional economics,* p. 361.

58. My analysis found that black legislative representation was one of the best predictors of early state adoption of enterprise zone programs (Hansen, *Political Economy,* chap. 4). Black legislators have also pushed for minority set-asides in state contracting, although their ability to do so has been limited by the Supreme Court's 1989 *Richmond* decision.

59. Hansen, S. B. (1989). Targeting in economic development: Comparative state perspectives. *Publius, 19*(2), 47-62.

2

The Conceptual Evolution of Enterprise Zones

STUART M. BUTLER

It is not difficult to trace the origin of the term *enterprise zone*. It appeared first in a speech on June 20th, 1978 by Sir Geoffrey Howe, then a leading opposition politician in the British House of Commons who later became Chancellor of the Exchequer (equivalent to Treasury Secretary) and Foreign Secretary in Margaret Thatcher's Conservative government.[1] Howe's speech was concerned with a familiar theme— urban blight. Although most politicians in Britain, and for that matter in the United States, usually proposed a new government program in speeches on that subject, Sir Geoffrey argued instead for a radically different approach. A far better policy, he declared, would be to remove as much government as possible from a number of small areas in the most derelict and depressed sections of Britain's cities. Within these enterprise zones, occupying perhaps a square mile or so, taxes and government regulation would be virtually eliminated to create the most attractive possible environment for free enterprise to flourish. Private enterprise would thereby be encouraged to revive areas in which government development programs had so dismally failed.

This free-market approach to urban development soon caught the imagination of scholars and politicians on the opposite side of the Atlantic. Early in 1979 the conservative Heritage Foundation, a Washington, D.C. think tank, published a paper summarizing the Howe enterprise zone proposal and calling for a similar urban strategy in the United States.[2] The paper was read enthusiastically by then-Congressman Jack Kemp, a New York Republican, who in turn persuaded South

Bronx Democrat Robert Garcia to cosponsor legislation refining the basic British enterprise zone idea. This congressional "odd couple" thus set in motion what turned out to be an intense debate over urban policy in America.

Like most ideas and people crossing the Atlantic, the enterprise zone concept changed a great deal once it landed in America, even though the essentials remained intact. During the last decade, as the proposal has become law in more than half the states and continues to be hotly debated in the U.S. Congress, it has evolved into a loose term covering many variations of the original idea. In some cases the result has been a refinement of Howe's enterprise zones; in others the radical elements of the concept have been ignored and the term used merely as a fashionable catchphrase to repackage old urban development ideas.

An appreciation of the conceptual evolution of enterprise zones is necessary to an understanding of the zone programs at the state level and the continuing debate over a federal program. Tracing that evolution is useful as well for a much wider purpose, because the proposal was the culmination of several new lines of thinking on urban policy, and the debate over enterprise zones has served as an umbrella for a national debate on new ways to save declining urban neighborhoods.

The Roots of
British Enterprise Zones

Sir Geoffrey Howe delivered his 1978 enterprise zone speech in London's depressed docklands district. The area at that time epitomized the decay seen in many of Britain's older port cities: derelict Victorian warehouses that once bustled with the country's trade, but now had yielded that role to smaller ports; crumbling tenements whose residents had long ago left for better prospects elsewhere. To Sir Geoffrey, the continuing decay of the area, just a stone's throw from London's throbbing financial district, symbolized the utter failure of government to trigger economic activity in blighted neighborhoods despite huge expenditures on sophisticated development programs.

That failure suggested two things to him. First, that policymakers should admit they did not have the solution to inner-city decline and that many of their attempts to impose universal solutions actually had made things worse. Instead they should select a few areas where their past failures were most pronounced and try radically different approaches simply to see which worked best. "The idea [of such enterprise zones] would be to set up test market areas or laboratories in which to enable fresh policies to prime the pump of prosperity, and to establish their potential for doing so elsewhere."[3]

Second, the dismal record of centrally planned economic development efforts suggested to Howe that instead of trying to micromanage economic activity with special grants and regulations, forcing entrepreneurs to work within an official straitjacket, government instead should simply create the best possible conditions for private enterprise in a set of inner-city zones. It should drastically cut taxes and regulations, and then stand back and allow entrepreneurs to pursue profit with the minimum of restriction. Howe's model for this approach was Hong Kong and the other free trade zones around the world. In these zones—usually located in places with little or no natural resources, he noted—a policy of very low taxes, minimal economic regulation, and few restrictions on land use, had produced staggering rates of economic growth and job opportunities for millions of people. Why not try the same strategy in declining urban neighborhoods; why not, in short, try to create mini-Hong Kongs in Britain's inner cities?

Sir Geoffrey Howe was given the opportunity to put his enterprise zone idea into practice just a few years later, when the Conservatives won the 1979 general election. By the end of 1980, legislation had been enacted to create enterprise zones and by the following year a dozen had been designated.[4]

The idea of cutting taxes and regulations to stimulate economic development within depressed neighborhoods has been the central element in the enterprise zone strategy as it evolved on both sides of the Atlantic. Howe's original proposal, however, and the subsequent legislation establishing the program, envisioned a collection of zones significantly different from the image in the minds of most American proponents.

Most importantly, the British enterprise zone program was and is intended to generate activity in abandoned industrial areas, virtually—indeed, ideally—devoid of population. The zones were not seen as tools to revive depressed neighborhoods, like New York's South Bronx (considered by U.S. advocates as the archetypal candidate for an enterprise zone), but were conceived more as inner-city industrial parks. The British imagined them as small areas in which there would be rapid industrial development, serving as the nucleus for the general economic revival of a metropolitan area. People eventually might come to live in an enterprise zone, much as immigrants gravitated to Hong Kong, but they were not to be a tool to reinvigorate specific small communities.

That original purpose can be seen in the legislation establishing enterprise zones in Britain. With the objective of rapid industrialization in mind, the program exempts industrial and commercial buildings from property taxes, but not residential buildings. The enterprise zone package also provides for a one-year tax write-off for all spending on business-related buildings and machinery within a zone, and if proposed construction or rehabilitation meets basic use guidelines, virtually no zoning restrictions apply. In addition, the zone legislation gives an exemption from customs duties for all imported materials used to manufacture goods that subsequently are exported. This last provision was not included merely as an afterthought, as a link to the free trade zone antecedents of the enterprise zone, but because many of the British zones have in fact been established in derelict port areas. One aim of the enterprise zones has been to breathe new life into abandoned warehouses and silent wharves.

Needless to say, huge tax breaks of the kind given in the program are only useful to a taxpayer with a huge tax bill from which to deduct them. Therefore, the British zones have been attractive, in the first instance at least, to large-scale property developers rather than to small entrepreneurs. Moreover, little could happen in most of the sites chosen for zones without first an injection of enormous amounts of private investment, because the zones were designated either on largely vacant land or, more usually, in old industrial areas needing major demolition and new construction. The entrepreneurs being sought as the pioneers in Britain's enterprise zones, in other words, were major corporations able to commit huge sums to pay for bulldozers and new buildings, not local small businessmen with a few tools who were willing to make do with a damp basement or abandoned store front.

Enterprise Zones in America

When the enterprise zone concept was first unveiled in the United States, in 1979, it was hardly surprising that the radical free market development strategy should appeal to conservatives like Jack Kemp and Ronald Reagan. To both these politicians, the proposal was, in effect, a supply-side program to save the inner cities: It was the urban complement to the general conservative strategy of cutting taxes and regulation to stimulate economic growth. Kemp eagerly adopted the proposal and introduced an enterprise zone bill in May 1980, and Ronald Reagan adopted enterprise zones as the centerpiece of his urban proposals during the 1980 election. Enterprise zones became official Reagan Administration policy in 1981.

More surprising was the liberal reaction. Within one month of Kemp introducing his bill in Congress, he had persuaded South Bronx liberal Democrat Robert Garcia to join with him on a slightly modified bill. By 1981 a remarkable bipartisan coalition had assembled to support the enterprise strategy, including leading congressional Republicans and Democrats, the Reagan Administration, the congressional Black Caucus, the National Urban League, the NAACP, and the National League of Cities.

To be sure, some of the liberal support after the 1980 election was triggered by the feeling that an enterprise zone program was the only approach likely to be acceptable to the tax and budget cutting Reagan Administration and the Reagan-dominated Congress, but there were deeper reasons for the remarkable coalition. For one thing, urban Democrats like Garcia had seen one expensive government program after another introduced into their districts, including Model Cities, urban renewal, and urban development action grants. Some had a marginal impact, but others, such as urban renewal, literally had destroyed neighborhoods and left wastelands. Despite the plethora of federal programs, places like the South Bronx continued to deteriorate. By 1980 there was a greater willingness among liberals to try a bold change in direction, at least in a few experimental areas.

The other reason a bipartisan coalition was possible was that the original British proposal was substantially modified in its American reincarnation. While the basic idea of cutting taxes and regulations to boost inner-city redevelopment in a small number of selected areas remained the core of the enterprise zone concept, the aims and legislative ingredients in the early U.S. proposals were shaped by a significantly different view of urban development from that held by Sir Geoffrey Howe. This distinctly American view of the purposes of an enterprise zone program sat better with most liberals that did the industrial park theme in the British zone program. Admittedly, not all American supporters of enterprise zones have shared exactly the same vision—indeed there has always been a fierce internal debate within the enterprise zone coalition—but it is fair to say that the development of the concept in the United States has been strongly influenced by the approaches to economic development discussed below.

The Primary Aim of Enterprise Zones
Should be the Economic Improvement
of Poor Neighborhoods

The British program is based on the notion that vacant sites make the best enterprise zones, with the zones acting as a focal point for the economic improvement of a wide area. Although job opportunities for poor families close to an enterprise zone are seen as an important consequence of the zone program, they are not the primary objective. In the United States, by contrast, most supporters of the enterprise zone idea have seen it as a tool to resuscitate specific poor neighborhoods, creating jobs primarily for local people. Thus the quintessential enterprise zone has been assumed in America to comprise a distinct neighborhood, not an entire city nor a vacant area.

There has been less agreement, however, regarding the idea of restricting enterprise zones to urban settings. Certainly the original British proposal was aimed at reviving cities (even though some of the British sites are in open areas on the edge of cities), and leading American supporters of the idea, such as Jack Kemp, always imagined heavily blighted, crime-ridden inner-city neighborhoods as the principal targets for enterprise zones. Similarly, most of the scholarly work contributing to the proposal assumed the purpose was to resuscitate urban areas. Nevertheless, there have always been certain proponents of enterprise zones in the United States who envisioned the concept also applying to small rural towns with chronic economic problems. Although the majority of enterprise zone proponents may be skeptical of the applicability of zones to rural areas, politics has decided otherwise. To secure political support at both the state and federal level, enterprise zone advocates generally have accepted the principle of reserving a certain proportion of zone designations for rural locations.

Underpinning the choice of objective is a basically optimistic impression of poor neighborhoods and poor people; one that is shared by conservative as well as liberal backers of enterprise zones. For politicians and scholars at both ends of the spectrum, the assumption is that there is enormous latent potential within even the most blighted neighborhoods. Currently, that potential is smothered in red tape, excessive taxation, and a culture of welfare dependency. But with the right incentives, the argument goes, the dormant human and capital resources of a South Bronx can be brought to life. Liberals, more than conservatives, tend to feel that other ingredients than incentives are necessary to trigger growth, but both agree that enterprise zones should be a tool to revive a neighborhood, not one to destroy it in order to start again.

Furthermore, basing growth on existing but unused or underused resources means that the enterprise zone proposal in the United States has been seen as a device to improve a neighborhood without having to divert people and economic activity from elsewhere. It is not, as Jack Kemp puts it, an exercise in "zero sum economics" but an attempt to create genuinely new economic activity. For this reason, Kemp and other conservative proponents maintain, the tax reductions in an enterprise zone should not be viewed as leading to a reduction in net government revenues. If cutting tax rates triggers indigenous activity in a depressed neighborhood where virtually no taxes were being paid, then the government would receive a fraction of something rather than all of nothing.

This notion that an enterprise zone program would be a catalyst for indigenous economic activity also suggested to most of its proponents that enterprise zone designation would be temporary for a neighborhood. The special tax and regulatory status would be like an economic "jump start" for an area, to ignite local resources and overcome obstacles arising from years of blight and crime. Economic growth itself, however, would gradually eliminate the obstacles and lead to self-sustained improvement. At that point, according to proponents, the area could safely be taken off the "endangered list" and returned to the regime of taxes (and possibly regulations) prevailing in adjacent non-zone areas.

Moreover, while supply-siders in the Reagan Administration in general opposed the idea of legislation committing the government to raise tax rates in the future, there was a widespread countervailing principle held by many Reaganite Treasury officials that the federal tax system should be neutral and not fine-tuned to benefit particular areas of the country. Thus the idea of ending tax breaks in enterprise zones was not opposed by the same officials who could be counted on to attack any move to raise general tax rates. Indeed, most supply-side economists at the Reagan Treasury were either lukewarm or hostile to the enterprise zone proposal, believing it to be a distortion of basic conservative tax principles.

No real consensus has emerged on what would constitute an ideal time limit. The benchmark for the British zones, contained in the 1980 legislation, was 10 years, although the precise period was left open to agreement between the national government and the local jurisdiction. Federal legislative proposals in the United States have also included similar time limits.

The emphasis on existing neighborhoods and the local population can be seen in the design of enterprise zone legislation, particularly at the federal level. Absent, for instance, are the deep tax incentives of the British program, intended to spur major physical development. Instead, the federal bills and most state measures have contained a variety of provisions aimed at fostering modest improvement of existing commercial structures. Unlike the British program, U.S. proposals also have included incentives to rehabilitate existing housing. And perhaps most important of all, the federal bills have all included deep tax incentives to encourage businesses to recruit labor, particularly low-skilled or disadvantaged workers. The British program contains no such incentives—British enterprise zone firms, in fact, are given every incentive to employ machines rather than people.

Community Institutions Are Crucial to Economic Development

American proponents of enterprise zones also have been strongly influenced by the argument that urban economic development initiatives for poor people can only succeed if their designers recognize and build upon the institutions that exist within a community. This view of urban development is in stark contrast to much of the thinking in the 1950s and 1960s, when the prevailing view was more that carefully planned physical redevelopment is the key to urban revival and that people could and should be moved around to fit within newly built neighborhoods. On the contrary, countered such urban writers as Jane Jacobs, in her books The Death and Life of Great American Cities and The Economy of Cities, successful urban development depends on complex social relationships within a community.[5] Ignore these relationships, and treat residents simply as individuals who happen to live in a certain geographic area—worse still, physically disrupt a neighborhood and its institutions—and development initiatives are virtually guaranteed to fail.

The principal theme of Jane Jacob's work is that diversity is needed for an inner-city neighborhood to be economically and socially vibrant. This means the mixed use of buildings, leading to a variety of economic activity, making the area better able to adapt to changing economic conditions, and to a flourishing street life throughout the day, reducing the incidence of crime. It also means recognizing that neighborhood organizations are crucial to the development process, mobilizing local people to tackle crime and other social problems that discourage enterprise.

This emphasis on preserving and strengthening community institutions has been a strong theme in enterprise zone proposals in the United States, although it was completely ignored in the design of the British zones. In the zone selection criteria contained in the Reagan Administration proposals, for instance, the Administration stressed that it would look more favorably on applications from cities that demonstrated they were taking steps to include neighborhood-based organizations in the development process.

The argument that strengthening community institutions is essential to economic development in poor communities also is an answer to the perennial question asked of antipoverty programs: Should the emphasis be on people or places? The answer implied in the enterprise zone strategy is that in a very meaningful sense people cannot be separated from place, and that an antipoverty strategy needs to treat individuals in the context of their community. Thus, in order to improve the condition of the poor, the enterprise zone strategy assumes that the focus must be on poor communities.

Small Businesses Should be Favored over Large Ones

The third influence on the evolution of the American version of enterprise zones has been the thesis that small enterprises are the key to economic growth, particularly in depressed urban neighborhoods. Proponents of enterprise zones argue that there are several reasons why a program should be geared to small firms.

The first is that a solid body of evidence points to the conclusion that small firms are overwhelmingly the most important generators of new jobs. In extensive surveys covering 80% of U.S. firms, for instance, David Birch of the Massachusetts Institute of Technology has found that about two thirds of all net new jobs are created by firms with less than 20 employees. In poor urban neighborhoods, small firms turn out to be the only net producers of jobs. The best job generators of all tend to be young small firms. By contrast, Birch points out, very large firms tend to be net destroyers of jobs.[6]

Birch also found that in comparing job losses throughout the nation, the curious fact is that the rate of job terminations tends to be remarkably similar—about 8% each year—in growing and declining areas. The crucial difference explaining growth and decline is the rate of formation of new firms. This implies that the primary objective of government development officials would be to institute policies that are likely to increase the start up rate of new firms, rather than measures designed mainly to retain existing employers in an effort to save jobs. This conclusion, of course, runs against the thinking of many officials. Development strategies aimed at reducing the loss rate of jobs, declares Birch, are "as futile as telling the tide not to go out."[7]

The second reason for targeting small firms in an enterprise zone strategy is that small enterprises fit better within an approach based largely on stimulating local activity within existing buildings. Small entrepreneurs in poor neighborhoods establish small firms, not *Fortune 500* corporations. Small firms also tend to fit more easily into existing structures; large firms tend to need new facilities. Small entrepreneurs are also more inclined to recruit local, unskilled labor and take the risk of operating in a marginal neighborhood. Executives from large corporations are disinclined to do so.

Enterprise zone proposals at the federal level have stressed incentives that are more likely to appeal to smaller firms, although there continues to be a vigorous debate about how small firms can, in fact, be induced by tax incentives to open their doors. It is pointed out by small-business people themselves that reductions in corporate income tax rates are not a major factor in their decisions to start a firm or to expand, because most make so little net profit in their early years that income tax rates are irrelevant. On the other hand, these entrepreneurs point out that two of the most important determinants of their success or failure are everyday operating expenses, including the cost of labor, and their ability to obtain capital for the start-up phase and for later expansion.

The architects of enterprise zone proposals have sought to fashion tax incentives that might address these needs of smaller firms. Thus the earliest version of federal legislation, introduced by Kemp and Garcia, included employment tax credits not only to induce firms to hire local labor, but also to reduce the largest operating cost of most small firms. Later federal versions have continued such credits for the same reasons. Similarly, the most important federal bills have all included tax incentives to encourage investors to risk modest amounts of money in small enterprise zone firms. Among these have been incentives to purchase stock in such firms, and the rapid depreciation for tax purposes of limited amounts of machinery placed in enterprise zone firms. The plan advanced by the Bush Administration, and designed by Housing and Urban Development (HUD) Secretary Jack Kemp, also eliminated capital gains for certain investments in an enterprise zone.

State enterprise zone programs have focused in varying degrees on stimulating the growth of small business. Typical incentives include partial relief from property taxes and inventory taxes, as well as steps to speed up and simplify the process needed to acquire a permit to open a business. In addition, the federal proposals have sought to induce states to include such actions by noting in the designation language that applications with measures to help small business would receive more favorable treatment.

Enterprise Zones and the
Politics of Federalism

The evolution of the enterprise zone idea in the United States has not been shaped only by American views of the nature and objectives of urban development. It has also been influenced by the peculiar politics and institutional arrangements of the American system of federalism.

When the enterprise zone concept was first introduced in the United States, it aroused interest almost exclusively at the federal level. With the exception of a narrowly defeated attempt at legislation in Illinois, it was legislative proposals at the federal level that constituted the template both for the debate over enterprise zones and for the design of legislation at the state level.

State legislation, however, was viewed as an essential complement to a federally designed program. There were two principal reasons for this. The first was that given the shared responsibilities for taxation and regulation, it would require state as well as federal legislation to bring about the reductions in tax and regulatory barriers envisioned in the proposal. The second reason was that the enterprise zone approach, from its very inception in Britain, was to be experimental in nature. The idea was to trigger slightly different approaches in different places, adapted to local conditions and drawing on local creativity. This required innovative state and local initiatives blended with a national framework of incentives established at the federal level.

Inducing states to cooperate by cutting their own taxes and regulations was not a simple task, however. State politicians and development officials had become accustomed in the 1960s and 1970s to a particular form of federal-state development program: In return for a certain set of actions by a state or city, federal cash would flow—but the enterprise zone proposal involved no cash. The federal government simply would reduce its tax rates on certain depressed areas if the state, and perhaps the local government would do likewise. It was not at all clear to some development officials schooled in the more traditional what they had to gain from such a novel arrangement.

Nevertheless, there was sufficient interest in the enterprise zone concept among state and local politicians, as well as organizations with an interest in urban affairs, for there to be strong pressure for federal enterprise zone designations and the tax incentives that would accompany the zones. But perhaps not surprisingly, state and local officials were far more interested in federal tax cuts in their cities than in reducing their own taxes or assembling a package of possibly expensive initiatives.

The relatively strong demand for a federal designation permitted congressional and administration architects of legislation to use a limit on the number of federal zones to force complementary state action. Thus federal legislative proposals have all included some limit on the number and size of possible designations, and guidance on actions at the state and local level that would improve the chances of selection by federal authorities.

Reagan-supported legislation introduced during the first term of the administration, for instance, required states to submit a proposed *Course of Action* with their application for a federal designation. If the application were accepted in the competitive process, the Course of Action then in effect would constitute an agreement by the state to undertake the actions. Although the legislation did not specify precisely what should be in such a state commitment, it noted that the plan might include such items as reductions in taxes and regulation, proposals to privatize municipal services in the zone, and steps to include community organizations in the development process.

In the first two years of the Reagan Administration, several states, including Connecticut, reasoned that the best way to increase the chances of selection for the federal program—passage of which was widely assumed to be a foregone conclusion—would be to enact a state program in tune with the basic elements of Reagan-supported congressional legislation. Thus the eligibility criteria of most state measures mirrored those in the federal legislation (based on UDAG criteria), and the tax, regulatory and other measures included in legislation and programs at the state level, broadly conformed to most people's best guess of a package likely to win applause from federal officials administering an enterprise zone program.

Enterprise zone legislation, however, never did pass Congress during the Reagan Administration, other than a token and toothless measure, devoid of any tax incentives, signed into law in 1988. At the time of writing, with the Bush Administration well into its second year, enterprise zone legislation has yet to pass Congress (although the prospects for passage seem better than at any time since the early Reagan years).

The precise reasons why legislation with such wide bipartisan support became stalled in Congress are complex and still disputed. But with the chances of a federal program becoming bleaker during the Reagan Administration, the enterprise zone concept slowly and almost imperceptibly underwent another stage in its evolution. It has changed from a federally inspired concept, in which state and local governments were to play very much a supporting role, into what is today a series of state programs in search of supporting federal tax incentives.

This change in the federal-state relationship regarding enterprise zones, with the states in the vanguard, has had a profound effect on the structure of state zones. As other chapters in this volume show, there is now a remarkable variety of state enterprise zones. Some may be considered enterprise zones in name only, because they include major government spending programs and development planning that are the antithesis of the whole concept. But others are relatively bold experiments in using tax and regulatory incentives to create an environment conducive to enterprise development in depressed areas. In this sense one of Sir Geoffrey Howe's original purposes for enterprise zones is being fulfilled: Enterprise zones at the state level are indeed a set of laboratories in which a wide variety of economic development strategies are being tested, and where successes and failures will serve as a guide to better policies in the future.

Notes

1. Howe, G. (1978, June). Speech at a meeting of the Bow Group, London, England.

2. Butler, S. M (1989). *Enterprise zones: A solution to the urban crisis?* Washington, DC: Heritage Foundation.

3. Ibid.

4. For background on the development of the enterprise zone concept in Britain and the United States see Butler, S. M. (1981). *Enterprise zones: Greenlining the inner cities.* New York: Universe.

5. Jacobs, J. (1961). *The death and life of great American cities.* New York: Random House; Jacobs, J. (1969). *The economy of cities.* New York: Random House.

6. Birch, D. (1979). *The job generation process.* Cambridge: Program on Neighborhood and Regional Change.

7. Birch, D. (1980). *Job creation in cities.* Unpublished manuscript, MIT, Program on Neighborhood and Regional Change, Cambridge, MA, p. 11.

3

Enterprise Zones and Federalism

ENID BEAUMONT

The continuously changing balance of power and responsibility among federal, state, and local governments is an important aspect of American society. During the past decade, changing federalism policies and the federal budget deficit have increased the responsibilities of state and local governments. At the same time, increasing federal regulation has reduced state discretion.[1] State and local governments have undertaken new programs with their own revenue while, at the same time, Congress has been increasing the number of rules and mandates on intergovernmental programs.

Enterprise zones in the United States have developed at the state and local level, without national incentives, legislation, or regulation. It is important to explore the meaning for federalism of a program that was suggested through the introduction, but not passage, of federal legislation. During that decade, state and local governments moved to create Enterprise Zones in 37 states and the District of Columbia. There are over 2,000 zones on paper and, according to the best estimates, there are 400 to 500 that are active, recognized, and have local commitment. Now that federal legislation that would fund 50 zones over the next four years might pass Congress, it is important to focus on the impact that a federal program would have on the already existing and operating zones.

There is a wide diversity among zones in terms of criteria used to create them, administrative practices, relationship to other government programs, size, scope, and complexity. Arguments are extant about how to measure their achievements, the costs/benefits that they entail, and why the original idea of reducing government involvement seems to have worked out in an opposite manner. Although some opponents continue to speak of zones as potentially dangerous dens of deregulation, more typically zone "designation has been the impetus for beneficial re-regulation with the targeted areas."[2] State and local governments in the United States have acted independently and established Enterprise Zones, which may now receive an overlay of federal legislation. The dimensions of such federal legislation should be quite different because of these initiatives at the state and local levels.

Federal Roles in the Intergovernmental System

Within the federal system, the federal government can play a variety of roles from coercive to cooperative. In the last decade, in spite of contrary rhetoric, Congress and the executive branch have leaned more and more toward the coercive mode in many programs. Under the Constitution, "states possess few powers that are immune from congressional interference and attributes of traditional state sovereignty are subject to direct regulation by the Congress."[3]

The Congress usually plays one of three roles in the federal system to influence behavior at the state and local levels: facilitator, initiator, or inhibitor.[4] As the *facilitator* of programs, Congress provides financial and program assistance to promote a program. As *initiator,* it provides through partial preemption statutes the framework for new regulatory programs. As *inhibitor,* Congress employs its total preemption powers to nullify state and local regulatory laws and rules. Although the current intentions of the federal government are to operate as a facilitator, in a cooperative and mutually supportive mode with regard to Enterprise Zones, that is not the usual way in which the federal government behaves toward state and local governments. There seems to be a drive toward the inhibitor mode through mandates and preemptions in order to influence state and local governments.

The Enterprise Zone concept was raised to national prominence during the presidential campaign of Ronald Reagan, as a concept in which less governmental action would be the hallmark of success. The idea was that private enterprise could solve the problems of distressed areas. The legislation was introduced early in 1981 by Congressman Jack Kemp (Republican) and Robert Garcia (Democrat). It appeared that the goals of the two were divergent and that "enterprise zones for Kemp seemed to represent job creation, but for Garcia, the concept promoted more generally inner city revitalization."[5] The difference in goals, the poor response of Congress, the conflict of theory, and the lack of experience all combined to stop passage of any federal legislation.

The federal government, however, continued to demonstrate interest in the Enterprise Zone idea both in Congress and in the Executive branch. There are many programs that are proposed in Congress that are not subsequently initiated at the state and local level. The variety of practices at the state and local levels are truly an American adaption of the concept of Enterprise Zones. Had the federal government acted in 1981, there would be much more standardization and much less learning.

Action by State and Local Governments

Why did state and local governments move so rapidly toward Enterprise Zones? The original motivation would appear to be anticipation of federal legislation. States moved to be ready to take advantage of any federal incentives that would be established.

The early states adopting an Enterprise Zone program were Florida, Louisiana, Connecticut, Missouri, Ohio, Pennsylvania, and Rhode Island. It is evident that zones have been motivated by the possibility of federal legislation. This is clearly reflected in Rhode Island and Texas legislation that delays implementation until federal legislation is enacted. Both of these states have or are changing this provision. In fact, specifically being UDAG eligible is a zone designation criterion in eight states, illustrating the influence of possible federal involvement:

1982: Connecticut, Missouri, and Ohio
1983: Kansas
1985: California
1988: Tennessee, Texas, and Wisconsin.

A second reason for the growth of enterprise zones seems to be their usefulness as a tool for development. State and local government officials have developed a variety of organizations that facilitate the sharing of information across jurisdictions. With the increase in both face-to-face meetings and modern methods of communication, ideas travel easily. The Enterprise Zone idea can be adapted to the needs of particular jurisdictions. It is difficult to find another example of such an idea that has been adopted so extensively so quickly without direct federal impetus. The National Association of State Development Agencies (NASDA) provides an ongoing source of information and assistance for states in the development and implementation of their programs. HUD itself concluded that zone designation appears to produce positive and tangible impacts and that such designation appears more important in generating new investment than the specific package of incentives offered.[6]

A third reason for the growth in the zones is related to the continued effort of the federal government to monitor and publicize the program. In this case, one half-time federal executive provided information and evaluation services that have had a positive effect. HUD operates a clearinghouse to share information about the state programs and has played a leadership role in developing data regarding programs. HUD has spurred and encouraged the development and growth of state zones. It has also provided technical assistance to a number of state legislatures which was instrumental in moving state legislation forward. With private sector funds, HUD, the Legislative Commission of Public Private Cooperation, and the New York Association of Renewal and Housing Officials, Inc. sponsored the Conference on Rebuilding New York—The Case For Enterprise Zones in the New York State Senate Chambers. This seminar is believed to have contributed to the eventual adoption of the program in New York.

Another probable reason for the growth in the zone concept, is state leadership in the field. The emergence of states as leaders in this movement may be attributed to Washington's inactivity. Whether government's actions or nonactions helped spur the explosion of state enterprise zone programs, the bottom line—state leadership in implementing such programs—remains the same.[7] The growth of zones occurred as state governments have taken on the role of economic activist.[8] The 1980s have been a decade of enormous innovation as the states dealt with the economic transition of the past decade. Enterprise zones were used by some states as part of this transformation, such as the creation of public venture-capital funds, stimulation of technological innovation, and the development of public investment funds.

The Federal Research Role

One of the most interesting aspects of Enterprise Zones as a federalism issue, is the continued presence of the federal government in zone activity without legislative authority. HUD has carried out and published the first set of case studies, which provides empirical information regarding the operation of locally designated state zones. HUD has developed the only national data base reflecting economic activity in state enterprise zones. HUD has played a leadership role in developing data regarding the state programs and in conducting, sponsoring, summarizing, and analyzing the research that has been conducted.

In addition, The Congressional Research Service (CRS) has conducted two studies of state and local progress at the request of Congress. Congress also requested a recent study by the General Accounting Office (GAO) of Maryland's enterprise zone program. In what has become perhaps the most controversial and quoted evaluation, GAO found little or no program-related effect on employment based upon a study of three zones in Maryland. The CRS and GAO studies are critical of Enterprise Zones. GAO suggests that a modest demonstration program might be more useful than the large scale efforts proposed in several bills because "the Maryland experience does not show that enterprise zones are effective."[9]

Their pessimistic findings are in contrast to most of the empirical studies conducted at the state and local level, which are more positive about the outcomes of zones. A recent study in New Jersey found that the return was $1.90 for every dollar invested.[10] Usually, when the federal government is interested in an area, it provides grants-in-aid, tax subsidies, loans, and loan guarantees. Such assistance is accompanied by regulations, and often by mandates directing certain behavior by state and local governments. In the case of Enterprise Zones without any federal financial incentives, state and local governments have innovated. It might be expected that the federal government would quit the field, leaving the issue to state and local governments.

The Federal Government's
Mixed Signals

Enterprise zone legislation, passed by Congress in 1987, created 100 federal zones but has not been implemented. HUD has until January,

1991 to designate these zones. The federal government accepted applications for this program and interest was expressed by a large number of jurisdictions. It would have been an interesting facet of federalism, if these federal zones had been created, to study their effect on communication and in coordinating other federal programs without any tax incentives. However, when Jack Kemp became Secretary of HUD he was not satisfied with the federal approach because there were no incentives attached to the program. A concerted effort is being made in the 101st Congress to attach tax incentives to the legislation, which include:

- A refundable wage credit for low-income zone employees;
- Expensing of investor purchases of small zone stock; and
- A zero capital gains tax rate on tangible zone assets.[11]

Willingness to use tax expenditures is a very mixed signal from the federal government: In the last decade, the federal government has moved to eliminate tax expenditures. For state and local governments, the changes have been very difficult and include the elimination of sales tax deductions from federal income tax calculations. There have also been complicated restrictions on the issuance of tax-exempt bonds by state and local governments that have substantially raised the costs for a variety of capital expenditures. Pressures in each presidential budget to eliminate or restrict a variety of mortgage revenue bonds and industrial development bonds have created conflict over the use and purpose of such tax expenditures. If the elimination of more state and local tax expenditures are suggested, some argue that all tax expenditures should be considered for elimination.

Given their choice, state and local governments would prefer direct funding through the use of general revenue sharing and other grant programs such as UDAG and CDBG rather than the creation of additional tax expenditures of unknown cost. While CBO has indicated that it cannot "cost out" the federal enterprise zone issue, some have suggested that the zones as introduced in the 101st Congress would be very expensive to implement. One Treasury estimate of current legislation is $1.04 billion over four years. GAO puts the figure at $4.75 billion over six years. Secretary Kemp believes that the program will pay for itself with the increased taxes that will be generated by additional economic activity. "My personal opinion is that enterprise zones in the long run will actually raise money."[12] The administration's revenue estimates assume no change in levels of national economic activity as a result of enterprise zones. Another source suggests that President Bush's more modest tax incentive version designating 50 zones over four years would total $1.8 billion.[13] Still another study by CRS states clearly that "even taking into account these potential increases in economic activity in EZ's, the EZ program is not a Federal revenue raiser."[14] The answer is obviously not in about the costs and benefits of this program. The appeal of tax expenditures is that they do not affect current budget deficits or calculations, and new direct appropriations that do so are scarce at this time.

Because the Enterprise Zone initiative appears to be one of the few state and local programs that is attractive to the administration, it is anticipated that state and local governments would be receptive but not enthusiastic. This lukewarm approach has characterized the reception of state and local governments toward federal involvement in enterprise zones since they were first suggested in the early 1980s.

Zones Used by
Other Federal Programs

It is interesting to note that the creation of state and local zones has had a bearing on other federal agencies and become a factor in their program administration on a voluntary basis. The Economic Development Administration has provided a funding priority for state zone projects. The Farmer's Home Administration regards zones as valuable resources in rural development. HUD grantees support zones with community development block grant funds.[15] The Small Business Administration (SBA) has established small business incubators in zones. The administration proposal suggests establishing local coordinating councils of federal agencies to support the objectives of federal zone legislation and to provide technical assistance and waiver of rules to support zone objectives.

Many local governments and states have incorporated other forms of assistance in their zone programs. These include public works projects, job training, and priority for other programs.

States have also paved the way by being first to include rural as well as urban areas; being first to include incentives beyond tax and regulatory relief; and working actively with local governments to provide incentives such as business fee reductions.[16]

The need for local involvement is apparent. Some localities have abated property taxes on improvements in the zone and others ask for local commitment to issue revenue bonds as a condition for zone designation. Any federal program will have to take the need for local involvement into consideration, which is difficult to determine from the national perspective.[17]

What a Federal Program Should Be Like

Any federal program that comes after such activity at the state and local level should understand and build upon that experience. Recent experience with programs regarding the homeless and child care, however, illustrate a lack of building upon state and local experience. A federal overlay to Enterprise Zones is not an initiating role any longer. Can a small demonstration program of 50 zones over a four year period really facilitate the enterprise zone programs now in effect? Regardless of the benign intent of the current federal sponsors, some change toward uniformity is to be expected with the advent of federal incentives. With only a small number of zones placed upon the large number of state and local zones, the impact could be minimal unless a coercive mode was employed. This also leads to the question of whether federal zones are needed at all. If they are established, they must be crafted with a sensitivity not at all common in the federalism arena, which tends to move toward the more coercive roles limiting the state and local diversity and flexibility.

State and local governments are fighting to avoid federal mandates in many areas. The need for sensitivity to achievements at subnational levels is understood at the federal level, but how to obtain enough state and local input into the design of a federal program is quite difficult. This is particularly true for Enterprise Zones, which now exist in so many states and localities in widely varying form. As early as 1986, HUD's Secretary Pierce noted that there was a wide body of knowledge from several years of experimentation by the states:

It is critical to learn from this experience. State and local officials would probably agree that the state programs would be strengthened by an overlay of federal incentives. The Administration continues to support the enterprise zone concept, and will look forward to working with the 100th Congress in developing a set of incentives that complement the state programs.[18]

Little has been done to define what type of a program would complement state programs. It is interesting to explore some of the parameters of such a program.

Designation of Zones

Subnational enterprise zones have been in existence for almost a decade. Their designation by state and local government take a variety of forms that best meet the needs of each jurisdiction. In the scramble to achieve federal designation and incentives, much of the experimentation at the state and local level could be ended. An option to have states and local governments independently designate zones might reduce some of the unanticipated consequences of federal decisions. The administration has stated that the nomination of a zone must be jointly requested by a local and state government but that designation will be based on the Secretary's assessment of the relative merits of the local/state strategies.

Mandates

In testimony concerning Enterprise Zones in October 1989, Secretary Kemp identified some key objectives for the federal legislation that would have major impact on the current state programs. These are:

- Focus on creating new small businesses;
- Avoid the type of complex, capital based tax incentives that appeal only to large businesses;
- Recognize that competition for designation is critical;
- Focus on neighborhood development, renovation and indigenous businesses.[19]

HUD wants to keep federal rules and mandates out of any federal overlay: Sometimes even the best intentions could have a perverse impact on current programs. For example, the competition criteria might prove controversial. Some of the outstanding programs were not designated through a competitive program. Kemp argues:

> Federal tax incentive should act as a catalyst for other State, local and private sector efforts to cooperate to restore vitality and economic buoyancy. In a competitive process, those States and localities which offered the strongest package of incentives and initiatives would receive preferential selection for zone eligibility.[20]

One begins to see the outlines of the federal selection criteria that will influence state and local zones in particular directions that have not all been evaluated or proven. Some zones have relied upon large business involvement and would suffer in a program emphasizing small business. Kemp argues for preference when states and localities offer relief from land use regulations, zoning laws, and real estate taxes, building codes, and rent control. He places other emphasis on coordination with community drug enforcement, anticrime efforts and improved services and neighborhood infrastructure. Should such emphasis turn into mandates, in order to obtain federal zone designation, then the freedom and ingenuity with which these zones have been conceived and operated could be diminished. This was noted in testimony indicating that "state and local programs are a necessary prerequisite for the success of a federal tax incentive program. Reliance on the state and local supervision and initiative should continue to be the theme of the perfecting amendments."[21]

For example, a recent review of state enterprise zones by the National Association of State Development Agencies notes that enterprise zone managers stress the importance of linking the zone program with other state and local economic development programs in order to promote investment.

> Equally important, though, is that the local development agency (or enterprise zone association) work hand-in-hand with businesses by helping them to secure financing, obtaining job training for employees, and informing them of the state and local incentives their company can take advantage of.[22]

This report stresses that the zones have grown rapidly because offering a full range of incentives including tax credits, job training, and low-interest financing can target business investment to economically distressed areas which in turn helps create jobs and pump money into sluggish economies.

Using Green and Brintnall's classification of program by major objectives provides informative insight into the possible impacts of a federal zone program. By stressing those programs that emphasize more than job creation, the Southern states would do very poorly in a national competition because their practice tends to stress narrow, job creation objectives and they do not incorporate community development objectives into their programs. Those states with strong interest in additional objectives, such as Illinois, Kentucky, Indiana, and Texas would be expected to do well in such a competition.[23] In a recent HUD study, states were categorized according to program goals. In 22 state programs, 7 states listed neighborhood revitalization as a goal in addition to promoting investment and creating jobs. These states would have an advantage in any competition in which such a goal was emphasized. They include Connecticut, Illinois, Maryland, Minnesota, New Jersey, New York, and Virginia.[24] Although the administration has announced that designation of zone will take geographic distribution into account, emphasis on statements such as "other factors determined essential to support Enterprise Zone activities and encourage livability or quality of life"[25] have the potential to substantially change current zone behavior.

Although there is some discussion in zone literature about the importance of improving the quality of life, most of the emphasis has been on the economic development and job creation aspects of zones. The broader mandate of the federal legislation would place more emphasis on social goals. The measurement of the social welfare results of enterprise zones has also proven difficult.

The federal government has been a positive facilitator of zones but federal zones could cause this to change because of the intense competition and the tendency to surround programs with regulations. "The national government has played an active non-programmatic role in promoting enterprise zones through coordination and dissemination of information on state activities."[26] The loss of this federal support through information and evaluation would weaken state and local zone efforts.

The American Association of Enterprise Zones (AAEZ) suggests a federal policy that would provide basic support for all state-designated zones, plus a set of incentives to be granted through a national competition.[27] The objectives are to promote employment of the disadvantaged, encourage manufacturing, encourage exports, and promote reinvestment in distressed areas by banks. It is to be noted that AAEZ's two-level proposal targets existing federal economic development programs to reinforce the states' zones in addition to other new incentives. They argue that the zones already designated by the state would be the ones from which the federal zones would evolve.

> We do not want the federal program to go through a separate process and redesignate 100 new zones. We think that the states and the cities, having worked together for the last three or four years, have really identified the communities that need and can develop the right programs for their cities. Therefore, what is essential is that the federal program provide additional benefits that would really make the program a total success. We don't want competition with a whole new set of zones.[28]

AAEZ also suggests that the Administration issue an executive order requiring the coordination of federal economic development policies and programs in those states where a program has been implemented. They might not respond favorably to the current Administration proposal to create federal coordinating councils to perform this role.

The problems of designation and competition will be difficult to solve. Should the funds and designation go to those who have been the most successful already or should there be targeting for those who are most deserving and are, perhaps, in the 13 states that have not yet established zones. What will be needed will be sensitivity to establish federal incentives that complement state programs. The language used by Secretary Kemp would suggest more elaborate goals that those now being used in a more focused way by state and local officials.

Targeted Federalism

Congress is not comfortable with targeted federalism, so it is to be expected that there will be a move toward more than 50 zones accompanied by a reduction in benefits. This is illustrated by the last 30 years of experience with urban programs. After the major city riots in the mid-60s, Congress responded with urban legislation. There were 44 federal grant programs for the cities in 1960 that expended $3.9 billion annually. By 1968, there were over 500 grant programs expending $14 billion, which grew to $26.8 billion by 1974. *Model Cities* was a program that used federal funding as a stimulus to local involvement in reviving the inner cities. At first, cities were to compete for 3 designations as a Model City. While still in the planning stage, the program grew to 10. Congress determined then that each state should have at least one site. By the time the legislation passed in 1966, the number of cities had been increased to over 120—but the funding request was cut from $2.3 billion for over three years to $900 million for two years.[29] Model Cities was eventually abandoned in favor of general revenue sharing, now eliminated, and Community Development Block Grants which struggle for survival. Block grants and general revenue sharing dispersed federal dollars to an ever larger number of communities under formula and less and less targeted to distressed communities. While the Urban Development Action Grants of the Carter Administration tried to focus on severely distressed cities and urban counties, one quarter of the funds were to go to non-metropolitan areas of 50,000 or less. Because there are already a large number of zones in 700 jurisdictions, the possibility is strong that Congress will be tempted to widen the number of zones eligible for federal incentives. In fact, in recent discussions in the House Ways and Means Committee, 100 federal rural zones were proposed. In the debate between a targeted demonstration program with high incentives and a wide program with minimum incentives, Congress will tend toward the latter. Whichever is adopted, the potential of growing regulation and mandates would not be surprising.

State and Local Interest Group Policies

The five major organizations representing the chief elected officials of state and local government—the National Governors' Association, the National Conference of State Legislatures, the National Association of Counties, the National League of Cities, and the United States Conference of Mayors—all have passed resolutions supporting the enactment of federal Enterprise Zone legislation. All, however, indicate caution in the design of that legislation in terms of designation of zones, relationship to state and local governments, and criteria. Several suggest that such legislation should not substitute for other federal support for distressed areas. None comment on the number of zones to be established, but it is to be expected that the number will emerge as a consideration.

In terms of substitution for other programs:

> National League of Cities: An Enterprise Zone program can be a useful addition to existing programs, but it must not be a substitute for them. Moreover, without adequately funded EDA, UDAG, CDBG and related programs, an Enterprise Zone program is likely not to be successful.[30]

> National Association of Counties: Adoption of federal enterprise zone legislation should supplement, and not substitute for other federal development programs.[31]

On the question of how the designations should be made, several of the organizations have indicated that they should be strongly influenced, if not determined, by state and local governments:

> National Association of Counties: The selection of federal enterprise zones should assure local control and should not be contingent upon the willingness of local governments to match federal incentives through local tax abatement.[32]

> National League of Cities: Cities that are eligible for UDAG should be eligible to apply for Zone designation. . . . States should be encouraged to provide additional business investment incentives and Enterprise Zone Programs for local governments, but should not have veto power over eligibility or application procedures.[33]

> National Governors' Association: Federal enterprise zone legislation should set broad geographic targeting guidelines within which states can certify locally developed zone boundaries. A package of complementary federal, state, and local incentives; investments; and services should be developed for each designated zone and should be negotiated in a cooperative agreement among all affected levels of government. The success of a federal program will depend upon the ability to leverage the existing and future state and local efforts directed at these same goals.[34]

> United States Conference of Mayors: Supports an expanded concept of enterprise zones, which would include grants to provide additional social services in these areas, such as job training, adult education, school improvement, anti-drug programs, and child care . . . all cities should be

eligible to apply for these resources, provided that basic thresholds of need are met for specifically designated areas.[35]

Conclusions

Placed in the state and local cauldron, enterprise zones have turned out differently than expected. There are more of them, they are in a wider range of areas, their boundaries vary, they do myriad activities, their goals vary, they are government infused rather than deregulated, they are rural and urban and diversified. This lesson in federalism needs to be understood prior to the passage of federal legislation. Enterprise Zones are a small part of the renewal that has occurred at the state and local levels at the time of diminishing resources allocated by the federal government to subnational governments for domestic purposes. State and local governments have marshalled a variety of resources from many pieces of legislation, and, working with the private sector, have turned an idea into reality. This reality should be protected and nurtured.

The analysis raises questions as to the future role of the federal government. The federal government has made a marked contribution to the development of zones at the state and local government level through its information and evaluation services. One approach is simply to continue these services because the Enterprise Zone concept has already achieved remarkable success. Because these zones will be in existence for some time through state legislation, continued information and evaluation services would be the least obtrusive way to encourage this development without changing its character and probably all that is necessary.

If federal zones are established, however, the legislation needs to take into account the state and local experience, especially in terms of designating zones only in full consultation and partnership with state and local governments.

If zone designation is all that is really needed to encourage economic activity in distressed areas, then this goal has been achieved and additional federal involvement is not required. In addition, given the differences in the research concerning the results of zones, it would seem inappropriate to initiate federal zones. It is certain that additional and more sophisticated research would be useful to assist the country in understanding how to improve conditions in distressed areas. Such information and research would be a tremendous contribution to federalism.

If federal zones are established, their impact should be closely monitored and evaluated. It is hoped that such zones would be developed in the most cooperative, facilitating mode, with awareness of the need to avoid restrictive rules, regulations, and mandates that would adversely affect innovation at the state and local levels.

Notes

1. See U.S. General Accounting Office. (1990). *Federal-state-local relations: Trends of the past decade and emerging issues.* Washington, DC: U.S. Government Printing Office, p. 2.

2. Wolf, M. A. (1989). An essay in re-plan: American enterprise zones in practice. *Urban Lawyer, 21,* p. 42.

3. Zimmerman, J. F. (1989, July). *Federalism theory in the post Reagan era.* Paper presented at Die Geschwister-Scholl-Institut für Politische Wissenschaft, University of München.

4. Ibid.

5. Green, R. E., & Brintnall, M. A. (1988). Comparing state enterprise zones programs: Variations in structure and coverage. *Economic Development Quarterly, 2,* p. 51.

6. U.S. Department of Housing and Urban Development. (1986). *State designated enterprise zones: Ten case studies.* Washington, DC: U.S. Government Printing Office.

7. Friedman, M. (1989, August). Enterprise zones spur business growth. *Area Development,* p. 137.

8. Osborne, D. (1988). *Laboratories of democracy* Boston, MA: Harvard Business School Press, p. 1.

9. See U.S. General Accounting Office. (1988). *Enterprise zones: Lessons from the Maryland experience.* Washington, DC: Program Evaluation and Methodology Division, Report 89-2.

10. Rubin, M. (1990). Urban enterprise zones in New Jersey: A case study. *New Jersey Department of Transportation.*

11. See The President's Enterprise Zone Initiative Fact Sheet, March 29, 1990.

12. Jack Kemp, testimony on enterprise zones, October 1989.

13. Hornbeck, J. F. (1989, October). State enterprise zones and economic redevelopment: Implications for the federal program. *Congressional Research Service,* p. 18.

14. Zimmerman, D. (1989, June). Federal tax incentives for enterprise zones: Analysis of economic effects and rationales. *Congressional Research Service,* summary.

15. Henry, D. L. (1987, August). Enterprise zones offer site incentives. *Area Development.*

16. Friedman, M. Enterprise zones spur business growth, p. 96.

17. See Department of Housing and Urban Development, Enterprise Zone Notes (Fall 1986), p. 13.

18. Pierce, S. R., Jr. (1986). Enterprise zones three years later. *Economic Development Commentary, 10* (Winter), p. 4.

19. Jack Kemp, Testimony.

20. Ibid.

21. Charles Harr, Testimony to Committee on Ways and Means, U.S. House of Representatives (October 19, 1989), p. 4.

22. Friedman, M. (1988). Enterprise zone roundup. *National Association of State Development Agencies* (October), p. 4.

23. Green & Brintnall, Comparing state enterprise zone programs, p. 60.

24. Ibid.

25. President's Fact Sheet.

26. Green & Brintnall, Comparing state enterprise zone programs, p. 52.

27. Hatras, D. (1987). Enterprise zones. *Business Facilities, 20* (May).

28. Ibid.

29. Marshall, P. G. (1989). Do enterprise zones work? Editorial Research Reports. *Congressional Quarterly* (April), p. 236.

30. National League of Cities, National Municipal Policy (1989), p. 45.

31. National Association of Counties. Resolution 2F. on Enterprise Zones adopted July 18, 1989, p. 27.

32. Ibid.

33. National League of Cities, p. 46.

34. National Governors' Association. Policy positions 1989-1990. Adopted August 1989, p. 250.

35. United States Conference of Mayors. Resolution No. 41 adopted June 1989, p. 74.

4

Enterprise Zones Through the Legal Looking-Glass

MICHAEL ALLAN WOLF

Introduction: Law's Necessity

In order to progress (or decline) from grand theory to nuts-and-bolts reality, any economic development or revitalization program must first be shaped in the crucible of law. It takes statutes and regulations to create the framework for the most mundane and the most innovative programs. Legislative acts and administrative rules are a reflection not only of the desires and prejudices of the lawmakers who craft and enact them, but also of the limitations posed by certain fundamental values—such as nondiscrimination, due process, and fair dealing—that are enshrined and protected by state and federal constitutions and by centuries of Anglo-American common law.

The purpose of this chapter is to explore how law has shaped one specific economic development experiment—Enterprise Zones (EZs). As other contributions to this volume indicate, the original proponents of EZs indulged in grand visions of government-free havens to stimulate entrepreneurship and increased employment for the nation's forgotten regions. Taxes would be driven down, financing made easier, and regulations eliminated, ushering in a new pro-business climate.

This attitude was summed up perhaps best (and most enthusiastically) by President Ronald Reagan in his State of the Union Address

AUTHOR'S NOTE: Professor Wolf thanks Kirsten Barron and Niall Paul for their skillful research assistance in preparing this chapter.

in 1982, at a time when federal EZs seemed just beyond the political horizon:

> A broad range of special economic incentives in the zones will help attract new business, new jobs, new opportunity to America's inner cities and rural towns. Some will say our mission is to save free enterprise. Well, I say we must free enterprise so that, together, we can save America.[1]

Somewhat surprisingly, given the president's powers of persuasion, the Reagan years would end without the passage of anything more meaty than the skeletal federal program authorized in Title VII of the Housing and Community Development Act of 1987.[2]

Still, the EZ concept did not languish. The nation of EZs dreamed about by the staunchest zone proponents was realized not through legislation handed down from Capitol Hill, but through state and local efforts in every region of the nation. The Bush years began with active zone programs in two thirds of the states, and with rumblings in a handful of others. In a reversal of governance trends experienced over the past several decades, the states and localities have led the way in EZ experimentation, so much so that House Ways and Means hearings on the concept in October 1989 focused in large part on developments and results in state-authorized zones.[3]

The multi-jurisdictional reality of American EZs has made it difficult to isolate and study any one course of development. Scholars and other observers instead talk in terms of patterns of program components and groupings of states;[4] broad generalizations concerning tools, goals, and results are hard to come by and problematic when proffered. It is thus not surprising that the best quantitative work on EZs has been the studies of individual states.

The natural starting point for state studies is a discussion of the statutory proposals as they make their way through the legislative process. Early on in the history of American zones it became apparent that much of the original theory would not become legislative reality. Inevitably, politics intruded, adding rural and suburban components to what was first conceived of as an inner-city scheme, or assuring influential interest groups that certain regulations would remain untouched. This chapter will explore some of the ways in which EZ statutes reflect these and other political pressures and compromises.

The law in place—statutory, common, and constitutional—has exerted a profound influence as well. In many instances dramatic evolution in legal principles has created a much more positive medium for fostering experimentation than existed just two or three decades previously. In other cases—such as the availability of incentives, the selection of targeted areas, and the eligibility of program participants—real and perceived legal barriers have retarded innovation and experimentation. This chapter will examine some of the positive and detrimental interactions of law and EZs in the formative stages.

Law's effect does not end upon enactment of a zone program. Court disputes and attorney general opinions, though by no means legion, have had an impact on EZ developments as well. A short review of these challenges reveals the continuing, generally supportive, influence of law, as zones have moved through the implementation and operational stages.

The chapter closes with some thoughts concerning future interactions of law and EZs, as state zone programs enter maturity or near renewal, and in the event substantive federal legislation emerges (or even dominates). As the new century dawns, the marriage of law and EZs may well serve as a paradigm for other public/private partnerships, particularly if certain remaining barriers can be overcome.

From Theories to Statutes: Politics Shapes the EZ Concept

I have noted elsewhere the dramatic contrasts between the earliest EZ "paradigm"—that is, zones in theory—and the "second generation of enterprise zones"—that is, zones in practice. As the 1980s began, the leading EZ proponents in this country, advocates such as Stuart Butler of the Heritage Foundation, Representatives Jack Kemp and Robert Garcia, and President Reagan, envisioned "a *federal, supply-side, anti-regulatory, conservative-Republican* program to attract *new, small* business to the *inner city*." By the end of the second Reagan term, a new model had emerged: EZs

> at their most effective are *state and local, public-private, reregulatory* partnerships, passed and endorsed by *liberals, moderates,* and conservatives of *both* parties, designed not only to attract small, *moderate,* and *larger* employers, but also to *retain existing* businesses in urban, *rural,* and *suburban* areas.[5]

Politics is the single most important reason for this gap between idea and reality. Early on, EZs fell victim to the partisan struggles between the Republican White House and the loyal opposition on Capitol Hill. With hindsight, we have little trouble understanding why federal EZs— a new program creating new tax loopholes and anticipating revenue losses—would fail in a political milieu characterized by tax reform fights and budget crises. President Reagan's repeated calls for zone legislation were effectively silenced by congressional opponents like House Ways and Means Chair Daniel Rostenkowski, who only begrudgingly scheduled hearings in late 1983 on a number of EZ proposals (including the administration's) and who consistently refused to budge when it came to including zone tax incentives in legislation headed for the House floor.[6]

There were, too, internecine battles that debilitated administration efforts to present a united front on federal EZs, such as the Department of Treasury's consistently high tax expenditure price tag and the inability of Senate Republican leadership to force the issue with House conferees. The insubstantial Title VII program emerged almost by happenstance, rather than as a result of direct pressure from the executive branch. It was thus up to states and localities to fashion their own zone programs, often in anticipation of a federal program that always seemed just beyond the horizon.

Another key shift occasioned by politics came in the reorientation of state EZs from a novel *supply-side showpiece* to another in a growing number of public-private partnerships. The earliest state proposals, often inspired by the model bill circulated by the American Legislative Exchange Council (ALEC), talked of freeing businesses from the fetters of government and the oppressive burdens of taxation.[7] Although such rhetoric might have been appropriate for describing the status of the private sector vis-à-vis the federal bureaucracy, the situation on the state and local levels was quite different.

The major problems faced by businesses located or interested in many economically depressed areas are often inadequate (or non-existent) infrastructure, government indifference or animosity, and insufficient access to capital from traditional lenders. Moreover, although the state and local tax bite can be significant in dollar terms— particularly when property taxes are part of the calculus—the percentages involved are often quite small when compared to marginal federal tax rates that, as recently as five years ago, approached the 50%

level. Therefore, in order to make the EZ package more attractive and effective, sales, property, personal and corporate income, franchise, and other tax concessions were combined with targeted government expenditures for infrastructure improvements; loan guarantees, subsidies, and creative devices such as tax increment financing; and regulatory streamlining like one-step permitting and much-needed rezoning of designated areas.

The wholesale deregulation foreseen by ALEC and other EZ hardliners was never realized. As zone bills made their way toward enactment, provisions designed to eliminate rent control, building codes, and licensing made way for more temperate language endorsing regulatory revisions as long as health and safety remained protected.[8] In this manner, those responsible for crafting actual EZ statutes have ensured a creative role for the public partner, a role that was hardly envisioned by original zone proponents.

As EZs ran the state legislative gauntlet, there occurred another fundamental departure from the vision of Stuart Butler and other earlier advocates who spoke of EZs as a tool for revitalizing inner-city pockets of poverty, who dreamed of using zone incentives to recreate the kinds of urban villages that Jane Jacobs and others so fondly recalled.[9] The geographic reorientation of federal EZ proposals came early; by 1982 the Reagan Administration had incorporated rural zones into its own bill, following the lead of Wes Watkins (House) and John Danforth (Senate).[10] To this day, rural set-asides are a consistent feature of congressional and executive offerings.

State zone statutes reflect as well the political influence of rural and suburban lawmakers who are quick to point out that economic distress does not end at the boundaries of the central city. Although some early EZ statutes might have referred to *Urban Enterprise Zones,* a careful look at designation criteria reveals a broader approach.[11] Today, in states such as Arkansas, Colorado, Maine, Vermont, and Utah, the central thrust of the program is nonurban, reflecting the special needs and desires of lawmakers and their constituents.

One final example of the ways in which the political process has shaped the legal framework of EZs is the manner in which state legislators have expanded the categories of businesses eligible to receive program benefits. Much early zone rhetoric was influenced most significantly by the findings on job generation of MIT's David Birch; EZ advocates hoped that zone incentives would serve to create the proper environment for the conception and incubation of new, small businesses.[12]

The redevelopment problem faced in many states considering EZs was not only the absence of new businesses in the burned-out ghetto, but also the retention of one or a handful of key employers in a community teetering on the edge of distress. Such diverse needs may breed either stalemate or compromise, depending on the obstinacy and comparative strengths of the political actors. In New York, for example, years of frustration for zone proponents ended with a creative solution: an Economic Development Zones program with enough designations and incentives to please lawmakers from small cities upstate and the devastated neighborhoods of New York City.[13] The Empire State's experience is far from unique, given the widespread use in other states of zone incentives by existing businesses seeking to maintain or expand their investment and employment levels.

The EZ statutory framework forged by the compromises and concessions of politics might vary from state to state, sometimes dramatically. What most, if not all, zone enabling acts have in common is a realistic approach to addressing the serious challenge of economic hardship. For, after all, one role of the legislator is to turn the ethereal dreams of theorists and ideologues into the corporeal blueprints that guide the officials charged with implementing the popular will.

Important Precedents: The Law as a Breeding Ground for Innovation

It might appear that EZs came out of nowhere onto the legislative scene in the early 1980s. On the contrary, the stage had been set over the course of the previous three decades, an evolutionary period during which public-private partnerships in three key areas—economic development, housing, and revitalizations—achieved legal legitimacy and public approval. EZs fit into a well-established and widely accepted pattern.

Economic development partnerships between the public and private sectors have been significantly advanced over the past 30 years by an expanded judicial and legislative appreciation of the notion of *public purpose*. Judges have come a long way since *Loan Association v. Topeka*,[14] an 1875 United States Supreme Court case that invalidated a

Kansas bond program designed to aid a "manufactory of iron bridges." Justice Samuel F. Miller's rationale for the Court's refusal to find a public purpose ironically serves as an accurate prediction of the overwhelming popularity, a century later, of the use of industrial revenue bonds as tax-exempt obligations:

> If it be said that a benefit results to the local public of a town by establishing manufactures, the same may be said of any other business or pursuit which employs capital or labor. The merchant, the mechanic, the inn-keeper, the banker, the builder, the steamboat owner are equally promoters of the public good, and equally deserving the aid of the citizens by forced contributions.

By the 1980s the problem faced by Congress was reining in bond issues—particularly private activity bonds—that were perceived as subject to local abuse and as drains on the United States Treasury.[15] Despite such concerns over individual manifestations, however, the public-private economic development partnership per se runs little risk of dissolution imposed from outside (particularly judicial) forces.

Favorable tax treatment—the key to industrial revenue bonds (IRBs)—has also been employed to address the alarming gap between housing needs and affordable housing availability in this country. The most popular tax incentives include the nearly ubiquitous mortgage interest deduction and more targeted attempts such as accelerated depreciation, low-income housing tax credits, and mortgage subsidy (or revenue) bonds.

As with IRBs, the judicial imprimatur was often sought and secured for these public-private partnerships. In *State v. Housing Finance Authority*,[16] for example, the Florida Supreme Court in 1979 affirmed the validation of a county's mortgage revenue bond program. The court noted with approval the state legislature's "finding that there was a shortage of housing and capital for investment in housing in this state . . . [and] that such shortage could not be relieved except through the encouragement of investment by a private enterprise." Nor was the court troubled by the fact that a private party might be the "primary beneficiary" of the bond issue, so long as "the public interest, even though indirect, is present and sufficiently strong." Such accommodation by the courts has become familiar in the area of housing and economic development incentives, as judges view themselves more and more as facilitators rather than as guardians of the public coffers.

Area revitalization—an area at the essence of the original EZ concept—has also benefited of late by judicial tolerance and encouragement. Following the lead of the United States Supreme Court in the 1954 urban renewal case—*Berman v. Parker*[17]—state and federal judiciaries have expanded the notion of *public use,* the constitutionally mandated prerequisite to the exercise of the government's eminent domain (or taking) power. In *Berman,* Justice William O. Douglas, writing for the majority, in effect merged the notions of public use and public purpose, and narrowed the judicial role considerably: "Once the question of the public purpose has been decided, the amount and character of land to be taken for the project and the need for a particular tract to complete the integrated plan rests in the discretion of the legislative branch." The Supreme Court's message was loud and clear: The judiciary would not block the use of eminent domain for the public cause of urban renewal, even if private parties might incidentally benefit.

In the early 1980s, observers of taking law witnessed the flowering of this concept of judicial deference, as illustrated by three leading cases. In *Poletown Neighborhood Council v. City of Detroit,*[18] the Michigan Supreme Court (with two justices dissenting), answered the following question affirmatively:

> Can a municipality use the power of eminent domain . . . to condemn property for transfer to a private corporation [General Motors] to build a plant to promote industry and commerce, thereby adding jobs and taxes to the economic base of the municipality and state?

An ethnically diverse neighborhood (Poletown) was thus sacrificed for a higher cause, a cause deemed important by local legislators.

Not long afterward the California high court, in *City of Oakland v. Oakland Raiders,*[19] allowed the city's eminent domain action to proceed to trial, despite the football team's insistence that the Raiders were not the kind of property that should be subject to the sovereign's eminent domain power. The court inquired rhetorically: "In this period of fiscal restraints, if the city fathers of Oakland in their collective wisdom elect to seek the ownership of a professional football franchise are we to say to them nay?" Although the city's taking attempt ultimately failed, the legal victory was an important one for states and localities throughout the nation who feel cheated and used by private companies that abandon the community.[20]

In the third case, *Hawaii Housing Authority v. Midkiff,*[21] the United States Supreme Court deferred to state legislators who, in a plan designed "to reduce the perceived social and economic evils of a land oligopoly," authorized the authority to condemn property currently occupied by certain tenants and, in return for compensation paid to the landlords, transfer fee interests to those tenants. Justice Sandra Day O'Connor noted that "the Court has made clear that it will not substitute its judgment for a legislature's judgment as to what constitutes a public use 'unless the use be palpably without reasonable foundation.' " As in *Poletown* and *Oakland Raiders,* the judicial branch—an institution that but a half-century ago might have called a halt to this scheme in the name of "free alienation," the sanctity of private property, or the limited powers of government—allowed the experiment to proceed.

There are direct connections between EZs and these preexisting public-private partnerships. Some state zone enabling statutes, for example, stress the availability of tax-exempt bond issues.[22] Also, EZ efforts have been coordinated with eminent domain efforts and with programs designed to increase the affordable housing stock and improve the quality of existing housing in depressed areas.[23]

The precedential value of such experimentation in public and private sector roles in economic development, housing, and revitalization is even more significant than these direct links. By the time EZs hit the legislative agenda as the "hot" new program of choice, lawmakers, bureaucrats, and, perhaps most importantly, the courts were used to the idea of tampering with traditional public and private roles in the name of the commonweal.

This is not to suggest that there were (and are) no legal barriers to EZ innovation. As the author has noted elsewhere, there are

> six important areas in which current or potential EZs may conflict with federal and state constitutional, common law, or legislative mandates [including] . . . unconstitutional taxation and financing schemes, questionable preferential hiring requirements, anticompetitive decision making, equal protection violations, deregulatory complications, and eminent domain problems.[24]

Sometimes a difference in the wording or meaning of state laws can lead to a variation in the components of zone programs. The most notable example is in the area of property tax incentives. Real property tax abatements, reductions, and exemptions are a popular feature of many EZ packages, but are absent altogether from a number of state programs. This disparity can be seen as the direct result of a strict interpretation of the "equal and uniform" provision found in a number of state constitutions.

Almost without exception, those responsible for crafting EZ enabling legislation have steered clear of legal pitfalls. Still, there are serious questions concerning the fairness of a program that singles out a limited number of geographic areas—and the businesses and residents who happen to be located inside—for special treatment. Because of the great deference granted state and local legislators over the past few decades, those mounting a legal challenge to a program already in place would face significant obstacles. Luckily, however, lawmakers in some cases have included some significant checks on potential abuse, such as designation procedures for noncomplying zones and businesses, carefully drawn qualifications for targeted employees that include nongeographic criteria, and provisions requiring businesses located in EZs before designation to increase employment or capital investment before qualifying for zone incentives.[25]

Today, we can observe nearly 40 variations on the EZ theme in state codes from every region of the country. The similarities and differences that arise in these variously named programs—from *enterprise zones,* to *economic development zones,* to *job opportunity zones,* and beyond—are thus as much a product of general trends in, and jurisdiction-specific variations of, the law in place as they are reflections of the political give-and-take from which the statutes emerged.

EZs at the Bar:
The Experiment Unimpeded

Although courts and other legal arbiters have been far from overwhelmed by challenges to EZ programs, over the past decade there have been a few dozen reported opinions by judges and attorneys general regarding the legitimacy and operation of zone programs. From that limited body of evidence, it can be said confidently that the precedents discussed above have served EZs well: In only a very few instances have legal decision makers cried "foul." The great majority of cases and attorney general opinions have either affirmed the legality of the state program or simply answered inquiries concerning EZ statutory or administrative provisions.

The opinions fall into three general categories—validity, governmental authority, and eligibility. For the most part, courts and attorneys general have affirmed the power of state legislatures to create EZs.[26] A 1982 Virginia attorney general opinion, for example, stated that proposed EZ legislation would not be prohibited by either federal or state constitutional and statutory law. Attorney General Mary Sue Terry reasoned, in part:

> The creation of . . . tax incentives is well within the power of the General Assembly so long as the Assembly's action is reasonable. Here the desirability of promoting economic strength in certain underdeveloped areas manifestly provides a basis for concluding that the action is reasonable. State and federal constitutional prohibitions against special legislation or denial of equal protection do not prohibit classification for tax purposes, and the necessity for and reasonableness of classifications are primarily questions for the legislature.[27]

Terry did, however, note an inconsistency between the act's unemployment tax credits and certain provisions of the Federal Unemployment Tax Act.

Other decision makers concur with Terry's general approval. State Attorney General Michael Turpen concluded that Oklahoma's EZ act—a statute that "includes sufficient qualifications, requirements and governmental controls for achieving its public purpose [increasing employment]"—did not, on its face, violate three key provisions of the state constitution.[28] Nor, according to the Oregon attorney general, did that state's program, allowing for enhanced police and fire protection within designated zones, violate the state constitution's privileges and immunities clause.[29] These and other legal officials have allowed legislators and administrators to proceed with fine-tuning the often unique set of incentives packaged together under the EZ label.

As EZs moved out of the enactment phase, a number of additional questions have arisen, questions concerning government authority to implement this new development tool. Who is qualified to serve on the bodies responsible for overseeing the EZ experiment?[30] What is the relationship of political subdivisions to state zone authorities, to qualified businesses, and to competing local government units?[31] What roles do the governor and state agencies play in the EZ process?[32] What effect does amendment of the EZ enabling statute have on participating concerns?[33]

Variations in state legislative language can, of course, lead to different legal conclusions. Assistant Attorney General Thomas Gay, in his November 2, 1984, reply to an inquiry from Arkansas State Senator Cliff Hoffman, noted that a city could be "selective in waiving the sales tax for one qualifying business applicant and not waiving the sales tax for another."[34] A contrary holding appears in a Louisiana attorney general opinion from 1988: "A local governing authority has no power to choose where, when, whom and how much of the local sales and use tax to be exempted."[35] This diversity—the EZ experiment progressing in what Justice Louis Brandeis called the "laboratory of the states"[36]— is one of the beneficial by-products of the failure of Congress and the White House to come to agreement on federal EZs, a program that would instead feature a single statutory framework, one group of regulations, and, eventually, a uniform set of interpretations.

The third, and most numerous, set of reported opinions goes to the heart of the matter, at least as far as private sector participants are concerned. On several occasions, judges and attorneys general have been asked to respond to specific inquiries concerning the eligibility of businesses that are considering, or already taking advantage of, EZ incentives.[37] Such inquiries can lead to an exploration of legislative history or analogous cases, as judges and attorneys general attempt to discern the meaning of terms such as "primarily nonretail" and "new buildings or structures or additions."[38]

Because the legislative record is often sparse (or nonexistent), and because precedents are rare in this new area, legal decision makers run the risk of defeating the intended (though unstated) reasons for promulgating EZ programs. For example, in *C.W.O., Inc. v. Commissioner of Revenue*,[39] a 1986 Minnesota Tax Court case, Judge Carl A. Jensen ordered approval of the company's EZ tax credits. The Commissioner's position was that C.W.O.—a company that had purchased the equipment and remaining business of a financially strapped company called C.W. Olson, Inc.—had shifted jobs from Minneapolis and Garfield to Montevideo, thus violating the statutory prohibition of credits to businesses transferring employment from one part of the state to a designated EZ. Judge Jensen noted that C.W.O., "despite its deliberately similar name . . . [was] an entirely new corporation with new and different stockholders," and that "whether the credits were given or not, the jobs . . . were already lost."

There are some troubling aspects to this case, such as the fact that one Olson officer (a 7.5% shareholder of C.W.O.) was hired by the new company, and the fact that the sale was at first contingent on securing EZ credits. It is quite possible that this move involved just the kind of intrastate incentive-shopping that state lawmakers sought to prevent. There is also the nagging question of whether the interests of former employees in Minneapolis and Garfield were considered adequately by the court. Even so, it appears that the overriding goals of the EZ program were better served by the court's understanding view.[40]

The interaction of the judicial, legislative, and administrative branches will continue as long as EZs remain operative. Questions of validity will come up as each new state program is enacted, and as each new zone wrinkle is fashioned. Inter- and intra-governmental disputes promise to spawn even more inquiries to legal officers. Lawyers, accountants, and other advisers will zealously continue to pursue favorable treatment for their business clients, and judicial arbiters will continue to play a role in resolving ambiguities and inconsistencies. There is every indication that that role, despite the occasional caveat, will remain a supportive one.

Shaping the Law to Come: EZs and the New Public-Private Partnership

EZs have evolved into a creative, provocative, and at times important economic development and revitalization tool for several states and localities throughout the United States. Businesses that choose to locate in zones often cite the EZ incentives as a key—though not often decisive—factor. Government officials have employed EZs in a decided effort to enhance a pro-business atmosphere for potential and existing employees. The future promises additional designations in states with programs, and more programs in states currently outside the EZ fold.[41]

This chapter has demonstrated how the law has shaped the EZ experiment to this point—how political compromise has given rise to a new EZ paradigm, how judicial deference has cleared the way for new public and private roles, and how legal arbiters have generally allowed the zone experiment to proceed. The chapter concludes with some preliminary thoughts about the future relationship of law and EZs, and considers how the zone experience can be translated in shaping those public-private partnerships on the horizon.

There is little chance that state (and federal) lawmakers will be relieved of significant budgetary pressures in the foreseeable future, or that the political winds will suddenly shift so that active government controls are viewed as favorable, or even benign. It is therefore quite likely that lawmakers, public policy experts, and others interested in effective governance will continue to explore public-private partnership mechanisms. Those responsible for shaping these new partnerships (including, of course, the public-private joint ventures given birth by any substantive federal EZ program that might materialize) should heed the state and local EZ experience for lessons in three key areas: accountability, bureaucratic coordination, and monitoring.

As with a purely private partnership, the participants in the EZ joint ventures look for assurances that each side will remain committed to the original goals and promises. Unfortunately, two legal principles stand in the way of a lasting and effective partnership, a relationship in which each party is truly accountable. First, several legal principles—such as the rule that governments may not bargain away the police power—may operate in such a way as to remove the public partner's obligation to live up to the arrangement.[42] Recently, however, particularly in the area of conditional zoning and land-use development agreements, courts have become more accepting of formal contracts between governmental units and their private partners.[43]

The second potential legal trouble spot is the protection of the private partner's privacy interest in financial and investment information. A 1983 Louisiana attorney general opinion, for example, states that the Department of Commerce must keep such information confidential to protect companies considering relocating to the state in order to take advantage of EZs and other programs.[44] This wide-reaching legal protection of the expectation of privacy may prevent the public sector from making a full investigation of such key claims as financial exigency that justify the availability of EZ incentives that would otherwise be inaccessible to an ongoing concern. In the future, courts should consider granting greater access to internal financial information, but *only in limited circumstances,* in order to enable public officials to make an informed decision as to the distribution of costly tax expenditures.

Bureaucratic coordination, like accountability, is a goal that EZs have yet to reach with any marked success. Too often revenue officials, eager to collect the highest possible tax payment, gloss over or refuse the tax incentives advertised and promoted by the commerce or economic development department responsible for administering EZs.

There have also been instances of localities clashing with their neighbors, with other political subdivisions, and with state bureaucrats over the location, value, and operation of zones.[45] From the beginning, state lawmakers should provide for a smoother transition from statute to partnership in action, even if it means stepping on a few departmental toes.

Those eager to learn from the EZ experience will find it hard to locate solid, empirical data indicating success or failure.[46] Monitoring is, unfortunately, too often an afterthought, perhaps because there is no tangible pay-off in a direct expenditure for a careful study. Savings over the long run are often hard to sell at the state capitol (and in Congress). If EZs are to inspire additional public-private partnerships, academics, private business, even the press, should call for monitoring up front, so that all interested observers can keep track of the joint venture's progress.

If EZs and the law are to continue their happy (and healthy) relationship, these and other modifications should be the subject of debate on popular, political, legal, and academic levels. Only if the process of innovation continues to evolve will EZs be worthy of the deference and indulgence they have received to this point.

Notes

1. Reagan, R. (1982). Address before a joint session of Congress reporting on the state of the union. *Public Papers of the Presidents, 1,* 76.

2. Housing and Community Development Act of 1987, Pub. L. No. 100-242, tit. VII, §§ 701-706, 101 Stat. 1815, 1957-64 (1988).

3. Gray, T. (1989). Enterprise zones: Bipartisan Comity or Washington Comedy? *Tax Notes, 45,* 378-380.

4. See, for example, Brintnall, M., & Green, R. (1988). Comparing state enterprise zone programs: Variations in structure and coverage. *Economic Development Quarterly, 2,* 50-68.

5. Wolf, M. (1989). Enterprise zones: A decade of diversity. *Economic Development Quarterly, 4,* 3-14.

6. See Boeck, D. (1989). The enterprise zone debate. *Urban Lawyer, 16,* 71-173.

7. American Legislative Exchange Council. (1982). Enterprise zone act. In *The source book of American state legislation,* 1983-1984, pp. 33-44. Washington, DC: Author.

8. See, for example, *Ky. Rev. Stat. Ann.* § 154.695(2) (Michie/Bobbs Merrill 1987).

9. Butler, S. (1981). *Enterprise zones: Greenlining the inner cities.* New York: Universe, pp. 82-84.

10. Boeck, Enterprise zone debate, 89-90.

11. For example, Virginia's Urban Enterprise Zone Act (1982), stated "the governing body of *any* county, city or town may make written application to the Department to have an area or areas declared to be an Urban Enterprise Zone." *Va. Code Ann.* § 59.1-274 (1987) (emphasis added). In 1988, the statute was renamed the Enterprise Zone Act.

12. Butler, *Enterprise zones,* 77-80.

13. "Such zones designated shall be, as far as practicable, equally distributed between urban, suburban and rural areas." *N.Y. Gen. Mun. Law* § 960(d) (McKinney Supp. 1988).

14. 87 U.S. (20 Wall.) 655 (1975).

15. See Staff of Joint Committee on Taxation, 99th Cong., 2d Sess. 1987. *General Explanation of the Tax Reform Act of 1986.* Washington, DC: Committee Print, p. 1151.

16. 376 So.2d 1158 (Fla. 1979).

17. 348 U.S. 26 (1954).

18. 410 Mich. 616, 304 N.W.2d 455 (1981).

19. 32 Cal.3d 60, 646 P.2d 835, 183 Cal. Rptr. 673 (1982).

20. Haar, C., & Wolf, M. (1989). *Land-use planning: A casebook on the use, misuse, and re-use of urban land.* Boston: Little, Brown, p. 816.

21. 467 U.S. 229 (1984).

22. See, for example, *La. Rev. Stat. Ann.* § 1789 (1987).

23. See *City of Duluth v. State,* 390 N.W.2d 757 (Minn. 1986) (approving use of eminent domain to enhance border city EZ); *Ill. Ann. Stat.* § 612(a)(13) (Smith-Hurd Supp. 1987) (authorizing local zone organizations to provide services for "rehabilitation, renovation, and operation and maintenance of low and moderate income housing").

24. Wolf, M. (1986.) Potential legal pitfalls facing state and local enterprise zones. *Urban Law and Policy,* 77-130. See also *Davis v. City of Portsmouth,* 579 F.Supp. 1205 (E.D.Va. 1983) (dismissing action based on allegations that EZ program amounted to racial discrimination).

25. See, for example, *N.Y. Gen. Mun. Law* § 969 (McKinney Supp. 1988) (dedesignation of zone); *Ohio Rev. Code Ann.* § 5709.64 (Baldwin Supp. 1987) (employee targeting criteria); *Mo. Ann. Stat.* § 135.225(7) (Vernon Supp. 1988) (criteria for expanded facilities).

26. The only major exception is a 1983 opinion by Tennessee Attorney General William Leech that "blew the whistle on the 'Local Enterprise Zone Act of 1983,' citing state constitutional strictures. He was particularly concerned with the 'troublesome constitutional question . . . presented by the tax exemption provisions of the proposed legislation.' " Wolf, Potential legal pitfalls, p. 82. State lawmakers revised the EZ proposal and the enacted program contains no such offending provisions. See Op. Tenn. AG No. 85-236, Aug. 30, 1985: "The 1984 legislation either deletes or amends the provisions considered objectionable by this office and provides a constitutionally valid scheme for the economic development of enterprise zones."

27. Op. Va. AG No. 623, Sept. 2, 1982.

28. Op. Okla. AG No. 83-218, Feb. 24, 1984.

29. Op. Ore. AG No. 5909, Dec. 12, 1985. The clause reads: "No law shall be passed granting to any citizen or class of citizens privileges, immunities, which, upon the same terms, shall not equally belong to all citizens."

30. See, for example, *Legislative Research Committee v. Brown,* 664 S.W.2d 907, 920, 924 (Ky. 1984) (invalidating selection procedures and membership provisions of several state boards, including Enterprise Zone Authority); Op. Ky. AG, Sept. 10, 1982 (officials of Urban County Government may be appointed to zone authority).

31. See, for example, Op. La. AG No. 86-663, August 28, 1986 (state may exempt zone businesses from taxes imposed by school board); Op. La. AG No. 88-440, October 26, 1988 (locality cannot compel EZ business to hire local workers exclusively); Op. Ark. AG No. 84-204, Nov. 2, 1984 (city cannot waive local sales imposed by county-wide election); Op. La. AG No. 83-471, July 25, 1983 (school board is not "governing authority" under EZ act); *Gay v. City of Springdale*, 298 Ark. 554, 769 S.W.2d 740 (1989) (court rejected challenge to annexation based on city's desire to acquire contiguous, EZ-eligible tracts).

32. See, for example, Op. La. AG No. 86-474, August 25, 1986 (governor's approval); Op. La. AG No. 85-848, November 26, 1985 (Board of Commerce and Industry may not delegate to staff the power to approve EZ applications); Op. Ore. AG, Nov. 10, 1986 (department's rule on building additions exceeds scope of enabling statute).

33. See, for example, Op. La. AG No. 88-405, Sept. 15, 1988 (renewal of EZ contract governed by terms of original state legislation).

34. Op. Ark. AG No. 84-204, Nov. 2, 1984.

35. Op. La. AG No. 88-440, Oct. 26, 1988.

36. *New State Ice. Co. v. Liebmann,* 285 U.S. 262, 311 (1932) (Brandeis, L., dissenting).

37. See, for example, Op. Ill. AG No. 85-014, July 19, 1985 (letter from Boone County State's Attorney includes details of a local corporation's "plan to change its production facility substantially").

38. Op. Ore. AG, December 3, 1987; Op. Ore. AG, June 24, 1986.

39. 1986 WESTLAW 9364 (Minn. Tax 1986).

40. See also Op. La. AG No. 86-15, Jan. 30, 1986 ("So long as the reopening of the Amex plant meets the [EZ Program] requirements . . . , and the closing and reopening was not fraudulently conceived to 'reap' the benefits offered by the Program, then the reopening . . . may be considered . . . as a new business and new jobs.")

41. States like New York continue to designate additional zones according to the statutory timetable, while Illinois and others have increased the maximum number of designations. Legislative interest is currently stirring in New Mexico, Massachusetts and Iowa.

42. See generally Reynolds, O. (1982). *Handbook of local government law.* St. Paul, MN: West, pp. 648-655.

43. See Wegner, J. (1987). Moving toward the bargaining table. *North Carolina Law Review, 65,* 957-1038.

44. Op. La. AG No. 82-860, January 14, 1983.

45. Generally, however, EZs have fostered a spirit of cooperation, as public and private participants move toward common goals. See Wolf, M. (1989). An essay in re-plan: American enterprise zones in practice. *Urban Lawyer, 21,* 29-53.

46. One of the few quality pieces is Rubin, M., & Armstrong, R. (1989). *The New Jersey urban enterprise zone program: An evaluation.* Report prepared for New Jersey Department of Commerce, Energy and Economic Development.

5

Framework for a Comparative Analysis of State-Administered Enterprise Zone Programs

MICHAEL BRINTNALL
ROY E. GREEN

The enterprise zone concept has had an unusual history in the United States. It was originally taken from foreign experience, raised to national prominence during the 1980s as a philosophical illustration of a wider strategy for economic and social policy, and adopted by state and local governments as a platform for experimentation and initiative.

Three major policy streams have influenced these developments, converging in the states to create both commonalities and differences in state enterprise zone initiatives. Each policy stream represents a different focal point or vantage from which American policymakers have acted. Analysts should be aware of this background to assess the evolution of the concept since its introduction.

Specifically, the different policy streams that have guided development of enterprise zone programs are the following:

AUTHORS' NOTE: This chapter was adapted for this volume from an original article published by the authors. Brintnall, M. & Green, R. E. (1988). Comparing state enterprise zone programs: Variations in structure and coverage. *Economic Development Quarterly, 2,* 50-68.

- the analytical/theoretical evolution that focuses on why the concept is expected to work, based on economic theory and the concept of public-private partnerships;
- the political/philosophical base of the issue that focuses on why the concept is considered a good idea, valued whether it has substantial economic benefits or not. This perspective relates the enterprise zone idea to prospects for more limited government intervention into economic affairs, and to the operations of the federal system;
- the legislative/programmatic focus that addresses how state and local government have adapted the concept to their own agendas.

Early evidence suggests that enterprise zone programs within the states have been influenced by all three of these policy streams.

We believe that these three policy streams are important starting points from which to raise several basic questions about the state experiences with the enterprise zone concept. The questions include asking: along what dimensions do state programs vary the most and the least; what is the balance of economic versus political objectives; to what extent do the novel features of the enterprise zone concept become subverted to existing state practices; how are individual states with operating programs arrayed along these dimensions; which state enterprise zone programs conform the most closely to narrow ideas about economic growth and which incorporate broader community development themes?

We have identified seven key dimensions on which we believe actual state programs are likely to vary and along which they can be compared. These dimensions are derived from a review of the policy streams that we contend have influenced the various state enterprise zone programs, and from our direct experience with federal and state efforts. These dimensions, and their relationship to the policy streams generating the enterprise zone idea, are as follows:

(1) *The extensiveness of state and local government intervention in program management.* In a pure sense, the economic and political ideas behind enterprise zones call for very limited government intervention, in deference to market forces. As a general pattern, however, many state governments are adopting a more activist orientation to economic development and program management, and may be expected to steer enterprise zones aggressively.

(2) *The degree of private-sector cooperation and involvement in program design and zone management.* Enterprise zones are often defined as a subset of a larger realm of public-private sector cooperation in achieving public policy aims. This cooperation is central to the enterprise zone concept. But the way that the public-private sector relationship is institutionalized in the design and operation of the program may vary widely within the states.

(3) *The degree to which the goals of the enterprise zone program extend beyond job creation to incorporate broader social and community development objectives.* Creation of new jobs and business ventures is an objective of all enterprise zone proposals and programs. Some programs, however, may go beyond the concerns of employment, tax rates, and general business activity to include concerns for a community's overall infrastructure, facilities, or the delivery of social services.

(4) *The extent to which the state's program is tolerant of risk.* Enterprise zones are intended to encourage risk-taking by participating entrepreneurs within targeted areas. But we expected to find variation in a state's willingness to share in that risk, in the state's willingness to test enterprise zone applicability in a variety of intra-state economic, social, and political contexts, and to allow the zones to persist for a long term without substantial oversight.

(5) *The extent to which the state program meets the expectation for being innovative.* The enterprise zone concept's most basic promise is that it will go beyond repackaging economic techniques that have been tried in the past. It seems reasonable to expect, however, that state programs would vary in providing new incentives previously unavailable for local development in the state or initiating activities in which the state does not previously have experience.

(6) *The emphasis placed by the state government on the enterprise zone program as a marketing device for economic development.* The business community frequently charges that it is often unaware of the availability of economic development incentives that might influence business location or expansion decisions. As a consequence it seems plausible that some states may actively market their enterprise zone programs.

(7) *The level of internal political consensus that characterized the enactment and implementation of each state program.* Critics have challenged the enterprise zone concept in many ways. They have questioned, for example, whether it is truly a significant or innovative tool for economic development and whether it creates new economic opportunity or merely redistributes what already exists. The degree of support and consensus behind the program ideas, in states with widely varying objectives and

public policy traditions in the first place, is likely to be highly varied. This in turn is likely to cause major differences in what the states attempt to do.

The Structure of State
Enterprise Zone Programs

Our first step in classifying different state program types was to examine closely what each state was actually doing. We then identified patterns of program design and operation, beginning with a look at variation in program structure. Later we related this variation to differences in state program goals, techniques, supports, and eventually performance.

Initial focus was on two dimensions of state program structure. The first looked inward within state government to the degree of agency involvement in program management. The second looked outward to the involvement of the private sector in design and management. We discuss each of these below, and then combine them to provide a core framework to classify state enterprise zone program style.

The analysis was based on a survey of state enterprise zone directors conducted in the Fall of 1985. Seventeen states (representing 18 different programs) out of the 24 states with legislation enacting programs at the time responded to our lengthy mailed questionnaire.[1]

Enterprise zone programs are changing constantly, and many additional states have enacted and implemented programs since our survey. Others have changed their programs since we surveyed them, and some have enacted programs yet to be implemented. The Florida program, for example, has gone through two substantial reformulations since our study. Because of this, the classifications in this chapter are not intended to pinpoint what any particular state is doing right now. They are useful as a complement to existing program descriptions and analysis by identifying variations in the way state programs are structured and what they have been attempting to accomplish. The case studies that follow in this book provide depth and analysis within this framework.

State Management

Classic treatments of the enterprise zone concept have suggested that zone programs are largely *self-executing*, not calling for active public oversight or reviews. This perspective has followed from both the economic and political implication of the free market orientation of the concept. Some states, however, have deviated from this principle. Enterprise zones have not emerged in a vacuum, and many states have embraced the enterprise zone idea with the arms of their own management experience and philosophy. We expected a major dimension in program operations to reflect variation in the degree the state actively manages its enterprise zone program and requires local governments to manage their zones. The index of management activism that we established was based on six indicators from our survey:

- whether the state required a local plan for each zone;
- the frequency with which the state modified or expected to modify local zone applications;
- whether the state required local managers be appointed;
- whether the state provided training for local managers;
- the frequency with which the state provided or expected to provide technical assistance to local zones; and
- whether public reports about the zones were required.

The states with the most management involvement, as indicated by having a score more than one standard deviation above the average score on the index, were Illinois, Missouri, California, Mississippi, and Indiana. States with especially low scores on this index were Georgia and Kansas. The state with the score closest to the average for all states on this score was Pennsylvania. Table 5.1 lists all states in our sample on this indicator by their standard score. A negative number indicates lower than average management involvement, and a positive number indicates higher involvement.

Public-Private Cooperation

A second key dimension to understanding enterprise zones is the extent to which private-sector groups are active participants in the development and operation of the program. Public-private cooperation is of course central to the enterprise zone concept. Whether this private-sector role occurs openly through private assistance in managing the program itself or behind the scenes through rational action within the marketplace in response to the enterprise zone incentives is an open

Table 5.1 Degree of State Management Involvement

State	Score
Georgia	−1.5
Kansas	−1.3
Tennessee	−0.9
Arkansas	−0.9
Texas	−0.8
Florida	−0.8
Kentucky	−0.6
Maryland	−0.4
Louisiana	−0.3
Pennsylvania	0.0
Virginia	0.2
Minnesota	1.0
Indiana	1.1
Mississippi	1.1
California	1.1
Missouri	1.3
Illinois	1.5

question. We based our index of public-private cooperation on five indicators, as follows:

- whether there was a state advisory group for the program;
- the number of nongovernmental groups reported to be actively involved in program design;
- the average importance of the role played by such groups in design as reported by the state program director;
- whether the program required consensus agreements be established with citizen groups within each zone; and
- whether public-private business partnerships were required within each zone.

The states with especially high levels of public-private cooperation were Indiana and Kentucky. States that were especially low were Georgia (allowing zones only in Atlanta), Missouri, Louisiana, and Minnesota. The state with the score closest to the middle of the index, a sort of "median" state, was Kansas. Table 5.2 lists all states in our sample on this indicator by their standard score. A negative number indicates lower than average degree of public-private cooperation, and a positive number indicates higher cooperation.

Table 5.2 Degree of Public-Private Cooperation

State	Score
Georgia	−1.4
Missouri	−1.3
Louisiana	−1.1
Minnesota	−1.1
Florida	−0.8
Mississippi	−0.6
Arkansas	−0.3
Texas	−0.3
Virginia	−0.3
Kansas	0.0
Maryland	0.4
Illinois	0.6
California	0.8
Tennessee	0.9
Pennsylvania	1.0
Indiana	1.6
Kentucky	1.9

Classifying States

The management and the public-private dimensions, we believe, distinguish the two major components of variation in the enterprise zone concept. They reflect the degree of internal state effort directed to the program, and the degree of external, private, involvement. As we expected, they were independent dimensions. The correlation between the two indexes is small (.1).

By cross-classifying these two indexes, we identified four types of enterprise zone programs within the states: an *activist* program with high levels of state management and of private group involvement; a *managed* structure, with high levels of state management and low levels of private group involvement; a *private* structure, with low levels of state management involvement and high levels of private group participation; and a *hands-off* structure, with low levels of both state management and private group involvement in the program.

States were assigned to each group by classifying them as high or low on each index based on their score relative to the average score. Figure 5.1 is a plot of each state, based on the standardized score of each index.

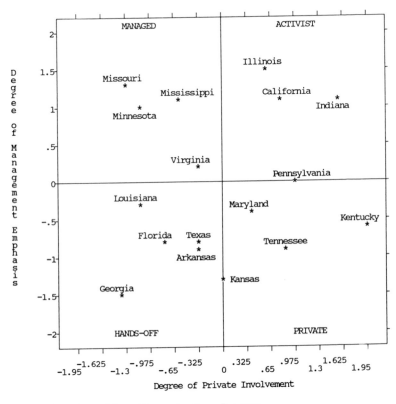

Figure 5.1. Type of State Enterprise Zone Program

Describing Program Variation

We were interested in whether differences in state enterprise zone programs correspond with other differences in state demography and policy experiences. In particular, we wondered whether the same factors that are related to whether a state has a program at all were also related to the kind of program a state implemented.

Although we found some characteristics that differentiate states with hands-off, private, and managed program structures, the major distinctions set activist programs apart from these others. Each of the key demographic factors is discussed separately below. Many of them are highly interrelated. Given the few states with enterprise zone programs, it was not possible to identify the multivariate effects.

Region was a major factor distinguishing types of enterprise zone programs. Not only were Southern states more likely to have enterprise zone programs, but their programs tended to be different from those in other regions. Half of the Southern enterprise zone programs we studied were of the hands-off structure, with low management involvement and less private involvement. None of the Southern programs were identified as activist.

Activist states were also clearly different in other ways. The activist states were larger. They had a distinctly higher *liberalism* score, which is a record of prior policy activism.[2] On average, the activist states were above the average for the United States on this score. States with the other three types of enterprise zone program structures were below the average for the nation. Activist states had higher unemployment rates than the other states, had existing programs targeting aid to distressed areas, and had Republican governors.[3]

States may be influenced in adopting and designing enterprise zone programs by what their counterparts are doing. We asked whether the design of state programs was influenced by enterprise zone programs in other states, and by the federal enterprise zone proposals. About half the states reported some or a great deal of influence from other states. Those reporting such influence tended to be those adopting a hands-off type of program structure, and were clustered together in the South. Commonalities shared by the Southern programs may have arisen both because of common circumstances and because of diffusion of ideas and approaches among them.

About two thirds of the states reported some or a great deal of influence from the federal initiative in their program design. There was no difference in program types adopted by states reporting such influence. Perhaps not surprisingly, at the time of our survey in 1985, states with Republican governors reported strong influence from federal initiatives twice as often as states without.

A state's political structure was also associated with variation in program structure. States with strong interest groups and weak political parties were far more likely to have adopted hands-off or private program types. States with strong parties and weak interest group domination tend to have managed or active programs.[4] In general, we believe the measure of interest group and party strength was more a

Table 5.3 Characteristics of States at Time of Enterprise Zone Diagram Enactment by Type of Enterprise Zone Program as of Fall 1985

Program style	Number of states	1983 Population (average)	Percentage in South	"Liberalism" score	Percentage Republican governors	1983 Unemployment rate
Hands-off	5	7780	80	−0.87	0	9.2
Private	4	3782	50	−0.23	25	9.1
Managed	4	4313	50	−0.62	25	9.2
Activist	4	13508	0	0.61	100	11.0
Unclassified	13	3652	15	0.37	31	9.2
No Program	20	3028	15	0.02	20	8.9

SOURCE: Sources of data for table are cited in text.

reflection of a general level of political development and differentiation in the state than a specific indicator of interest group involvement in the enterprise zone program alone.

Table 5.3 summarizes key data for states exhibiting each of the four enterprise zone program types, for states without zone programs at all, and for states with zone programs for which we did not have data to classify a program type.

Other Dimensions of State Activity

Our research looked at several other dimensions of state program activity as well. We developed indices for each added dimension in a manner analogous to that described above for state management and public-private cooperation, and related the resulting scores to program structure and state characteristics. Several of these other dimensions are the following.

Program Objectives

We classified program objectives by whether the state articulated an explicit interest in community and neighborhood development as well as job creation. We found a relationship between what states have done in the past, and what they attempt to do with their enterprise zone program. States that have targeted aid for community development before also tended to adopt a broader range of objectives for the enterprise zone program. This linkage appeared to be specifically related to community development activity, because there was not any relationship between enterprise zone program objectives and the more general liberalism score.

We also found that variation in program objectives was not tightly determined either by state characteristics or by program structure. Program objectives themselves are variable. Any attempt ultimately to assess the impact of enterprise zone programs must account not just for what the state actually did, but for what it hoped to do.

Initiative

Another program dimension we measured was the extent to which states employed new initiatives in their programs. For this we considered whether incentives were designed explicitly for enterprise zones, and whether the state actively reduced regulatory burdens in the areas, instead of repackaging existing activities.

We found that states with a high level of policy activism across the board also had a higher degree of new initiatives in their enterprise zones. States with more active types of program structure also tended to have a higher degree of new initiatives. On the other hand, new programs with little involvement of state agencies or private sector groups tended as well to have few new tools with which to work.

Evaluability Assessment of State-Administered Enterprise Zone Programs

One of the major reasons for the lack of evaluation research on state-administered enterprise zone programs has been that the concept's integral components have not been sufficiently defined. Policymakers and analysts have thus had difficulty establishing criteria for individual or comparative analysis of state programs. We had in this chapter conducted an initial evaluability assessment of state enterprise zone programs by attempting to bound and refine the concept through actual program analysis from two perspectives: the potential users of evaluation, and the evaluator.

We still believe that the classification of state enterprise zone programs that we began in 1985 continues to have value in at least two related aspects. It offers an important benefit as a baseline for comparison of state activity in current policy decision making within states. It also can help to provide a standard to compare and assess future evaluation studies of state programs similar to those reported in the next section of this volume.

State enterprise zone programs are fundamentally different from each other—in management style, program goals, and so forth—but these differences are not always apparent and officials in the states may not even recognize them. The typologies begun in this chapter can help officials in states without programs to identify states with a style they would like to adopt, to use as models. They can assist states with on-going programs to identify others with similar strategy or structure to compare program experiences and to place into proper context the experiences of neighboring states that may have different types of programs in place.

There are two ways in which the matching of program styles can take place. One way is for policymakers to identify the type of program they are interested in—such as active or passive management, broad or narrow objectives—and then to identify from the classifications suggested here a state or states that fit the criteria. Another approach, perhaps more responsive to the way state by state interaction really takes place, is for policymakers to identify individual states with which they feel comfortable making a comparison, and then checking the typologies suggested here to see what kind of program operations those states might have. In either case, we believe an important use of the classifications is to help those interested in this level of policymaking to find each other, and to help analysts understand more accurately what each state is really trying to do.

Another use of the classifications is to guide future impact evaluation studies. We have found that there are dimensions to the enterprise zone concept that can be overlooked in an evaluation that focuses solely on economic achievements. The zone concept has political and management dimensions, as well as an economic one. The politics and management of zones are not just design considerations—although our study shows considerable variation in them. They are also program goals themselves. An important question to be answered about enterprise zone programs is whether states find they must trade off achievements in one of these dimensions—economic, political, management—for achievements in the others, and if so, how they do it.

The findings in this study show that program goals and program design of state programs do vary. We were able to identify some factors that appear to account for this variation. For example, major differences existed between activist states and others. Activism in turn was associated with increased innovation and reduced risk. Much more remains to be learned about how enterprise zone programs work, however, and what they accomplish.

What Comes Next?

We encourage the reader, in the next section of this volume, to look at a set of in-depth, singular, and comparative case studies, for greater understanding of other sources of variation among the states. The breadth of economic objectives adopted by a state is an example of what to look for. We found in our research that a state's decision to broaden program goals beyond job creation by incorporating community development objectives was not correlated with state characteristics or management style.

There is no single path to be followed for evaluating state enterprise zones. It is unrealistic to expect there will be a comprehensive national evaluation that might internalize the between- and within-state variations in approaches to each program's important dimensions. Further, there are many different kinds of questions to ask about the programs, which require different research designs to implement.

Therefore, we have included in the following section three case studies (Florida, Maryland, and New Jersey) and two comparative assessments (one by Elling and Sheldon on enterprise zone programs in Illinois, Indiana, Kentucky, and Ohio; and another by a team of researchers headed by Rodney Erickson at Pennsylvania State University that includes a nation-wide 17 state program analysis). Many of these states represent programs that we had identified from our 1985 survey as being different programmatic types. All four types of state enterprise zone programs are represented by one or more of the studies. All of these studies are based on information collected since our survey was done, giving the reader an opportunity to assess changes that may have occurred in program structures and operations.

Notes

1. The states responding to our survey were: Arkansas, California (2 programs), Florida, Georgia, Illinois, Indiana, Kansas, Kentucky, Louisiana, Maryland, Minnesota, Mississippi, Missouri, Pennsylvania, Tennessee, Texas, and Virginia.

2. The measure includes Walker's index of innovativeness, the McCrone-Cnudde Scale of antidiscrimination provisions, average AFDC payments, earliness of ratification of the ERA amendment, number of state consumer-oriented provisions, and percentage of federal Title XX social service program funds actually spent in 1976. Klingman, D., & Lammers, W. (1984). The general policy liberalism factor in American state politics. *American Journal of Political Science, 28,* 598-610.

3. Sources of data for these measures are: U.S. Bureau of the Census. (1984). *Statistical abstract of the United States.* Washington, DC: U.S. Government Printing Office; Council of State Governments. (1984). *Book of the states.* Lexington, KY: Council of State Governments; and U.S. Advisory Commission on Intergovernmental Relations. (1985). *The states and distressed communities: The final report.* Washington, DC: U.S. Government Printing Office.

4. Interest group and party measures come from Sarah McCalley Morehouse's study of state government; because interest group and party measures are almost perfectly negatively correlated, we have treated them here as essentially the same measure. Morehouse, S. M. (1980). *Politics, parties and policy.* New York: Holt, Rinehart and Winston, 107ff.

PART TWO

The Practice of
Enterprise Zones

Section A

Case Studies of Individual State Enterprise Zone Programs

6

Florida's Enterprise Zone Program:

The Program After Sunset

WILLIE LOGAN, JR.
LEE ANN BARRON

Enterprise zones in Florida have undergone extensive changes in the first decade of their existence, evolving from *slum and blighted areas* to *superzones*. Florida's Legislature asserts that it enacted the nation's first state enterprise zone program during its 1980 legislative session. Although the enterprise zone program is one of the most heavily studied economic development programs in the state, concern for accurate and reliable information on the effectiveness of zone incentives continues to worry state officials.

The State of Florida currently maintains 30 approved enterprise zones eligible for various tax credits and exemptions, regulatory relief, and preference in grant and loan programs. The existing zones were chosen by a competitive process in 1986 based on physical and socioeconomic distress (65%) and local participation (35%). Tables 6.1 and 6.2 identify the specific factors used in selecting Florida's enterprise zones. All zones and their accompanying incentives will sunset on December 31, 1994.

The competition for Florida's enterprise zones was conducted within population categories, guaranteeing the creation of both urban and rural zones. Although not required by legislation, Florida's zones are geographically distributed throughout the state. Figure 6.1 contains a map reflecting the location of the state's approved enterprise zones. Legislation dictated the creation of up to six zones in each of the following population categories:

(1) Communities having a population of less than 7,500 persons.
(2) Communities having a population of 7,500 persons or more but less than 20,000 persons.
(3) Communities having a population of 20,000 persons or more but less than 50,000.
(4) Communities consisting of census tracts in urbanized areas having a total population of 50,000 persons or more but less than 125,000 persons.
(5) Communities consisting of census tracts in urbanized areas having a total population of 125,000 persons or more.

Rule 9B-37, Florida Administrative Code, required that population categories be based on 1980 U.S. Census data in order to provide standardized information.

Benefits provided to Florida's approved enterprise zones include:

(1) The Enterprise Zone Jobs Credit which permits a corporate income tax credit equal to 15% of the wages paid to enterprise zone residents, Aid to Families with Dependent Children (AFDC) recipients, or economically disadvantaged persons.
(2) The Enterprise Zone Property Tax Credit, which provides a corporate income tax credit equal to 96% of the ad valorem taxes paid on the property.
(3) Eligibility for the Community Contribution Tax Incentive Program. Corporations contributing to approved nonprofit organizations conducting eligible community development projects in enterprise zones or other eligible areas receive a corporate income tax credit equal to 50% of their donation.

Table 6.1 Enterprise Zone Scoring Factors

Distress Criteria (65%)

---

1. The percentage of housing units in the area built more than 30 years ago.
2. The percentage of year-round housing units in the area that are vacant rental housing units.
3. The percentage of housing units in the area that lack some or all plumbing facilities.
4. The per capita income in the area.
5. The percentage of change in per capita income in the area from the prior year to the current year.
6. The percentage of the population in the area that is over the age of 65 and the percentage of the population that is under the age of 18.
7. The unemployment rate in the area.
8. The percentage of the population in the area having incomes below the poverty level.
9. The per capita taxable value of property in the area.
10. The percentage of change in the per capita taxable value of property in the area from the prior year to the current year.
11. The per capita local taxes levied in the area.

Local Participation Factors (35%)

---

1. The adoption of the local option economic development property tax exemption.
2. The adoption of occupational license fee abatement.
3. The adoption of utility tax abatement.
4. The targeting of locally generated funds to be expended for capital projects in specified amounts to the area authorized to be an enterprise zone.
5. The eligibility of the area authorized to be an enterprise zone for the Urban Development Action Grant Program.
6. The commitment of specific additional local government services to the area authorized to be an enterprise zone.
7. The targeting of federal community development funds in specified amounts to the area authorized to be an enterprise zone.
8. The adoption of a community redevelopment plan and an ordinance funding a community redevelopment trust fund.
9. A commitment to reduce the impact of specific local government regulations within the area authorized to be an enterprise zone.
10. A commitment to issue industrial revenue bonds for projects located in the area authorized to be an enterprise zone.

Figure 6.1. Florida Enterprise Zones

(4) Eligibility for the Community Development Corporation Support and Assistance Program. Nonprofit corporations conducting community development projects in enterprise zones or other distressed areas are eligible to receive administrative grant funds and zero interest loans.

(5) Sales tax exemption for building materials used in the rehabilitation of real property in an enterprise zone. A refund of taxes paid on the purchase of building materials used to rehabilitate real property in an enterprise zone is available if the assessed value of the property increases by at least 30% over the prior year assessment.

(6) Sales tax exemption for business equipment used in an enterprise zone. This incentive provides a refund of taxes paid on the purchase of tangible personal property such as office equipment, warehouse equipment, and some industrial machinery for use exclusively in the enterprise zone.

(7) Sales tax exemption for electrical energy used in an enterprise zone. A 100% sales tax abatement is available to businesses located in an enterprise zone on the purchase of electrical energy. This abatement is only available if the municipality in which the business is located has passed an ordinance to exempt enterprise zone businesses from 50% of its municipal utility tax.

(8) The credit against sales tax for job creation in enterprise zones. This incentive reduces a business firm's sales and use tax by $100 for each eligible new full-time employee and $50 for each eligible new part-time employee hired.

(9) Various local incentives such as the economic development ad valorem tax exemption, municipal utility tax exemption, occupational license tax exemption, industrial revenue bonds, and targeting of state, federal, and local community development funds.

(10) Additional incentives and encouragements for development through state housing and community and economic development programs.

Florida's existing enterprise zone program is the product of prior experience with enterprise zones during the early 1980s. An examination of the legislative history of the early program provides great insight into the construction of the program that exists today.

Legislative History

In 1980, the Legislature passed three corporate tax incentives for use in economically disadvantaged areas of the state: the *Economic Revitalization Jobs Creation Incentive Credit,* the *Economic Revitalization Tax Incentive Credit,* and the *Community Contribution Tax Incentive Credit.*[1] These tax credits, introduced by Representative Barry Kutun, were limited to slum and blighted areas designated according to the procedures outlined in chapter 163, Florida Statutes. Additional incentives included expanded use of Industrial Revenue Bonds in slum and blighted areas, provision of grants and loans to nonprofit community development corporations, and the local option property tax exemption for economic development.[2]

In enacting the Economic Revitalization Jobs Creation Incentive Credit, the Legislature considered that approximately 1,700 jobs had been lost in the 1980 Liberty City civil unrest. Ensuring the reemployment of these individuals was crucial to the recovery of this economically depressed area.

The adopted legislation contained factors to measure the level of economic distress in areas seeking designation as a tax credit area; however, procedures for approval were not outlined—such as a competitive process or a minimum distress level. The analysis accompanying the proposed legislation incorrectly assumed that Dade County would be the only area to participate in the program, predicting an annual cost of $310,500; however, records of testimony by the bill's sponsor reveal that the program was presented to legislators for consideration on a state-wide basis. Program designers probably never expected that annual program costs would one day exceed $28 million.

The concept of enterprise zones was introduced to the Florida Legislature in 1981. Communities throughout the state had expressed interest in participating in the economic revitalization program. Many objected, however, to the requirement that eligible areas be designated as "slum and blighted". Therefore, House Bill 1201 was introduced which permitted communities to call the tax credit areas "enterprise zones". Under that legislation, a community could designate an area to be either a slum or blighted area or an enterprise zone. In either case, all of the tax credits authorized in 1980 would apply. This bill did not pass the Legislature.

The Legislature adopted the enterprise zone name in 1982 as proposed by the Committee on Tourism and Economic Development, with formal legislative findings, definitions, and intent language.[3] Unlike the 1981 proposal, all eligible tax credit areas were referred to as enterprise zones. Those areas that had been locally authorized as slum and blighted areas for participation were "grandfathered" into the new program. Today, the statutory definition of an enterprise zone still remains virtually indistinguishable from that of a slum and blighted area, the designation required to invoke authority for tax increment financing.

In 1983, the Florida Senate began expressing concern over the proliferation of enterprise zones. An analysis prepared for SB 1166 by Senator Meek stated

The Department of Community Affairs has, to date, designated 117 enterprise zones in Florida, which have a total population of 1,046,092, ten percent of the state's population. The Department is currently creating new zones at the rate of one or two a week.

This same analysis also pointed out the "highly targeted" nature of enterprise zone programs in other states. SB 1166, which proposed additional incentives for enterprise zones, did not pass.

Following the 1983 legislative session, the House Committee on Tourism and Economic Development conducted an interim study of Florida's Enterprise Zone Program. The study revealed that the average percentage of the population of a jurisdiction residing in an enterprise zone was 19.5%. Three local governments had designated their entire jurisdiction as an enterprise zone. Santa Rosa County's enterprise zone population comprised 75% of its residents and its zones covered 472 square miles. Although the report expressed concern over the indiscriminate approval of enterprise zones, it noted that areas receiving enterprise zone approval generally contained higher levels of distress than the jurisdiction in which they were located. The report concluded that:

(1) The large number of enterprise zone approvals undercut the value of the incentives offered because the same incentives were available in many areas, some of which were less distressed than others.
(2) Constantly changing or unpredictable boundaries contributed to uncertainty in the business community and wasted public relations resources.
(3) Few local governments offered their own incentives for development in enterprise zones after seeking approval for state tax credits.

The 1984 Legislature enacted most of the recommendations of the House Tourism and Economic Development Committee interim report in HB 1218 and scheduled the majority of the changes to take effect on January 1, 1987.[4] The bill prohibited the Department of Community Affairs from approving any new enterprise zones upon becoming law. At that time, the Department had approved 172 resolutions for approval effecting 136 separate enterprise zones concentrated into 61 cities and 11 counties. An average of 37.11% of the population of a designating local government resided in an enterprise zone. Each of these existing zones were scheduled to expire on December 31, 1986.

Although most economic development professionals agree that the number of zones under the old program was unmanageable, a sunset report of the program in 1986 by the House Committee on Tourism and Economic Development noted:

(1) Per capita income in the zones was less than 80% of the county or metropolitan statistical area (MSA).
(2) The percentage of persons with incomes below the poverty level was 125% of the level for the county or MSA.
(3) The percentage of families with incomes below the poverty level was 150% of the rate for the county or MSA.
(4) The percentage of housing more than 30 years old was 150% of the rate for the county or MSA.
(5) The percentage of housing lacking some or all plumbing facilities was 175% of the rate for the county or MSA.

In establishing the new enterprise zone program to take effect January 1, 1987, the Legislature prescribed a competitive selection process based on physical and socioeconomic distress and local participation. In addition, the legislation required that at least one local participation factor be offered by the local government and authorized the Department of Community Affairs to refuse approval to any area that was not contained within the 20% most distressed areas of the state. The additional incentives originally proposed in 1983 were authorized for the 20 new enterprise zones. According to the staff analysis for HB 1218, the new enterprise zone incentives were expected to cost the state less than $3 million in additional annual revenue loss.

The bill provided approximately three and a half years for the Department to develop its comprehensive distress indicator, the Community Conservation Index, draft rules governing the selection of the new enterprise zones, and accept and review applications. However, no staff or resources were provided to accomplish these tasks. In addition, the Department was required to develop a research design for use by the Auditor General in evaluating the program in 1990. Annual reports were required by the legislation to provide data on the effectiveness of the program.

Responding to local government and industry requests, the Legislature approved the creation of 10 additional zones for the new program in 1986.[5] This legislation also amended the maximum population requirement for the zones by permitting the population of the zone to be up to the percentage of families below the poverty level in the jurisdiction or 10% of the population of the district, whichever was greater.

The reduction from 136 zones of various sizes to 30 zones with increased incentives led Florida's economic development community to label the newly approved areas superzones. The redesign of Florida's enterprise zone program reduced total costs from approximately $28 million in 1986 to just over $10 million in 1988.

Revisions to the "New" Program

Despite a complete restructuring of the Florida Enterprise Zone Program in 1986 and extensive study of the program, additional legislative and administrative actions have been necessary to improve the program and allow it to operate effectively.

Concerned about the coordination of tasks among agencies involved in the program, the Department of Community Affairs sought the formation of an interagency task force. All departments cited with responsibility for the program in the Florida Statutes were asked to participate on the task force formalized by interagency agreement. These departments included:

(1) The Department of Community Affairs, responsible for the direct administration of the Enterprise Zone Program.

(2) The Department of Commerce, which generally serves as the first contact for businesses desiring to locate within the state and provides assistance to in-state businesses that could be seeking to expand.

(3) The Department of Labor and Employment Security, responsible for providing certifications to enterprise zone residents stating the tax benefits eligible to potential employers.

(4) The Department of Revenue, which receives and reviews all applications for tax credits and exemptions and collects state taxes.

(5) The Department of Health and Rehabilitative Services, which provides assistance to families through AFDC. AFDC recipients are eligible employees for business firms desiring to claim the Enterprise Zone Jobs Credit or the Credit Against Sales Tax for Job Creation, regardless of their residence.

In addition, staff of the appropriate legislative committees and the Department of State informally participate on the task force. This task force continues to operate as needed.

In 1988, while considering amendments to the job creation incentives, the Legislature recognized the need for resources to market the enterprise zone program and provide assistance to businesses and local governments. One professional staff position, one part-time clerical position, and $8,000 for the development of marketing brochures were authorized and appropriated by the Legislature on a recurring basis. Prior to that time, the program had been administered on a part-time basis by a single professional responsible for the administration of the Community Contribution Tax Incentive Program. Program marketing had been left exclusively to the participating local governments except for the provision of brochures in 1982 developed under a U.S. Department of Housing and Urban Development 107 Technical Assistance Grant.

Responding to constituent requests for additional enterprise zones, the 1988 Legislature also authorized the Secretary of the Department of Community Affairs to approve up to 20 additional zones "following a review of the effectiveness of the 30 enterprise zones approved prior to January 1, 1987." In order to complete the effectiveness review, the Department of Community Affairs enlisted the assistance of the interagency task force to prepare and analyze questionnaires and conduct on-site inspections. The task force split over a recommendation in support of the creation of the new zones and presented its factual report to the Secretary of Community Affairs without a recommendation. The Secretary delayed his decision and has not issued an opinion as of this writing. No new zones may be created after July 1, 1990.

Other changes adopted in 1988 included an expanded pool of eligible persons for the Enterprise Zone Jobs Credit and the Credit Against Sales Tax for Job Creation. Prior to 1988, business firms could claim these benefits when hiring residents of an enterprise zone or—if the business itself was located in an enterprise zone—a recipient of AFDC. Chapter 88-201, Laws of Florida, expanded the definition of new employee to include Job Training Partnership Act participants who were economically disadvantaged. *Economically Disadvantaged* was defined as a person who:

(1) Receives, or is a member of a family that receives, cash welfare payments under a federal, state, or local welfare program.

(2) Received a total family income for the preceding 6-month period not in excess of the higher of the poverty level as determined by the Office of Management and Budget or 70% of the lower living standard income level.

(3) Receives food stamps pursuant to the Food Stamp Act of 1977.

(4) Is a foster child on whose behalf state or local government payments are made.

(5) Receives Aid to Families with Dependent Children (regardless of the location of the business in an enterprise zone).

In order to reduce the economic impact to the state, the bill also reduced the amount of the Enterprise Zone Jobs Credit from 25% to 15% of the wages paid to the eligible employee. The Credit Against Sales Tax for Job Creation was similarly reduced from $130 to $100 a month for each full-time employee.

In early 1989, the House Committee on Small Business and Economic Development issued a report on all economic development grant and loan programs administered by the state. This report criticized state agencies for failure to implement the rule review and regulatory flexibility provisions of the Enterprise Zone Act. Section 290.013, Florida Statutes, states that each state agency rule adopted after January 1, 1987, when applicable, shall provide encouragements and incentives that will assist in the redevelopment of enterprise zones. Stating the need to provide tangible benefits to local governments, the report recommended establishing legislative preference for enterprise zones in competition for the state's economic development funds and resources. As a result, preference for enterprise zones was included in the Economic Development Transportation Fund.[6] An unsuccessful attempt was made to direct the state's job training funds available under the Sunshine State Skills Program to approved enterprise zones.[7] The Enterprise Zone Program is also linked to the Florida Safe Neighborhoods Program, an innovative crime prevention program designed to correct environmental design features of neighborhoods which contribute to crime.[8]

Initially, the Department of Community Affairs, the administrative agency with primary responsibility for the enterprise zone program, made only a cursory attempt to implement the rule review provisions, providing bonus points for limited categories of the Small Cities Community Development Block Grant; however, in 1988, the Department reevaluated its position and enacted several rules providing benefits to enterprise zones. The agency initiated an internal administrative procedure that required its bureaus to prepare a memorandum for each amended or new administrative rule, stating any positive or negative impact on enterprise zones. Following this initiative, bonus points were provided in the competition for funds under the Community Development Corporation Support and Assistance Program, the Housing Predevelopment Trust Fund, the State Apartment Incentive Loan Program, the Elderly Homeowner Rehabilitation Program, and the Florida Quality Development Program. In addition, the existence of a project in an enterprise zone serves as a "tiebreaker" for scoring under the Elderly Housing Community Loan Program.

The House Committee on Small Business and Economic Development intends to include preference for enterprise zones in other state programs whenever possible.

Despite criticisms of uncertain boundaries in the early program, the Legislature has twice yielded to local government requests and permitted amendments to enterprise zone boundaries. Barring additional legislative changes, the existing boundaries will remain stable through 1994.

Evaluation

One of the major criticisms of the "old" enterprise zone program was the lack of data for evaluation of the program. The State could not prove or disprove the effectiveness of the program due to the confidential nature of tax information filed at the Department of Revenue and the lack of reporting requirements. The 1984 revision to the program provided for the submittal of annual reports by all local governments participating in the program. Extensive reporting requirements were introduced to ensure that local participation promises were kept and that updates were provided on the level of physical and economic distress in the zones. The data provided by local governments in their reports is culminated into a comprehensive enterprise zone annual report.

Two local governments failed to submit an annual report after the first year of operation under the new program. The Legislature therefore enacted provisions for the rescission of enterprise zone approval for failure to submit the report.

The initiation in 1988 of a special form to be completed by business firms utilizing the enterprise zone benefits should provide detailed information on the extent to which credits are claimed and the areas receiving the greatest benefit from the program. State officials asserted that information on credits and exemptions utilized is essential to evaluate the effectiveness of the enterprise zone incentives, and pursued legislation to exempt this information from the confidentiality provisions generally granted to firms claiming tax exemptions. Submittal of these forms officially began in April of 1990 with the data expected to be reflected in the Department's Annual Report due March 1, 1991.

The Department's 1989 Annual Report notes a 32% increase in the number of businesses located in enterprise zones, rising from 25,542 in 1987 to 33,806 in 1989. Building permits issued for new construction between 1987 and 1989 total 2,954. An additional 11,334 building permits were issued for rehabilitation during the same period.

In addition to the annual report, the Auditor General is required to conduct a review of the program. This review, originally scheduled for 1990, has been postponed until 1992 to allow the use of 1990 census data.

As noted earlier, the interagency task force completed an effectiveness review of the Enterprise Zone Program in early 1989. Although the effectiveness report provided great insight into local government administration of the program, the report was prepared without benefit of the changes that took place in 1988 and did not provide conclusive results on the effectiveness of the enterprise zone tax incentives. Although the report was critical of local government administration of the zones, over 90% of the zones have developed brochures or other local marketing materials. The State does not fund the administration of the program by local governments. The report also revealed that during the first two years of the program, 41,689 jobs had been created at a cost to the state of $23.4 million or $562 per job. The on-site enterprise zone inspections convinced participants that all zone areas were the most economically distressed areas of the communities in which they were located. Although the population of the zones remained stable, substandard housing continued to be a major problem in the zones. The report also noted that the Enterprise Zone Jobs Credit was responsible for most employment improvements and that other enterprise zone incentives had not been widely used.

Possible Future Changes

At the request of the Department of Community Affairs, Representative DeGrandy filed HB 1821, which authorizes an Urban Demonstration Enterprise Zone Program, for the upcoming 1990 session. The bill provides for the creation of two urban enterprise zones from communities with populations greater than 50,000 persons. Enhanced state incentives and mandatory local incentives are provided for the demonstration zones as well as state funded, locally controlled nonprofit community development corporations to market and administer the zones.

In 1987, the Legislature made provisions for capital improvements funding for enterprise zones providing the applying community utilizes the innovative planning process of crime prevention through environmental design. Several enterprise zone local governments were awarded planning grants in 1988 and 1989 to prepare safe neighborhoods plans that demonstrate the relationship between criminal activity and environmental factors in the zone. During the 1989 session, the Legislature approved appropriations for safe neighborhoods capital improvements in three enterprise zone neighborhood improvement districts; however, these appropriations were vetoed by Governor Martinez. During the 1990 session, the Legislature will again seek appropriations for the three districts vetoed in 1989 and several additional enterprise zone neighborhoods.

Notes

1. Chapters 80-247, 80-248, and 80-249, Laws of Florida, respectively.

2. Chapters 80-250 and 80-287, Laws of Florida, and Senate Joint Resolution 9E, respectively. The Joint Resolution was implemented pursuant to chapter 80-347, Laws of Florida.

3. Chapter 82-119, Laws of Florida.

4. Chapter 84-356, Laws of Florida.

5. Chapter 86-152, Laws of Florida.

6. House Bill 1679 by the Committee on Small Business and Economic Development and Representative Logan.

7. House Bill 1702 by Representative Reddick.

8. Part IV of chapter 163, Florida Statutes.

7

Urban Enterprise Zones in New Jersey:

Have They Made a Difference?

MARILYN MARKS RUBIN

Introduction

New Jersey's robust economic growth in the 1980s was not distributed evenly throughout the state's 21 counties, but occurred, for the most part, in 7 of its southern and western counties—generally in newer suburban and rural communities. In contrast, older central cities, located primarily in the highly industrialized northeastern part of the state, experienced population losses and economic distress characterized by disinvestment and rising unemployment rates. In August 1983, in an effort to revitalize these cities, the New Jersey Legislature enacted The New Jersey Urban Enterprise Zones Act (P.L. 1983, ch. 302). This Act authorized the provision of State tax incentives and other benefits to encourage business growth in geographically targeted areas in distressed urban communities, i.e., in Urban Enterprise Zones (UEZs). The fundamental purpose of the Act, as stated in its preamble, was to "stimulate economic activity within zones so designated." [1]

New Jersey's Urban Enterprise Zone legislation was neither the State's initial attempt to target aid toward declining central cities, nor its first attempt to use tax incentives to encourage economic development. The Act did, however, represent a bipartisan effort by the State's Republican governor, and the Democratic leadership in the State Legislature, to ameliorate urban distress using tax incentives to private businesses rather than direct government subsidies to municipalities.

Notwithstanding skepticism among some legislators and other public officials about addressing urban distress and job generation through the supply-side approach, the UEZ Program engendered a great deal of enthusiasm among many politicians who saw benefits to their constituent municipalities of a UEZ designation. Thus, the original legislation, stipulating that no more than 2 zones were to be designated in any one year, was amended to accelerate the designation process. By the end of 1985, 10 zones were designated, the maximum number allowable under the UEZ Act. Additional pressure from some legislators and others to expand the maximum number of zones to 15 was diffused, primarily on the grounds that the existing program had not yet been evaluated.

An analysis of the UEZ Program conducted in 1986 had provided preliminary evidence that the UEZ Program was "creating new infusions of private capital, thereby bringing about the creation of new employment in New Jersey's most distressed urban communities."[2] However, incentives to businesses responsible for this capital infusion also constitute costs to government in foregone tax revenues. The question thus arose: what is the impact of the UEZ Program on New Jersey when benefits accruing from UEZ-induced economic growth are compared with costs associated with the Program?

This case study addresses the cost-benefit question by focusing on New Jersey's UEZ Program over a two-year period. Using survey data for 1987 and 1988, for almost 1,000 firms participating in the Program, and an economic model of New Jersey, the study estimates the cost-efficacy of the Program. Survey data and the economic model are also used to isolate economic growth attributable to the UEZ Program from that which would have occurred in its absence. The study's findings suggest that the UEZ Program is a cost-effective tool in the State's economic development arsenal, yielding $1.90 in State and local taxes for every dollar in tax revenues foregone by the state as a result of tax forgiveness to UEZ businesses.

New Jersey's UEZ Program may differ somewhat from programs in other states with regard to zone selection criteria, incentives offered, and administrative structure. The methodological approach described in this case study is, however, suggested as a way to evaluate any enterprise zone program that uses geographically targeted tax incentives to promote urban revitalization.

The New Jersey Urban Enterprise Zone Program: Administrative Parameters

In Brintnall and Green's comparative study of state enterprise zone programs, a framework was developed to classify and compare states with respect to: (1) the management dimension; and (2) the public-private cooperation dimension.[3] In their study, the *management dimension* reflected the degree of internal state effort directed to the enterprise zone program and the *public-private dimension* measured the degree of external, private involvement in the program. Although New Jersey was not one of the states included in the Brintnall-Green analysis, applying their typology to the State would position it just about at the midpoint of both the management and public-private sector continuums.

The following section of this chapter, which provides additional information on the administrative structure of New Jersey's UEZ Program, sets the framework within which the cost-effectiveness of the Program can be assessed.

UEZ Administration

General oversight of New Jersey's UEZ Program is vested in a nine-person Enterprise Zone Authority (The Authority), with four of the nine members State Cabinet officials who serve ex officio: the Commissioner of the Department of Commerce (Chair); the Commissioners of the Department of Community Affairs and the Department of Labor; and the State Treasurer. Each ex officio member has a direct or indirect role in the administration of the UEZ Program. For example, to be eligible to apply for UEZ designation, a municipality must be designated by the Commissioner of Community Affairs as an "area in need of rehabilitation."[4]

The Authority's remaining five members are appointed by the Governor with the advice and consent of the Senate. They are prohibited from holding any elective office or State employment. Qualifying credentials for the public members include training and experience in local government, finance, economic development, or volunteer civic service and community organization. The legislation does not specify the role of the public members, but each has generally brought his or her own agenda to The Authority depending upon the constituency represented.

Day-to-day operations of the UEZ Program are vested in the Office of Urban Programs (OUP) in the State's Department of Commerce. The OUP has primary responsibility for operationalizing the criteria used by The Authority in UEZ designation, and for reviewing municipal applications for such designation. Given OUP's responsibilities, it is not surprising that the real impetus for the cost-effectiveness study presented in this case study came from this part of State government. After conducting the preliminary UEZ evaluation previously discussed, and faced with legislation proposing additional zones, OUP recommended that an evaluation of the UEZ Program be conducted to ascertain its cost-effectiveness. The results of this evaluation are presented in later sections of this chapter.

In the following section of this chapter, the criteria that OUP uses to assess municipal applications for UEZ designation are summarized, as is the UEZ designation process.

The Zone Designation Process

The UEZ Act specifies how a specific area, within a qualifying municipality, is designated as an enterprise zone. First, the zone has to be designated (or be eligible for designation) by the State as an area in need of rehabilitation. Second, the municipality has to meet criteria relating to urban distress, as defined by The Authority.

In designating the first two zones, The Authority was constrained by the UEZ Act itself, which, by stipulating the precise criteria to be applied, effectively assured that the 2 most distressed cities in the State would be chosen, that is, Camden and Newark. The remaining 8 zones were selected, on a competitive basis, from 16 municipalities that met the distress criteria as defined by The Authority, and submitted applications for UEZ designation. These applications were in the form of a Zone Development Plan, adopted by the governing body of the municipality, and containing a description of zone boundaries and existing economic conditions in the city and in the zone. Each plan also had to provide a detailed prescription for economic revitalization of the proposed zone area.

As is the case with all states in Brintnall and Green's study, the overriding objective of New Jersey's UEZ Program is job creation, but an analysis of the factors used in New Jersey's UEZ selection process indicates that community and neighborhood revitalization efforts were also considered. Indicative of this additional focus by the State is the preference given to cities with Zone Development Plans that, among other factors, showed the greatest potential for addressing urban distress. This concern with neighborhood revitalization is not unexpected given the State's previous commitment to distressed areas. According to Brintnall and Green, one of the strongest factors influencing a state's interest in development objectives beyond job creation is "the presence of state development programs for distressed areas already on the books."[5]

All of the cities receiving New Jersey's UEZ designation were able to demonstrate a private sector commitment of resources to the development process. This commitment is seen by Brintnall and Green as central to the enterprise zone program concept.[6] Although an important factor in New Jersey's UEZ designation process, this commitment is not institutionalized. It is, instead, voluntary but seen by The Authority as a signal of the private sector's willingness to work with State and local government in revitalizing distressed areas.

Upon recommendation by the Department of Commerce's Office of Urban Programs, the cities selected by The Authority for UEZ designation were: Elizabeth, Plainfield, Jersey City, Kearny, Trenton, Bridgeton, Millville/Vineland (two-city, joint zone), and Orange. Cities not chosen were: Passaic, Paterson, Asbury Park, East Orange, Long Branch, and Hoboken.

Zone Benefits

Once a municipality is selected to be in the UEZ Program, businesses within the targeted area become eligible to apply for *qualified business* designation. This designation is based upon either a company's existence in the zone at the time of zone designation, or upon its meeting criteria relating to the hiring of new employees.[7] To remain in the Program, a business is required to maintain a specified employment level which must be reported, in the annual recertification process, to the Department of Commerce.[8]

With one exception, all major benefits available under the UEZ program accrue to qualified businesses in the zone. The one exception provides that projects in UEZ cities, regardless of where they are located, be given priority consideration in applications to New Jersey's Local Development Financing Fund (LDFF).[9] All UEZ businesses are permitted the least restrictive and time-consuming ways to conform with governmental regulations. The major benefits to UEZ businesses, however, are tax credits and exemptions that, using Erickson and Friedman's typology of incentives, can be classified as investment and labor credits.[10]

Illustrative of Erickson and Friedman's labor incentives, three of New Jersey's six UEZ benefits provide tax incentives to UEZ companies to hire so-called disadvantaged workers with specific characteristics, generally related to poverty and/or welfare status. Two of the labor incentives give companies tax credits of up to $1,500 to be applied against their State Corporation Business Tax liability. These credits are available to the UEZ company for each new full-time employee who was previously unemployed and/or receiving public assistance, and who meets specified residence requirements.[11] The third labor incentive entitles the UEZ business to an Unemployment Insurance Tax rebate for each new employee whose gross annual salary is less than $18,000.

Under the investment incentives, a qualified business may be entitled to exemptions from sales and use taxes on the purchase of all tangible personal property except motor vehicles. Moreover, the sale of materials, supplies, or services to a contractor, subcontractor, or repairman for exclusive use in erecting structures or improving real property within an Enterprise Zone is exempt from sales and use taxes.

The UEZ Act also authorizes the designation of certain Enterprise Zones in which retail sales (except sales of motor vehicles) are subject to sales and use taxes at 50% of the state's tax rate (currently 7%). The Sales Tax collections from UEZ businesses eligible for this incentive are deposited in the Enterprise Zone Assistance Fund (EZAF) and earmarked for spending in the zones for public improvements or for upgrading selected municipal services. The creation of the EZAF may be seen as further evidence of New Jersey's interest in overall community revitalization, rather than simply in the more narrowly defined job creation objective.

It should be noted that incentives to UEZ businesses are associated with employment and investment activity in a specific year. For example, Sales Tax exemptions for 1987 only relate to investments made in 1987, and Corporate Tax credits for 1987 are one-time credits for new employees hired in 1987. Although these credits may be carried forward on the company's tax return (applied against tax liability in a later year), they should be considered "one-shot," rather than ongoing, UEZ Program costs.

Table 7.1 Program Costs: New Jersey Urban Enterprise Zones[a]

Source of Cost	Cost (Dollars in Millions)
Sales Tax Exemptions	41.0
3% Sales Tax in 5 cities	9.7[b]
Corporate Tax Credits	0.2
Unemployment Insurance Tax Rebate	0.2
Administrative Costs	0.5
TOTAL	51.6

NOTES: a. Costs are calculated over the 1985-1988 period, but are primarily for 1987 and 1988 since 80% of total program costs are associated with the sales tax exemptions for investments made in these years.
b. This cost does not include the $9.7 million in sales taxes collected by the state government and placed in the Enterprise Zone Assistance Fund. Although a cost to the state's General Fund, the $9.7 million is not revenue foregone to the state's overall fiscal base, because it is placed in the Enterprise Zone Assistance Fund which is earmarked for use in the UEZs.

Program Costs

All of the tax incentives described above constitute costs to government in foregone revenues. Indeed, almost all UEZ Program costs are attributable to taxes foregone by the State as a result of tax exemptions and credits. Data on the actual dollar value of foregone revenues were available for some UEZ tax incentives, but not for all. For cost data not routinely available from state agencies, estimates were made specifically for this study, either by the New Jersey Division of Taxation or by the author.[12] Table 7.1 shows UEZ Program costs for each of the tax incentives.

The New Jersey UEZ Evaluation

On one side of the UEZ cost-benefit analysis are the costs portrayed in Table 7.1; on the other side are the benefits to the State in tax revenues resulting from the jobs and investment generated by UEZ businesses. To determine the cost-effectiveness of the New Jersey UEZ Program, costs were compared with benefits for 1987 and 1988 in a study conducted by the author for New Jersey's Department of Commerce.[13] The remaining sections of this chapter are based on the methodology and findings of this study.

Data Sources

New Jersey's governmental agencies collect only limited data on the UEZ Program. Therefore, the quantitative information necessary for the cost-benefit analysis was obtained from a mail survey sent to all qualified businesses that had been in the UEZ program for at least one full year as of June 30, 1988. Adjusting the survey base for business decertifications, moves, and mergers left a population of 976 companies that both met the full-year criterion and were still in the Program at the time the survey was administered.

The 49% survey response rate yielded a solid base of micro-level data. However, to assess the cost-effectiveness of the UEZ Program, data were needed for the entire 976 companies in the study, not just the 478 respondents. Acknowledging the nonrandom nature of the respondents, but faced with the need for micro-level data for nonrespondents, it was decided to use the company-specific data available from the New Jersey Department of Commerce as the basis for extrapolating characteristics of nonresponding firms.

As part of the UEZ Program's annual recertification process, the Department of Commerce collects information on jobs created and investments made for all firms in the Program. A statistical analysis of these data for 1987 and 1988 showed no significant difference between respondents and nonrespondents with respect to size (as measured by number of employees) or industry (as identified by four-digit standard industrial classification [SIC] codes).[14]

Given the results of this statistical analysis, and in the absence of any other available information, firm-level data for nonrespondents were extrapolated on the basis of industry-wide relationships for respondents. To illustrate: If responding firms in Industry A reported average annual per-employee earnings of $26,000, this value was assigned to nonresponding firms in Industry A. Actual and estimated firm-level data were aggregated to the industry level and used to estimate the benefits attributable to the UEZ Program, as described in the following section on methodology.

Methodology

Various analytic techniques have been used to evaluate state enterprise zone programs, including econometric modeling[15] and shift-share analysis.[16] Neither the regression analysis used in the econometric approach, nor the shift-share decomposition of economic change into its major components, produces a measure of the full impact of UEZ incentives. Such a measure would include direct increases in economic activity associated with UEZ firms, plus the additional or multiplier effects resulting from this activity as it ripples through New Jersey's economy.

In contrast with the econometric and shift-share approaches, the Input/Output (I/O) Model is able to estimate the full effects of economic change in a specific geographic area. The availability of a relatively recent I/O Model for New Jersey facilitated the implementation of this methodology for the UEZ evaluation summarized in this case study.[17]

The multiplier effect estimated in the New Jersey I/O Model results from the initial impact of the increase in economic activity of the businesses in the State's UEZ Program. All of this initial activity is defined in I/O terminology as the *direct impact* of the UEZ Program. Based upon respondent information and extrapolations for nonrespondents, it was estimated that in 1987 and 1988, the initial, or direct, impact of the 976 firms in the study was:

- 9,193 new jobs;
- $243 million in new payroll;
- $1,776.6 million in additional output by New Jersey firms; and
- $803 million in new capital investment.

The Input/Output Model

In an I/O model, which is essentially a method of mathematically representing an economy in a system of linear equations, the economy is disaggregated into individual industries which are bridged into Standard Industrial Classifications (SICs). The output of each industrial sector in the model is then described in terms of the quantities of this output consumed by its various intermediate and final users, within the framework of three matrices: the Transactions Matrix, the Direct Technical Coefficients Matrix, and the Matrix of Direct and Indirect Requirements.

The *Transactions Matrix,* which is the basic I/O construct, shows the interindustry transactions between and among different producing industries of the economy, for example, between the Iron and Steel industry and the Plastics industry. In the Transactions Matrix, each industry is shown both as a seller to other producing industries and as a buyer from these industries. Also shown in this matrix is the demand for the output of the producing industries, by all nonproducing industries, consumers, and government. The Transactions Matrix is used to derive the *Direct Technical Coefficients Matrix* (DTCM) and the *Matrix of Direct and Indirect Requirements* (MDIR). The MDIR is used to simulate the impacts of a wide array of *what-if* economic scenarios; for example, *what* will be the impact on the economy *if* there is an increase in output of the Iron and Steel Industry?[18] In this case study, the question asked is: *What* will be the impact on New Jersey's economy *if* there is a UEZ Program-related expansion in economic activity?

In the New Jersey UEZ evaluation, the three matrices discussed above describe the transactions among the state's producers, consumers, and government in terms of what they buy and sell to each other. These interrelationships are expressed in such a way that the impact of a change in demand for one product can be linked back to the changes in demand for all other product and service inputs that are required for its production. The I/O Model isolates all of the New Jersey-specific transactions that are required to produce the State's output and deliver it to final demand.[19] The Model stimulates a series of what-if scenarios to estimate the indirect and induced impacts of changes in the State's economy resulting from direct economic activity generated by the 976 UEZ businesses in the study population.

In this study, the direct economic activity is specifically defined as the increased output and investment attributable to the 976 companies. As these firms expand their output, they purchase goods and services from other firms located in-state and out-of-state. In turn, the in-state companies expand their output by buying additional goods and services within and outside New Jersey. Total State output thus increases in a multiplicative way, the value of which is estimated in the I/O model's *Output Simulation*. Investments by UEZ firms also have a multiplier effect on the State's economy, the value of which is estimated in the I/O Model's *Investment Simulation*. The output and investment simulations, which yield the indirect impacts of the UEZ Program, are described below.

The Output Simulation

The direct increase in total gross receipts of the 976 firms in the study, from the beginning of the Program to 1987 and from 1987 through the end of 1988, was estimated at $1.8 billion. In the I/O Model, gross receipts are set equal to total output, so that each industry's incremental change in receipts over the period was treated as expanded output—that is, production—by the appropriate I/O producing sector. Given this direct increase, the Model was used to estimate the multiplier effect of the initial $1.8 billion in output as it rippled through the State's economy.

The full effect of the $1.8 billion in direct output increases was calculated at $2.9 billion, for a multiplier of 1.61, so that each $1.00 of direct expansion in output by the 976 UEZ firms generated an additional $.61 in indirect output by other New Jersey companies. The employment multiplier associated with the added output was calculated to be 2.26, meaning that for every job added by the 976 firms, an additional 1.26 jobs were created in New Jersey.

The Investment Simulation

The second component of the indirect UEZ impact relates to the $803 million in capital investment expenditures made by the 976 UEZ firms in 1987 and 1988. This capital formation, however, is defined as final demand in the I/O Model.[20] As such, it is virtually absent from the Interindustry Transactions Matrix and thus from the two matrices derived from the Transaction Matrix. Therefore, the multiplier effect of the $803 million in investment had to be calculated in the two-step procedure described below, rather than directly in the I/O Model.

After identifying the *capital purchasing industries,* that is, the industries making the capital investment,[21] the estimation procedure involved attributing the dollar amounts of various types of purchased capital, such as equipment, to *capital producing industries.* This attribution was accomplished using a so-called *Capital Matrix,* in which various types of capital are attributed to each of 127 industries (the same 127 industries in the I/O Model).[22] The dollar value of the output of these capital producing industries was, in turn, used as input to the New Jersey I/O Model. Specifically, the output of the capital producing industries was assumed to expand in the New Jersey I/O Model, that is, each industry was assumed to create and put-in-place all of the capital purchased by the 976 UEZ firms.

The results of the two-step investment simulation showed that the direct $803 million in capital investment made by the 976 UEZ companies caused an indirect increase of $1.5 billion in New Jersey State

Table 7.2 The Impact of the UEZ Program on New Jersey[a] (Dollars in Millions)

Resulting From:	Impact Indicator		
	Output	Jobs	Taxes
Payroll Impact	$ 299.7	3,668	$ 36.04
Output Impact	2,864.7	20,755	141.09
Investment Impact	1,490.9	18,315	90.25
TOTAL	4,655.3	42,738	267.38

NOTE: The payroll and output impacts are based upon increments to jobs and output from the time the program began in each UEZ to 1987 and increments from 1987 to 1988. The Investment impact is based upon full 1987 and 1988 dollar values.

output. An additional 18,315 jobs were created by the capital-producing industries, as was $41.2 million in state and local taxes.

The Induced Impact of UEZ Activity

As previously noted, the direct economic activity of the 976 UEZ companies produces 9,193 jobs and $242.8 million in incremental payroll dollars. Most of this payroll becomes *disposable personal income* (DPI) that is spent by workers on goods and services produced within and outside of New Jersey. The induced impact of the UEZ Program is defined as the value of the activity resulting from the expansion of New Jersey firms to meet the additional demand for goods and services generated by increased worker spending.

This induced impact is calculated in two rounds of simulations: (1) the first round of induced effects are those associated with the DPI spending of the workers in the 976 UEZ businesses; (2) the second round of induced impacts are those associated with the spending of workers who were added in the indirect round of I/O simulations. Table 7.2 shows the induced impacts of the UEZ Program as calculated in the two rounds of DPI spending, as well as the direct and indirect impacts of the economic activity created by the 976 UEZ businesses in 1987 and 1988.

For purposes of this study, the impact summarized in Table 7.2 is defined as the total benefits of the UEZ Program to the State of New Jersey. Comparing these benefits with the costs arrayed in Table 7.1 shows that the UEZ Program had a substantial positive impact on the

Table 7.3 The Impact of the UEZ Program on New Jersey Attributable to Primary/Only Respondents[a] (Dollars in Millions)

| | Impact Indicator | | |
Resulting From:	Output	Jobs	Taxes
Payroll Impact	$ 110.5	1,353	$13.27
Output Impact	1,169.5	9,644	59.48
Investment Impact	433.5	5,283	25.22
TOTAL	1,713.5	16,280	97.97

NOTE: a. The payroll and output impacts are based upon increments to jobs and output from the time the program began in each UEZ to 1987 and increments from 1987 to 1988. The investment impact is based upon full 1987 and 1988 dollar values.

State, with benefits far exceeding costs. However, within the environment of New Jersey's rapid growth during the period of the study, it is doubtless that some of the job increases and taxes generated by UEZ firms would have occurred in the absence of the Program. The question to be answered is thus: How much of the activity summarized in Table 7.2 would not have occurred *but for* UEZ incentives? This but for question has long been raised in program evaluation, but generally has not been addressed in enterprise zone evaluations.[23]

In this study, responses to a question in the UEZ survey regarding the importance of UEZ incentives to business location/expansion decisions were used to address the but for question. Specifically, the UEZ firms were asked: "To what extent did UEZ tax benefits influence your decision to locate/expand your business in the Zone?" In the but for context, this question would translate to: "Would you have invested 'but for' the UEZ Program?"

Thirty-two percent of the firms in the study reported that the UEZ benefits were the primary or only reason for their increased/new economic activity. That is, they would not have increased their activity but for the Program.

To isolate the impact of the UEZ Program from general economic growth, the I/O Model was used to calculate the economic and fiscal impacts attributable solely to the 315 firms giving the *primary/only* response. Table 7.3 summarizes the direct, indirect, and induced impacts attributable to these 315 firms, as calculated within the New Jersey I/O Model.

Cost-Effectiveness
of New Jersey's UEZ Program

In calculating the cost-effectiveness of New Jersey's UEZ Program, direct, indirect, and induced economic impacts attributable to the 315 primary/only firms are treated as the Program benefits. It is assumed that the activity associated with the remaining 661 firms would have occurred even in the absence of the UEZ Program. However, Program costs are calculated as the full $51 million associated with the Program and summarized in Table 7.1, because regardless of the perceived importance of UEZ incentives, all firms, regardless of response, use them.

The cost-efficiency of New Jersey's UEZ Program was first evaluated by comparing Program costs and benefits with and without the multiplier effect. As shown in Table 7.4, ignoring the multiplier effect, the Program is not cost-effective with respect to taxes generated, yielding only $.70 in State and local taxes for every $1.00 foregone in State tax collections. When the multiplier effect is considered, however, the Program is certainly cost-effective, with every tax dollar given up by the State matched by $1.90 in State and local taxes generated by UEZ-related economic activity.

The New Jersey UEZ program was also evaluated with respect to the costs of the Program per job generated, an alternative way to measure cost-effectiveness. The study showed that, in the absence of the multiplier effect, the cost-per-job generated by the primary/only respondents was $13,000, making the Program competitive with, for example, the UDAG Program which is generally considered to be highly efficient.[24] When the multiplier effect is considered, New Jersey's UEZ Program obviously becomes an overwhelmingly efficient job generator at a cost of $3,000 per job.

Conclusions

Based upon the findings in this case study of New Jersey, the UEZ Program is a cost-effective economic development tool, leveraging almost $2.00 in State and local taxes for every $1.00 foregone in State tax revenues. The study also showed that the Program is an efficient way to generate jobs, even when the multiplier effects of UEZ business activity are not considered.

Table 7.4 The Cost-Effectiveness of the New Jersey UEZ Program[a]

Fiscal Base: Full program costs—taxes foregone and administrative costs—relative to the total of taxes generated by primary/only respondents (Dollars in Millions):

Costs	$51.6
Direct Taxes Generated	$38.6
Benefit: Cost Ratio	0.7:1
Total State and Local Taxes Generated[b]	$98.0
Ratio Benefits: Costs[b]	1.9:1

Economic Base: Program costs—taxes foregone and administrative costs—relative to the total number of jobs generated by primary/only respondents:

Costs (Dollars in millions)	$51.6
Jobs Generated: Direct Employment	3,948
Jobs Generated: Total Employment[c]	16,270
Cost/Job: Direct Employment	$13,070
Cost/Job: Total Employment[c]	$3,171

NOTES: a. Data used to calculate the values in this Table relate to increments to jobs, payroll, and output from the time the program started up in each UEZ to 1987 and from 1987 to 1988. Investment calculations are based upon full 1987 and 1988 dollar values. For program costs, 80% are for tax exemptions related to investments made in 1987 and 1988.
b. Total taxes generated by direct, indirect, and induced economic activity associated with UEZ firms, as estimated in the New Jersey I/O model.
c. Includes direct, indirect, and induced jobs as estimated in the New Jersey I/O model.

Despite the cost-effectiveness findings, a number of important unanswered questions remain. First, because the displacement of economic activity from non-UEZ areas to the UEZs is not considered, to what extent are the benefits to the State overstated? Second, because the reduction to the State in welfare and other costs associated primarily with dependent inner-city residents are not considered, to what extent are the benefits of the UEZ Program to the State understated? Although the data needed to address these issues were not available for this study, it is recommended that future research focus on them, thereby providing a more definitive answer to the cost-efficacy of enterprise zones as an economic development tool.

Notes

1. *The New Jersey Urban Enterprise Zones Act, N.J.S.A. 52:27H-60, et seq.*

120 Enterprise Zones in New Jersey

2. Brame, S. C. (1987). A preliminary assessment of New Jersey's UEZ program. Trenton: New Jersey Department of Commerce, Energy, and Economic Development, unpublished report.

3. Brintnall, M., & Green, R. (1988). Comparing state enterprise zone programs: Variations in structure and coverage. *Economic Development Quarterly, 2*(1): 50-68.

4. These municipalities are, by definition, eligible for state aid as per *N.J.S.A. 52:27D-178 et al.,* which provides for state aid to selected municipalities for services and to offset property taxes.

5. Brintnall & Green, Comparing state enterprise zone programs, p. 60.

6. ibid., p. 57.

7. A company becomes qualified: (1) if it is authorized to do business in New Jersey and is actively engaged in the conduct of a trade or business at the time of UEZ designation; or (2) if it moves into the UEZ after the date of (UEZ) designation and has at least 25% of its new hires meeting criteria relating to residence and unemployment and/or public assistance status.

8. Once a qualified business has met its statutory requirement for new hires, it must maintain its aggregate employment at the approved level throughout the duration of its participation in the UEZ Program.

9. The Local Development Financing Fund (LDFF) was established by the State of New Jersey to provide financial assistance to qualified commercial and industrial projects in selected communities, which, by definition, include UEZ cities.

10. Erickson, R., & Friedman, S. (1989). *Enterprise zones: An evaluation of state government policies.* Washington, DC: U.S. Department of Commerce, p. 37.

11. Credits against Corporation Business Tax liability are available for full-time employees who are residents of any of the 11 UEZ cities. For each employee who also meets specified unemployment/public assistance criteria, a $1,500 credit is available; otherwise a $500 credit is available.

12. Data on the Unemployment Insurance Tax Rebate were supplied by the NJ Department of Labor based upon information from actual UEZ business records. Estimates for the Corporation Business Tax Credits were made by the NJ Division of Taxation based upon tax returns of UEZ businesses. Costs associated with the Sales Tax exemptions were estimated by the author using survey responses regarding the tax-exempt value of investments made in the zones.

13. The evaluation study was conducted in 1988 and 1989 by the author and Regina Armstrong for Urbanomics, an economic consulting company, in conjunction with Richard Buxbaum and Battelle Laboratories of Columbus, OH.

14. Using a Chi-square analysis to test the null hypotheses of no relationship between business size and response and industry affiliation and response resulted in rejection of both hypotheses at the .001 level of significance.

15. See, for example, Erickson & Friedman, *Enterprise Zones,* for an illustration of the application of econometric analysis to the evaluation of enterprise zones.

16. See Rubin, B. M., & Wilder, M. G. (1989). Urban enterprise zones. *APA Journal,* (Autumn), pp. 418-431 for an illustration of the application of shift-share analysis to the evaluation of enterprise zones.

19. In input/output analysis final demand can be defined as the demand for the output of the producing industries by all sectors of the economy, that is, consumers, producers, and government.

20. Ibid.

21. In this study, firm-level data for UEZ companies making capital investments—that is, purchasing capital—are aggregated to the industrial sector level.

22. The Capital Matrix used in this study was constructed by Battelle Laboratories. The Matrix is 127 sectors square and incorporates considerable detail and variation in the types of capital purchases across industrial sectors.

23. One notable exception is the 1989 Rubin & Wilder study (Urban enterprise zones) in which it was found that enterprise zone incentives are cost-effective.

24. James, F. J. (1989). Testimony before the Ways and Means Committee of the U.S. House of Representatives, Hearings on the Administration's Enterprise Zone Proposal and H.R. 6, The Enterprise Zone Improvements Act of 1989.

8

Enterprise Zones:

Maryland Case Study

PATRICK G. GRASSO
SCOTT B. CROSSE

Although enterprise zone proposals have been on the federal legislative agenda for more than a decade, the real action has been taking place at the state and local levels. Partly in anticipation of eventual passage of federal incentives, three fourths of the states had enacted some form of enterprise zone program by the end of the 1980s. This pattern of activity has resulted in a variety of experiments in enterprise zone programs, providing in this case an example of what is often said to be an advantage of the U.S. federal system—the use of the states as laboratories for national public policy development.

The role of the states in promoting enterprise zones provides an excellent opportunity to use the tools of program evaluation to address the debate over whether to adopt a national enterprise zone program and, if so, what the scope and components of that program should be. As evaluations of the state programs are completed and reported, a picture is emerging of the extent of success of these programs and the factors that may have contributed to any such success. This chapter is intended to contribute to that body of evaluative information by summarizing some of the key findings of a U.S. General Accounting Office (GAO) study of enterprise zones in Maryland.[1] The study was conducted between 1986 and 1988 at the request of then-Representatives Robert Garcia and Jack Kemp, both of New York. It was designed to address a number of questions, but this chapter deals primarily with

122

only one: How much employment growth occurred within the enterprise zones?

The Maryland
Enterprise Zone Program

The Maryland enterprise zone program was among the earliest state programs, beginning operation in 1982. By 1989, 13 zones had been established around the state. The GAO study focused on three of the oldest Maryland zones, those in Hagerstown, Cumberland, and Salisbury, which became operational between December 1982 and December 1983.

The major features of the Maryland enterprise zone program at the time of the study are summarized in Table 8.1. Eligibility criteria were based on the level of unemployment, extent of poverty, prevalence of low-income families, and degree of population loss or physical disinvestment in the proposed zone area. To be designated an enterprise zone, an area would have to have at least one of the following: a high unemployment rate; a high poverty rate; a low average family income; *or* substantial population decline and property abandonment or property tax arrearage. (These criteria are quite similar to those in the Kemp-Garcia bill then pending before Congress, except that the bill also included minimum population requirements, a provision linking zone designation to eligibility under another community development program, and more stringent requirements for all but the income criterion. It also would have required the proposed zone area to meet *all* these criteria, rather than any one of them.)

Two types of incentives, aimed at stimulating employment and investment, were offered to firms participating in the Maryland enterprise zone program. On the employment side, participating firms were eligible for tax credits of various amounts, ranging from $500 to $3,000, for hiring unemployed workers to fill new jobs. The precise maximum amount depended on whether the worker was disadvantaged and whether he or she had previously worked for the firm making the claim. On the investment front, incentives included a property tax credit for increased assessments resulting from improvements, loan guarantees for long-term financing, increased loan limits for government land acquisition and development projects, and state redevelopment funds in excess of the normal maximum.

Table 8.1 Maryland Enterprise Zone Program Features

Feature	Requirements or Incentives
Eligibility and Duration	Area must meet at least *one*:
	Unemployment rate at least 1.5 times higher than national or state level
	Average income below 125% of national poverty level
	At least 70% of families below 80% of local median income
	Intercensus population loss of 10% and either chronic property abandonment or substantial property tax arrearage
	Designation effective for 10 years
	Maximum of 6 zones designated in any 12 month period
Employment Tax Credits	Up to $500 for each new job filled
	Up to $3,000 over 3 years for each new job filled by disadvantaged worker
	Up to $1,750 over 2 years for each worker rehired by firm after being laid off more than 6 months
Investment and Property Incentives	Property tax credit equal to 80% of increase in assessment value resulting from improvements for first 5 years; decreases by 10% per year for next 5 years
	Up to 100% guarantee for long-term loans to finance fixed assets, working capital, and government contracts
	Higher loan limits for local government land acquisition and development projects
	Funds equal to 25% over the maximum from state redevelopment fund

The Maryland enterprise zone program has been classified as *private* in terms of the typology that underlies this volume. That is, the program has been found to be below average in the extent to which the state government manages and requires local governments to manage the zones, and above average in the extent to which the private sector is actively involved in developing and operating them.[2] Maryland, however, actually scored rather near the average on both these dimensions. This is not to argue that the Maryland program was in any sense typical or representative of all state enterprise zone programs, but rather to note that it was not an extreme case, at least in terms of these dimensions.

Research Design and Analysis

To estimate the job creation effects of the Maryland enterprise zone program, GAO examined the employment patterns of firms participating in three zones. The analysis was designed to test whether there was either an abrupt or gradual increase in employment in each of the three enterprise zones in the period following implementation of the zones. In addition, GAO conducted a survey of firms participating in the enterprise zones program and other, nonparticipating employers to gather information on the importance of the proferred tax incentives in affecting business location and hiring decisions.

For each of the three enterprise zones, GAO identified each firm located within the zone boundaries. From among these, the firms actually participating in the program were selected for the analysis. The decision to focus on participants reflected the belief that, logically, any impact of the employment and investment incentives included in the program was most likely to be found among the actual participants. Indeed, for a firm to be certified by the local zone administrator as a participant it must provide evidence that employment or investment was higher in the year of application for incentives than it had been the previous tax year. Of course, this leaves open the question of whether such increased employment or investment was higher than it would have been in the absence of the program. The GAO study was designed to examine precisely the latter issue, at least insofar as employment was concerned.

For each participating firm in each of the three enterprise zones, GAO collected monthly data on the number of persons employed at the firm from the state's unemployment insurance system records. The data covered the period from April 1980 to September 1987, or a total of 90 monthly observations. These figures were aggregated for all the participants in each of the three zones to permit an analysis of the trend for total employment among zone participants in each zone over the 90-month period.

The analyses GAO conducted involved a comparison of the employment growth pattern among participating firms before implementation of the local enterprise zone with that among the same firms for the period after zone implementation. This analysis was based on interrupted time series (ITS) techniques in which a series of autoregressive integrated moving average (ARIMA) models was estimated.[3]

This type of analysis is designed to identify statistically significant changes in some variable, in this case the level of employment among enterprise zone participants after some intervention, in this case implementation of the zone. Various models were fitted to the data in order to test whether there was either a one-time shift in the level of aggregate employment among participants, or a change in the rate of increase in employment among those firms. In other words, the GAO analysis was designed to determine (1) if there was a sudden increase in the number of persons employed in participating firms following enterprise zone implementation, which would show up as an upward jump in the trend line at or somewhat after the date of implementation; or (2) if there was an increase in the month-to-month rate of growth in employment among participating firms, which would be indicated if the employment trend line were steeper after than before implementation.

In effect, this type of analysis uses information on the overall trend in employment in each zone as a predictor of what would have happened in the absence of the program, and compares actual performance to this trend. Because it takes account of the conditions in the specific zone area this approach has advantages over others that have been used, such as national employment trends, as used in at least one study.[4]

The statistical analysis of an interrupted time series involves the fitting of a series of models to the data until the simplest one that adequately fits the data is found. This is a useful alternative to other statistical techniques (such as classical regression models) in cases where there is little guidance from theory or prior research, but a long preintervention series of empirical data.[5]

In addition to this analysis, GAO conducted a survey of employers to collect information on the likely effectiveness of different tax incentives and other development strategies. Somewhat different versions of a mail survey instrument were administered to enterprise zone participating firms, nonparticipating firms located within the enterprise zone areas, and firms in a non-enterprise zone area. The overall response rate to this questionnaire was 54%; among enterprise zone participating firms it was 70%.

Analysis and Findings

Overall, GAO found that employment among participating firms in the three Maryland enterprise zones studied did increase by between 8% and 76% during the approximately four years following implementation of the programs. This growth, however, could not be attributed to the zone incentives. A detailed analysis of the patterns of employment growth and information provided by employers revealed that even in cases where there initially appeared to be an effect from the zone incentives no such attribution could be sustained.

To illustrate the analysis and findings, let us here concentrate on the Hagerstown case. A city of 34,000 located in northwestern Maryland, Hagerstown suffered seriously during the 1981-1982 recession, when local unemployment reached over 14%, and one major employer left town while another laid off a substantial number of workers.

Under these conditions, Hagerstown and surrounding Washington County jointly applied for enterprise zone designation under the state program in October 1982. The zone was designated by the state in December of that year, but implementation was delayed until a year later when city and county officials agreed on a package of local business incentives. These included tax credits and assistance to businesses seeking state aid, required by the state. The zone is an area of about 2,000 acres including the old central business district, several industrial areas near the edge of the city, and an industrial park located on county land. Within four years the Hagerstown enterprise zone had 64 participants, most of which applied for benefits within the first year of zone operation. Of these, 36 had been located within the zone boundaries prior to zone designation, 14 were businesses that moved into the zone, and 14 were newly started businesses.

An initial analysis of the employment growth patterns for the Hagerstown enterprise zone seemed to suggest that implementation of the zone did lead to higher employment levels. As shown in Figure 8.1, employment among participating zone firms began to increase erratically beginning about the middle of 1982. The enterprise zone was implemented in December 1983, as indicated by the vertical line in the figure. Then, in August 1984, employment increased by 16%, and in October

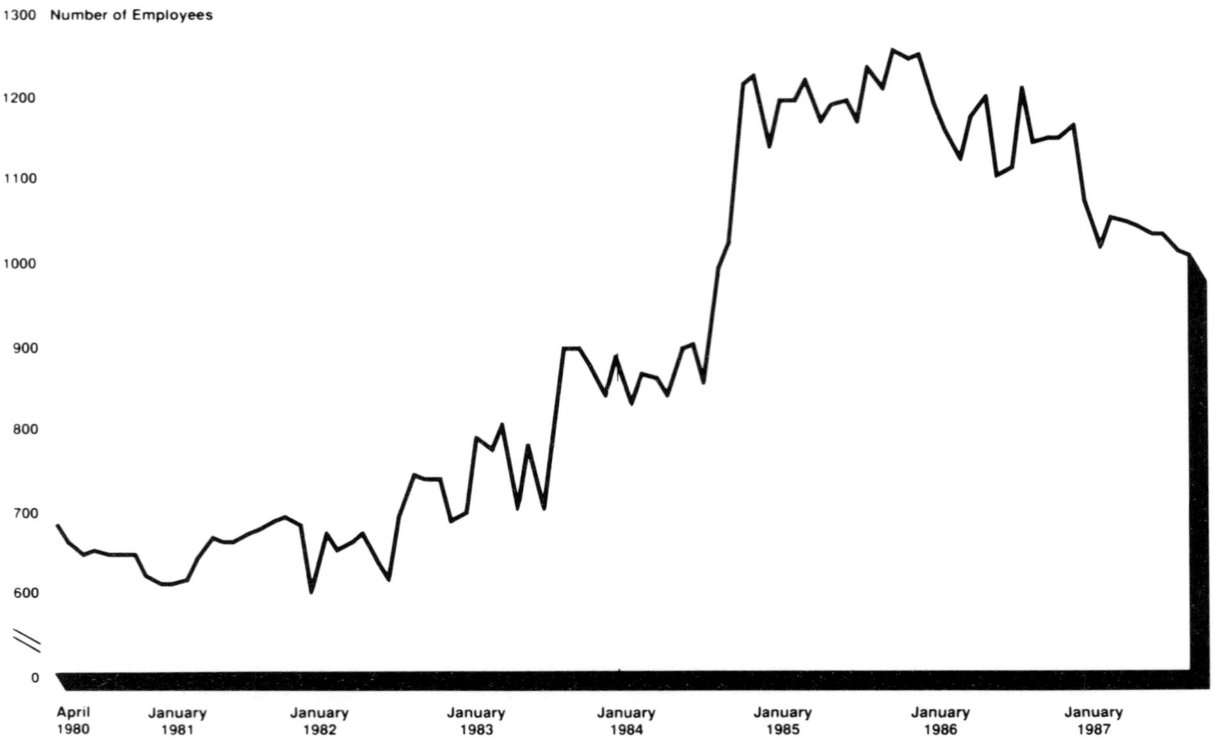

Figure 8.1. Number of Employees for Participants in the Hagerstown Enterprise Zone, 1980–1987[a]

a. The vertical line represents the intervention of the program.

128

of that year by 19%. Employment leveled off during 1985 and declined during 1986-1987.

The dramatic increases in August and October of 1984 were statistically significant. That is, even though employment was increasing before these months, the increases recorded at these times exceeded the rate of growth sufficiently so that the change cannot be explained by chance fluctuations alone. In standard ITS analysis, this is prima facie evidence that the enterprise zone program did lead to increased employment among program participants.

To insure that this initial conclusion could be sustained on detailed analysis, and to try to determine which zone incentives were the most important contributors to these results, GAO identified the specific firms associated with the employment increases. These companies then were contacted and asked about the factors affecting their location and hiring decisions at these times. It turned out that each of the two increases could be explained almost entirely by the actions of one firm.

The August increase was associated with a store that began full operation in Hagerstown at that time. Discussions with representatives of the company revealed that the firm was unaware of the enterprise zone incentives at the time of its decision to begin operations in Hagerstown, nor was it aware of the program at the time it hired employees. In fact, the firm learned about the program and the incentives available to participants only after it began operating in the city. Therefore, it is impossible to conclude that the enterprise zone incentives were responsible for the spurt of employment growth in August 1984.

Similarly, the October increase was accounted for almost entirely by the actions of one large employer, a multistate retailer that began operating in Hagerstown at that time. In this case the employer apparently was motivated primarily by the availability of a vacant retail facility in a location that constituted a hole in its east coast marketing network rather than by the enterprise zone incentives. The employer indicated to GAO that it likely would have located in Hagerstown even without the incentives. Once again, the evidence suggested that the impact of the program on employment growth was more apparent than real.

In both cases discussed above, the employers did claim the tax incentives available to enterprise zone participants. In neither case, however, could it be concluded that the decision to locate and hire employees in Hagerstown was a result of the enterprise zone program itself—rather, market forces seemed to be the major factors underlying these decisions.

The importance of this follow-up analysis can be seen by examining the employment growth pattern if we exclude the two firms discussed above. This is shown in Figure 8.2. Here we can see that among the remaining 62 participating firms in the zone, no dramatic increase in employment occurred following program implementation. Rather, the growth begun in 1982 continued at a fairly steady average rate through mid-1985 before declining. Neither a sharp one-time increase nor a major increase in the rate of growth (the slope of the line) is seen in the figure, a finding confirmed by statistical analyses that found no statistically significant increase in employment growth beyond the long-term trend after December 1983.

Similar findings emerged from GAO's analysis of the enterprise zones in Cumberland and Salisbury. In Cumberland, which implemented its program in December 1982, GAO first analyzed employment data with all participants included. No employment effects were found. But in this case one particularly large firm had a widely fluctuating employment picture, reflecting a pattern of lay-offs and rehires tied to changes in its industry. To insure that this was not obscuring zone-induced growth among the other participating firms, GAO also ran the analysis excluding this firm. No effects were found, however.

Salisbury's enterprise zone became fully operational in October 1983. Again, the initial analysis revealed no employment effects following implementation of the zone program. One large employer, however, had an erratic record of employment that seemed to be the result of reporting problems rather than actual changes in employment. Thus, again to insure that this problem was not hiding real employment effects, the analysis was rerun excluding this firm.

The results of this analysis seemed to indicate some positive effects on employment, with major increases in January 1984 (11%) and March 1984 (10%). These increases could be traced to six firms. One of these began participation in the program too late for the program to explain its hiring behavior. Four of the employers indicated that their increased hiring resulted from increased demand for their goods or services rather than the enterprise zone incentives. In the final case, the information was inconclusive, but this firm was responsible for only a small amount of employment growth in these months.

Thus, overall there was no evidence linking the observed employment growth following implementation of the Maryland enterprise

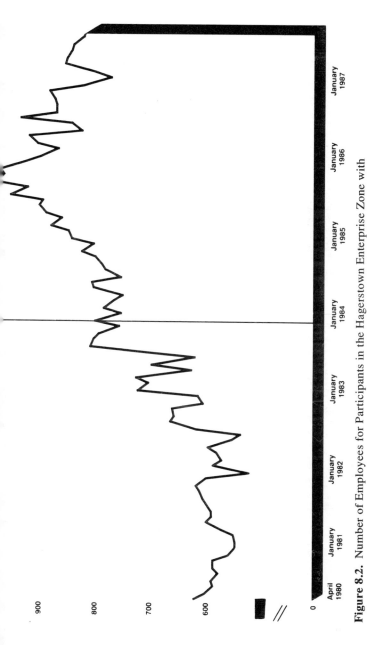

Figure 8.2. Number of Employees for Participants in the Hagerstown Enterprise Zone with Two Participants Excluded, 1980–1987[a]

a. The vertical line represents the intervention of the program.

131

Table 8.2 Employer Ratings of the Importance of Factors in Their Location and Hiring Decisions (in percentages)

Factor	Very Great/ Great Importance	Moderate/ Some Importance	Little or No Importance
Market Access	57	28	14
Government Cooperation	41	32	27
Site Characteristics	40	39	20
Community Characteristics	39	42	19
Transportation	38	37	26
Financial Health of Region	32	38	30
Real Estate Costs	31	38	31
Quality of Life	28	39	33
Miscellaneous Taxes	23	39	38
Regulatory Practices	22	43	35
Labor Force	21	33	46
Financial Inducements	14	27	60
Technical Assistance	5	28	66

$N = 468$

NOTE: Rows may not total to 100% because of rounding. Items are ordered by percentage citing each factor as of "very great" or "great" importance in the firm's location and hiring decisions.

zones in these three cities with the enterprise zone program and its related incentives. The GAO study included information that helps to explain why the incentives apparently did not stimulate growth. These data came from a survey of Maryland employers including both partic- ipants and nonparticipants in the Hagerstown and Salisbury zones, participants in the Cumberland and Park Circle (Baltimore) zones, and employers in Cambridge, a comparable area without an enterprise zone.

All of these employers were located in relatively depressed areas where the need for financial incentives to help the firms might be expected to be particularly strong. GAO asked the employers to rate a number of factors that have been cited as likely to affect hiring and investment decisions on a 5-point scale, from "very great" to "little or no" importance. The results of this survey are shown in Table 8.2, where the items are listed in the order of the percentage citing each as of great or very great importance in making location decisions.

The most important finding in the table for our purposes is that financial inducements, which include the incentives found in the enterprise zone program, are near the bottom of the list of factors, with only 14% of the employers citing these as very great/great important to their location decisions. Only technical assistance finished lower on the list. The most important factor, cited by 57% of the respondents, was market access. Broad factors such as government cooperation, community characteristics, and transportation also ranked high, as did the more narrow consideration of site characteristics. But most specific government-related factors, including miscellaneous taxes and regulatory practices, like financial inducements, fell far down the list.

These results are consistent with the findings of most other studies of business location decisions. In general, tax incentives are not among the most important cited for business location decisions.[6] There is some evidence, however, that once the general area for a business is selected (such as a metropolitan area) tax incentives may help to direct investment to a particular location within that area,[7] and that the effects of tax incentives have been stronger in recent years.[8] In any case, the literature suggests that the reliance on tax incentives alone for enterprise zones is unlikely to lead to very dramatic effects on employment within the zones.

The GAO study is generally consistent with the findings of other studies of the effects of enterprise zones. Sheldon and Elling[9] found in a four-state comparative analysis that the tax and regulatory components of enterprise zone programs have little or no effect on zone success, but administrative efforts and nonfinancial assistance are more important. Similarly, Wilder and Rubin[10] concluded that the success of the Evansville, Indiana enterprise zone in creating jobs resulted more from the marketing efforts of the zone administrators than from the tax incentives offered by the program.

Conclusions

This analysis provides no evidence that the Maryland enterprise zone program increased employment in the areas GAO studied. Of course, in establishing the enterprise zones Maryland was interested in goals other than new job creation—such as job preservation and community revitalization—that were not directly evaluated in the GAO study. Still, job creation is an important goal of virtually all state enterprise zone programs, so the lack of evidence of success in this area is important.

It appears that the lack of job creation associated with Maryland's enterprise zones may be a result of the incentive structure underlying the program. These incentives do not directly address the considerations that are most important to firms making location decisions. Without strong administrative action to sell the zone areas, it seems unlikely that firms will be induced to locate or expand in these locations. This suggests that the most important role of an enterprise zone program may be as a tool for marketing otherwise relatively undesirable areas to potential employers or as a means of organizing development activities in the community.[11]

Notes

1. U.S. General Accounting Office. (1988). *Enterprise zones: Lessons from the Maryland experience*. Washington, DC: Author.

2. Brintnall, M., & Green, R. E. (1988). Comparing state enterprise zone programs: Variations in structure and coverage. *Economic Development Quarterly, 2*, 50-68.

3. McCleary, R., & Hay, R. A. (1980). *Applied time series analysis for the social sciences*. Beverly Hills, CA: Sage. See also Cook, T. D., Campbell, D. T. (1979). *Quasi-experimentation: Design and analysis issues for field settings*. Chicago: Rand McNally, pp. 207-293.

4. Erickson, R. A., & Friedman, S. W. (1989). *Enterprise zones: An evaluation of state government policies*. Washington, DC: U.S. Department of Commerce.

5. This approach often is appropriate for the analysis of an ITS quasi-experiment, as in this case. GAO used the SAS/ETS program library to carry out the analysis. See SAS Institute. (1982). *SAS/ETS Users Guide*. Cary, NC: Author.

6. Wasylenko, M. (1981). The location of firms: The role of taxes and fiscal incentives. In R. Bahl (Ed.), *Urban government finance: Emerging trends*, pp. 155-190. Beverly Hills, CA: Sage; Howland, M. (1985). Property taxes and the birth and intraregional location of firms. *Journal of Planning Education and Research, 4*, 148-56; Carlton, D. (1979). Why new firms locate where they do: An econometric model. In W. Wheaton (Ed.), *Interregional movements and regional growth*, pp. 13-50. Washington, DC: Urban Institute.

7. Kale, S. R. (1984). U.S. industrial development incentives and manufacturing growth during the 1970s. *Growth and Change, 15*, 26-34.

8. Ledebur, L. C., & Hamilton, W. W. (1986). The failure of tax concessions as economic development incentives. In S. D. Gold (Ed.), *Reforming state tax systems*, pp. 101-117. Denver, CO: National Conference of State Legislatures; Netzer, D. (1986). What should governors do when economists tell them that nothing works? *New York Affairs, 9*, 19-36; Kenyon, D. A. (1988). Interjurisdictional tax and policy competition: Good or bad for the federal system? Manuscript prepared for the U.S. Advisory Commission on Intergovernmental Relations, Washington, DC, February; Newman, R. J., & Sullivan, D. H. (1988). Econometric analysis of business tax impacts on industrial location: What do we know, and how do we know it? *Journal of Urban Economics, 23*, 215-234.

9. Sheldon, A. W., & Elling, R. C. (1989, October). *The enterprise zone: A four state analysis of program success.* Paper presented at the Annual Meeting of the Association of Collegiate Schools of Planning, Portland, OR.

10. Wilder, M. G., & Rubin, B. M. (no date). *Targeted development through urban enterprise zones.* Bloomington: Indiana University School of Public and Environmental Affairs.

11. U.S. Department of Housing and Urban Development. (1986). *State-designated enterprise zones: Ten case studies.* Washington, DC: U.S. Government Printing Office.

Section B

Comparative Analyses
of State Enterprise Zone Programs

9

Determinants of
Enterprise Zone Success:

A Four State Perspective

RICHARD C. ELLING
ANN WORKMAN SHELDON

Introduction

Although more than three fourths of the states had Enterprise Zone
(EZ) programs by 1990, they have operationalized the concept in
diverse ways.[1] State programs typically include various classic EZ
elements such as a reduction in taxes, regulatory burdens, and other
business costs. Most have also seen fit to include provisions that
establish a more active or *interventionist* governmental presence, including the provision of loans and venture capital, land assembly to
facilitate new uses of land, and public investment in physical infrastruc-

ture. Economic development professionals argue that interventionist policies—along with factors such as proximity to markets, facility or utility costs, and the quality and cost of labor—may figure more prominently in the decisions of firms to begin or expand operations in given areas than do those business costs addressed by classic EZ program elements.[2] This chapter explores this issue by examining the significance of differing program components for the success of 47 enterprise zones in the states of Illinois, Indiana, Kentucky, and Ohio.

Research Setting and Data

In addition to similarities such as regional location and the importance of manufacturing to their economies, Illinois, Indiana, Kentucky, and Ohio are similar in having well established EZ programs.[3] In each of the states, eligibility for zone designation is limited to areas that are highly distressed.[4] The zones are quite small, as well. The median sized zone was 13.4 square miles in Kentucky, 7.5 square miles in Ohio, 5.0 square miles in Illinois, and just 3.0 square miles in Indiana.

The differences that exist in the state and local incentives and services available to qualifying firms and in how zone programs operate are of central interest in this study. Information on the provisions of the state-level enterprise zone programs in these four states was obtained from each state's enterprise zone law, from the National Association of State Development Agencies, and from telephone interviews with state enterprise zone officials.[5] Information about local EZ program components and about the economic development history of zones was initially gathered via a questionnaire mailed to local zone administrators in mid-1987, with follow-up telephone interviews as needed. In the summers of 1988 and 1989 zones were re-contacted to update existing data and to secure additional information on the dollar value of investment in them.

Zone economic activity is measured in several ways: the number of firms qualifying for EZ benefits as a result of investing in a zone, the total amount of such investment, the number of jobs created, and the number of jobs retained.

The next section of the chapter examines variation in the benefits, incentives, and services provided by the 47 zones along with other differences among them. We then detail the differential success of the zones. This is followed by an analysis of the impact of EZ program characteristics and other factors on levels of economic activity in the zones.

Characteristics of Illinois, Indiana, Kentucky, and Ohio Enterprise Zones

Even when the enterprise zone laws of two states appear to be similar, what is actually available in individual zones may be quite different. Although state law may authorize local zones to provide various kinds of incentives or services to firms that qualify, local zones may not be required to provide them or they may be free to add others. Because even within a given state zone comparability is not assured, comparison of local zone as well as state programs is important.

In Illinois, Indiana, Kentucky, and Ohio the central EZ concept—that a reduction in tax burdens will spur economic development in distressed areas—is widely embraced in the form of reductions in local property taxes (see Table 9.1). Other direct tax savings, such as reductions in local utility or sales taxes, are provided by a smaller proportion of zones. Provisions reducing future tax liabilities, although less common than up-front tax reductions, frequently exist. Substantial interzone and interstate variation is also evident.

Other benefits available to firms willing to invest in a particular zone include those that reduce costs of investment through fee waivers or reductions, below-market-rate financing, provision of venture capital, and *shopsteading*. Some local zones offer specific services designed to facilitate investment in the zone; most common is the provision of technical assistance.

Enterprise zone advocates stress the need to lift the "dead hand of government regulation," but great disagreement exists over the desirability of pursuing deregulation as part of state enterprise zone programs.[6] This deviation from the classic EZ model is clearly evident in Illinois, Kentucky, and Ohio.

Table 9.1 highlights the interstate diversity that exists in incentives, benefits, and services—but diversity also exists among the zones of a single state. Rarely is a benefit, incentive or service not offered by a few zones in every state.

Table 9.1 Incentives, Benefits, Services, and Other Provisions in Illinois, Indiana, Kentucky, and Ohio Enterprise Zones

	Illinois	Indiana	Kentucky	Ohio
Direct Tax Savings				
Property Tax Abatement/Reduction	94%[a]	90%	83%	100%
Sales Tax Abatement/Reduction	90%	0%	50%	0%
Utility Tax Relief	47%	10%	17%	8%
Other Tax Abatements	0%	50%	67%	25%
Longer Term Tax Savings				
Job Tax Credit	58%	90%	0%	17%
Other Tax Credit (Sales tax credit, etc.)	16%	40%	33%	0%
Nontax Direct Savings				
Fee Waivers/Reductions	63%	30%	100%	17%
Lower Cost Financing	63%	80%	17%	33%
Venture Capital	10%	10%	17%	0%
"Shopsteading"	53%	20%	33%	50%
Benefits/Services				
Deregulation	26%	60%	33%	0%
Technical Assistance	90%	90%	83%	33%
Aid with Regulatory Relief Applications	32%	50%	50%	8%
Other Components				
Infrastructure Improvements	63%	80%	33%	42%
Administrative Staffing Level[b] [2]				
Mean	12.2	42.8	13.5	9.8
Median	10.0	40.0	10.5	5.5

NOTES: a. Except for administrative staffing, table entries are the proportion of EZ administrators reporting that a particular incentive, benefit, service or activity was available to potential investors in the zone.
b. Number of hours of staff time per week devoted to administration of an EZ program. The range on this variable was from 2 to 60 hours per week.

Green and Brintnall have classified the enterprise zone programs of 17 states along seven dimensions.[7] One of these they label *state management involvement*. They note that "many state governments are adopting a more activist orientation to economic development and program management and may be expected to steer enterprise zones aggressively."[8] A second dimension, *public-private cooperation,* assesses efforts to stimulate public-private sector cooperation in the design and operation of the zone program. Based on these two dimensions, Green and Brintnall generate a fourfold typology of state EZ programs. Illinois' and Indiana's fall into the activist quandrant with high levels of both state management and private group involvement. The Kentucky program falls into the private quandrant with a low level of state management involvement but a high level of private group participation. Although Ohio was not part of the Green and Brintnall study, our research indicates it is an example of a hands-off state program in which both state management involvement and private group participation are low.

Interzonal variation on these two dimensions is possible within particular states as well. Local zone management activism might be manifested in several ways, but the staff available to operate the zone is surely one manifestation. No enterprise zone is self-executing. This is especially true for zones with interventionist elements that involve the provision of direct services. Firms, and especially those outside an area, must know that a zone exists. Marketing requires staff effort, but staff resources vary widely and are often quite limited (see Table 9.1).

As for efforts to encourage public-private cooperation, another deviation from the pure enterprise zone concept, involvement of public-private organizations—such as a special association formed for the EZ program or an economic growth corporation—in EZ operations is reported by 75% or more of the EZs in Illinois, Indiana, and Ohio, but by few of the Kentucky zones.

Finally, some enterprise zones engage in efforts to make the area more attractive to investors by improving its physical infrastructure. Although variation exists in efforts to improve streets, rail crossings, sewer systems and the like, some zones engage in such efforts in each state.

Economic Growth in Illinois, Indiana, Kentucky and Ohio Enterprise Zones

Substantial variation in zone economic activity exists across these four states.[9] The mean number of firms investing annually in Indiana's ten zones is ten times greater than the number investing in Ohio's zones

Table 9.2 Enterprise Zone Activity Controlling for Years of Zone Operation

	All Zones (N = 47)	Illinois (N = 19)	Indiana (N = 10)	Kentucky (N = 6)	Ohio (N = 12)
Number of Firms Investing in Zones Per Year, Per Zone					
Mean[a]	17	17	32	22	3
Median[a]	11	10	35	25	2
Range	1–69	2–69	16–49	4–39	1–14
C.V.[b]	0.99	1.14	0.31	0.57	1.25
Value of Investment Per Year, Per Zone (in millions)					
Mean[c]	$24.0	$33.0	$12.6	$13.3	$22.8
Median[c]	8.4	6.8	10.4	9.3	13.8
Range	0.7–218	0.8–218	5–26	0.7–31	1.2–55
C.V.	1.92	2.03	0.67	0.89	0.99
Number of Jobs Created Per Year, Per Zone					
Mean	175	201	243	119	102
Median	92	91	163	92	75
Range	1–694	10–694	62–596	21–272	0–358
C.V.	1.02	1.08	0.78	0.80	0.99
Number of Jobs "Retained"[d] Per Year, Per Zone					
Mean	334	269	240	84	600
Median	75	83	50	50	78
Range	0–3362	0–1200	6–1025	9–244	0–3362
C.V.	2.05	1.45	1.70	1.15	1.92

NOTES: a. Rounded to nearest whole number.

b. The coefficient of variation (C.V.) is calculated by dividing the standard deviation by the mean. A rough rule of thumb is that a C.V. of 0.30 or greater indicates fairly substantial variation and one greater than 1.00 reflects very substantial variation.

c. Rounded to nearest $100,000.

d. Based on local zone administrators' estimates of the number of jobs within the zone that would have been lost due to firms departing the area were it not for the availability of zone benefits.

(see Table 9.2). On the other hand, the median investment per zone per year in Ohio is more than double that occurring in Illinois' zones. These interstate differences suggest that variation in state level provisions affect EZ success. State differences may also reflect other economic advantages of a state or its general business climate.

Substantial variation also exists in the success of zones *within* a given state, with large coefficients of variation for each of the measures of economic activity in the states. Interzonal variation is such that, even in those states with less successful zones overall, there are a few that are more successful than many of the zones in the states that, on average, have the most successful zones. No other state can match the 40% of Indiana's zones that experienced annual investment of more than \$15 million. But one or more zones in each of the other states had this amount of investment. This suggests—state-level program differences notwithstanding—that there is something about zones that affects their ability to stimulate investment.

Firm Status and
Enterprise Zone Activity

Firms already operating in or near an EZ are more likely to take advantage of its benefits.[10] Such firms ought to be more aware of a zone's existence than those located some distance away. Existing firms may also predominate because many, planning to expand anyway and aware of the imminent designation of a zone, postpone investment until incentives become available.[11] Although some EZ advocates contend that enterprise zones are particularly valuable in stimulating entrepreneurship, those wishing to start a business may be least likely to know that a particular area is an enterprise zone. Others argue that EZ incentives will cause firms to relocate to a distressed area. Thus, the relationship between a firm's status and the likelihood that it will invest in a zone must be explored.

Firms already in business in the zones accounted for between 55% (Indiana) and 66% (Illinois) of those investing in them. Our data indicate the zones have had limited success in attracting outside firms—whether from elsewhere in the state or from other states. Only in Indiana was the median number of relocating firms attracted to a zone greater than three per year. Seven percent of the firms receiving EZ incentives in Illinois were relocating firms. The comparable figures are 14% in both Indiana and Ohio, and 16% in Kentucky.

New or start-up firms comprised between 21% and 31% of those qualifying for EZ incentives. This may seem a fairly impressive proportion, but even in Indiana—where such firms constituted nearly a third of those receiving benefits—the median number of new firms per zone was less than nine a year.[12]

Interzone variation within states in investment activity remains substantial regardless of firm status. Although subject to the parameters of the same state program, some zones are more successful than others in attracting particular types of firms.

Even if we assume that all of the development in the 47 EZs has occurred in response to the presence of zone benefits, most zones have experienced only modest success. Across the four states the median number of firms investing in a zone per year was 11. Over half of the firms receiving EZ benefits were already operating in a zone. The zones appear to be less effective than many EZ supporters predict in attracting start-up firms. Equally important is the finding that certain zones have been more successful than others in stimulating economic development of various kinds.

Determinants of
Enterprise Zone Success

Why are some zones more successful than others? What is the relative value of the classic components of EZ programs as opposed to the interventionist elements that many states also include in their programs? Is a hybrid zone, blending both types of elements, most efficacious? What combination of zone components is associated with greatest success in stimulating the expansion of existing firms within a zone versus stimulating new firms to begin operation, or in causing outside firms to either relocate existing operations or expand operations into the zone? Answers to questions such as these are essential to decision making about the enterprise zone economic development strategy.

In this section we use multiple regression techniques to assess the impact of a set of enterprise zone characteristics and differences suggested by the literature and economic development officials on the success of the 47 zones. Enterprise zone success (the dependent variable) is the number of firms qualifying for zone benefits by investing in the zone, measured on an annual basis. We do not use estimates of job creation, job retention, or total investment for two reasons. First, we have greatest confidence in the validity of zone administrators' reports of the number of investing firms. Second, attracting firms—especially start-up firms—is a major focus in economic development, stimulated by Birch's argument that economic growth is most strongly a function of an increase in the number of firms in an area—and especially of newly created firms.[13]

Because the number of zones in the study limits the number of independent variables that can be used in the regression analysis, we focus on the benefits, incentives, and services provided by the zones—along with two locally measured variants of the state-level dimensions of management activism and public-private cooperation identified by Green and Brintnall—that were summarized in Table 9.1.[14]

Classic EZ components include provisions for direct tax savings and are operationalized as the number of different abatements or reductions offered.[15] A second classic component—direct nontax savings—is operationalized as the number of such savings offered by a particular zone. A third element—deregulation—is operationalized as a dichotomous variable. Are such efforts present or absent?

As for interventionist components, management activism is operationalized as the hours of administrative staff time per week devoted to zone operations. The number of discrete services such as technical assistance, but excluding deregulation, that a zone provides is another interventionist component, as is the presence or absence of efforts at infrastructure improvement. Public-private cooperation is indicated by whether or not a public-private EZ organization is active in a given zone.

Zone success is a function of much more than just differences in the package of incentives, benefits, and services that each offers. Although these other factors will receive less emphasis here, they include differences in the objectives of zones, and a variety of *contextual* factors. Zones exist within municipalities as well as within the borders of a particular state. These larger jurisdictions offer various incentives and services to all firms, not just those that choose to invest in the zone. Hence, in our analysis we include measures of whether the broader community economic development program provides loans and/or assistance with site clearance and whether it provides any or all of the following services: streamlining the process for firms to receive assistance, aid in site selection, and aid with loan applications.

Other contextual factors include the regional location of the state or city in which a zone exists, the population of the larger jurisdiction from which a zone has been carved, the economic circumstances of that jurisdiction, its population demographics, and the like. Here we consider the population of the encompassing jurisdiction out of which a zone has been carved. A more populous community has more businesses, businesses that may be attracted to the zone. Moreover, larger communities may possess greater economic development resources that can aid in the attracting of outside firms to a zone. We also examine the impact of zone size—measured in square miles—on zone success on the assumption that larger zones can accommodate more firms, and especially those needing more space.

Because of the small number of states in the study, we have not developed measures of the dimensions on which the EZ programs in Illinois, Indiana, Kentucky, and Ohio differ at the state level. To control for the effects of such state level differences on local zone success, as well as for other unmeasured *state* effects such as *natural advantages* or *economic climate,* we use state dummy variables.

Determinants of Enterprise Zone Success: The Comprehensive Model

Tables 9.3 and 9.4 summarize the predictive power of a regression equation with eight independent variables that test the classic and interventionist models. Measures of contextual factors such as the direct nontax savings or other services provided by the economic development program of the community in which a zone was located, as well as the population of the community, are not included here because analysis indicated they had no explanatory power. The eight variables in the model account for approximately one half of the variance in the ability of zones to attract firms of all types. Although they account for a third or more of the variance in locating for new and expanding firms, this set of variables has much less explanatory power when relocating firms are considered.

As Table 9.4 makes clear, the explanatory power of the comprehensive model is heavily dependent on one or two interventionist enterprise zone components. Classic EZ program components matter little. Decisions by firms to invest are not influenced by the number of tax abatements or nontax savings available to them, nor does deregulation matter. Rather, overall zone success is linked to the administrative resources devoted to operating the EZ program and, to a lesser degree, to the services such as technical assistance that an EZ program provides.

Examining investment by firms of different statuses highlights some differences. Classic enterprise zone inducements sometimes are significant. Direct nontax savings are associated with investment by firms

Table 9.3 Comprehensive Model of Predictors of Enterprise Zone Success Standardized Regression Coefficients (Beta) for Zone Program Components and Zone Area, All Firms and by Firm Status[a]

Beta t	All Firms Probability		New Firms Probability Beta t		Expanding Firms Probability Beta t		Relocating Firms Probability Beta t	
Classic EZ Program Components								
Direct Tax Savings	.08	.58	−.07	.66	.23	.15	.03	.86
Direct Nontax Savings	.13	.38	−.16	.30	.29	.08	−.07	.71
Deregulation	.10	.55	.30	.07	−.05	.78	−.04	.84
Interventionist Components								
Staffing Levels	.65	.00	.35	.02	.64	.00	.41	.02
EZ Program Services	.11	.50	.41	.02	−.09	.60	.24	.22
Infrastructure Improvements	.02	.87	.01	.95	.03	.81	.12	.44
Activity of Special EZ Organization	−.21	.15	.02	.88	−.33	.04	−.11	.54
Other Factors								
Area of Zone	.07	.56	.01	.92	.06	.61	.15	.31
R^2	.51		.49		.44		.27	
Adjusted R^2	.40		.38		.33		.12	
F	4.88		4.55		3.77		1.79	
Sig. F, 8.38 d.f.	.000		.001		.002		.11	

NOTE: a. After extensive testing of other variables (e.g., city population, city economic development program components), classic and interventionist variables, as well as zone area, were entered through stepwise approach with very relaxed criteria (SPSS-PC) to permit all of them to enter the equation. This approach facilitates examination of best-fitting models while allowing for collinearity.

already in the zone and efforts at regulatory relief explain a small amount of the variance in the number of start-up firms. Direct nontax savings such as low cost financing matter for expanding existing firms, but they are negatively associated with investment by start-up firms. Investment by new firms, but not existing ones, is positively related to the availability of services such as technical assistance. Decisions of relocating firms are least well accounted for by the comprehensive model although there is a hint in the data that the availability of various services matters. These are the only firms for whom size of zone seems to matter. Perhaps this is because relocated operations

Table 9.4 Comprehensive Model for Factors Predicting Enterprise Zone Success, Variance Accounted for by Local Program Components and Zone Area, All Firms and by Firm Status[a]

	All Firms	New Firms	Expanding Firms	Relocating Firms
Traditional EZ Program Components				
Direct Tax Savings	.01	.00*[b]	.03	.00
Direct Nontax Savings	.02	.02*	.16	.00*
Local Deregulation	.00	.04	.00*	.00*
Interventionist Components				
Staffing Levels	.31	.25	.18	.16
EZ Program Services	.11	.18	.00*	.07
Infrastructure Improvements	.00	.00	.00	.00
Activity of Special EZ Organization	.04*	.00	.07*	.01*
Other				
Zone Area	.00	.00	.00	.02

NOTES: a. Each variable was entered stepwise with very relaxed criteria to ensure the inclusion of each in the model. The explained variance for each variable, considering the value of the previously entered variables(s) is its explanatory power within the whole set.
b. Indicates that this predictor was inversely related to number of investing firms in a zone.

require more land than do either start-up firms or firms expanding existing operations.

Best-Fitting Models of Determinants of Enterprise Zone Success

Table 9.5 presents the best-fitting model for the number of firms investing in an enterprise zone. This more parsimonious model achieves an adjusted R^2 of .44. Better staffed zones and those that offer more services to investing firms do best. Provisions that yield nontax direct savings are of value as well. The existence of a special EZ organization, something stressed by programs in some states and discussed in the HUD ten-case study as important, is negatively associated with zone success.[16] We have no satisfactory explanation for this. Although Wilder and Rubin attribute the success of the Evansville, Indiana, zone to

Table 9.5 Best Fitting Models of Determinants of Enterprise Zone Success

	B	S	Beta	Probability	
All Firms					
Constant	1.44	4.97	—	—	—
Staffing Levels	.64	.12	.68	.00	$R^2 = .49$
EZ Program Services	3.93	3.09	.17	.21	Adjusted $R^2 = .44$
Activity Level of Special					$F = 10.122$
EZ Organization	−2.22	1.23	−.23	.07	$p = .000$; 4.42 d.f.
EZ Nontax Direct Savings	2.99	2.28	.18	.20	—
Start-Up Firms					
Constant	−1.25	1.31	—	—	$R^2 = .46$
Staffing Levels	.14	.04	.42	.00	Adjusted $R^2 = .43$
EZ Program Services	2.47	1.03	.31	.02	$F = 12.586$
Local Deregulation	3.12	1.78	.23	.08	$p = .000$; 3.43 d.f.
Expanding Existing Firms					
Constant	−3.96	4.82	—	—	—
Staffing Levels	.39	.09	.60	.00	$R^2 = .43$
EZ Direct Nontax Savings	2.88	1.63	.25	.08	Adjusted $R^2 = .38$
Activity Level of Special					$F = 8.009$
EZ Organization	−1.97	.89	−.29	.03	$p = .000$; 4.42 d.f.
EZ Direct Tax Savings	1.85	1.32	.19	.17	—
Relocating Firms					
Constant	−.13	.66	—	—	$R^2 = .24$
Staffing Levels	.05	.02	.38	.00	Adjusted $R^2 = .20$
EZ Program Services	.82	.40	.27	.05	$F = 6.787$
					$p = .003$; 2.44 d.f.

the activity of such an organization, they note that these organizations, required by Indiana's EZ law, have been less useful in other Indiana zones.[17]

Best-fitting models for different types of firms are also given in Table 9.5. The most interesting aspect of the model for investment by new firms, aside from the fact that four variables account for more than 40% of the variance, is that efforts to reduce regulatory burdens do matter—a finding consistent with the arguments of EZ advocates. At the same time, availability of provisions that reduce a firm's taxes do not enter into this model. One reason for this, suggested by some economic development officials, is that a tax credit (a common form of tax incentive for firms) is of little value to a firm that has yet to show a profit. On the other hand, staffing levels—which indicate the availability of personnel to provide services such as technical assistance and help with various types of paperwork—appear to be important to those starting a business.

Although staffing is the strongest predictor of investment by existing zone firms, some support for the classic conception of an EZ is provided by the fact that the availability of various tax and nontax direct savings contributes to the likelihood that existing firms will invest in a zone. The four variable best-fitting model accounts for slightly less variance than in the case of start-up firms (adjusted R^2 of .37). A negative association between the presence of a special EZ organization and zone activity emerges only in the model for existing firms.

Classic EZ components are not included in the best-fitting model for firms that relocate operations to a zone (Table 9.5). Staffing levels and the number of other services provided by the EZ program are the only significant predictors. The explanatory power of the model for relocating firms is the weakest of the three. There are significant differences in the ability of states as a whole to attract relocating firms—largely relating to factors over which local and state policymakers have little influence. We think this accounts for the limited ability of zone programmatic components of any sort to explain variance in the number of firms relocating to a zone.

State Effects and Enterprise Zone Success

Although the best-fitting models account for a good deal of the variation in the success of enterprise zones, other factors are clearly at work. Interstate variation in zone success suggests that various state variables are also important. State enterprise zone programs differ in scope and direction and in the overall worth to the firm of EZ incentives. State differences in resources, taxes, and other business costs are probably related to the success of its zones as well. Given the fairly narrow range of variation in the states' enterprise zone programs, and the overlap of states in zone success, differences in state program provisions are probably not great enough to explain interstate variation. State effects may, therefore, reflect other differences that have been shown to affect firms' location decisions.

With regard to industrial firms at least, Rubin and Zorn argue that investment decisions are best explained by factors that are *uncontrollable*—in the sense that state and local policymakers can do little to affect them, especially in the near term.[18] Transportation, energy, and labor costs are examples of such factors. Only when such costs are relatively comparable between several locations, do costs that are more readily addressed through public policy, such as those affected by the provisions of enterprise zone programs, enter into locational decisions. The data in Table 9.2, as well as the results of a regression analysis using state dummy variables, make it clear that, for all firms, Indiana's zones have been the most successful, followed by those in Kentucky and Illinois. Illinois' zones rank second to those in Indiana in investment by expanding firms, however, although no differences exist among these three states in the number of start-up firms investing in their zones.

It is probably no coincidence that Rubin and Zorn's estimates of labor, transportation, and energy costs for representative firms in each of 20 SIC categories showed Indiana with the lowest or next to lowest uncontrollable costs among these four states in 16 of 20 categories, although Kentucky had the lowest or next to lowest costs in 12 categories. State differences in uncontrollable costs presumably matter most for firms that are considering interstate relocation of operations—firms that the Indiana and Kentucky zones were particularly successful in attracting. On the other hand, Ohio—whose EZs performed least well with respect to investment by relocating firms—had uncontrollable costs that never ranked lowest or next to lowest in any of the 20 SIC categories.

A more completely specified model of enterprise zone success would also have to enter terms for variables such as these—measured not only for states but for individual zones as well. When state dummy variables representing the combined effects of an enterprise zone operating in a particular state context are included, however, predictive power does not improve.

Implications for Economic Development

Although the 47 Illinois, Indiana, Kentucky, and Ohio enterprise zones generally experienced only modest success, some were more successful than others. Variation in investment activity is often due to factors that EZ programs do little to affect, such as broader market conditions or labor costs. Our findings provide only limited encouragement to those advocating the classic enterprise zone approach to economic development. The more successful EZ programs are hybrids that combine interventionist components with one or two elements of the classic EZ approach. Administrative resources matter more than any other factor in our multivariate analysis. Staff that can undertake marketing efforts, meet with firms, and provide supplemental services increase the utility of the traditional incentives that reduce business costs. The significance of competent management and administrative support for zone success has been pointed out by others.[19]

Our analysis also highlights the differential effects of specific EZ program components on the investment actions of firms of varying sorts. Proponents argue that enterprise zones encourage entrepreneurship and, indeed, one quarter of the firms that invested in the 47 zones were new firms. The economic development officials whom we consulted considered this to be a fairly low proportion, however, especially because such firms experience high failure rates. Moreover, interventionist elements of programs, not the business cost-reduction aspects, were most strongly associated with new firm investment.

Elements of the classic EZ model were most powerful in accounting for variation in levels of investment by firms already located within a zone, although administrative staffing again was the most important predictor of investment. The enterprise zone approach had least utility in getting firms to relocate. Even the best-fitting model, which consisted primarily of interventionist components, had little explanatory power. Tax reductions are of little consequence in part because they are so widely available and, hence, do little to differentiate a zone from any other location in the eyes of relocating firms. Even more important is that relocation is primarily driven by cost considerations that local or state policymakers are relatively powerless to effect. This is a major reason that great differences existed across the four states in the success of their respective zones in attracting relocating firms. Only if a zone located in a state with generally high labor, transportation, or utility costs could somehow reduce these to levels well below those of other areas of the state would relocating firms be inclined to consider locating there. As between two states that are comparable in other respects, however, the existence of enterprise zones in one but not the other *may* make a difference in the calculus of a relocating firm.

These findings on the limited efficacy of classic enterprise zone components reinforce those of other scholars, yet political support for the concept remains strong. Given such a climate of support, this research provides some guidance for state and local policymakers seeking to enhance the utility of enterprise zones as an economic development tool. Three points stand out.

First, zone programs should include those elements best suited to the circumstances of the particular types of firms they wish to attract. We believe that zones should target the needs of start-up and existing zone firms. Leaving aside the fact that competition for relocating firms is a zero-sum process from a national perspective, most of the expansion in areas experiencing higher rates of economic growth is unrelated to success in smokestack chasing. Instead it reflects the creation of new firms and the expansion of existing ones.

Second, what matters most for new and expanding firms is clearly the quantity and quality of administrative resources that support the program. Zones should place greater emphasis on levels of staffing and on the skills of those they employ to administer the zone.

Finally, because property tax relief is so generally available in enterprise zones, and abatements are frequently available from local governments for most firms anyway, it makes the most sense to expand other opportunities for direct savings for firms. Low cost financing, access to venture capital, expanding shopsteading programs, and providing fee waivers are some productive approaches. At the same time, for competitive reasons zones must continue to be able to offer property tax reductions to investing firms.

The evidence from this and other studies does not justify a categorical conclusion that the classic enterprise zone does not work. Within the limits of these data, however, we think the classic enterprise zone program is oversold. EZs that include certain of the classic elements along with benefits and services that require that government play a more active role do, however, appear to be relatively effective tools for economic development in distressed areas. This is particularly so when they are supported by the efforts of a sufficiently large and competent staff of economic development professionals. There is, of course, more than a little irony in the fact that the success of an economic development strategy long associated with political conservatives may ultimately depend so heavily on the efforts of bureaucrats for its success.

Notes

1. Green, R. E., & Brintnall, M. A. (1988). Comparing state enterprise zone programs: Variations in structure and coverage. *Economic Development Quarterly, 2,* pp. 50-68.

2. Rubin, B. M., & Zorn, C. K. (1985). Sensible state and local economic development. *Public Administration Review, 45,* pp. 333-339.

3. When data collection began in July of 1987 there were 59 zones in Illinois, 10 in Indiana, 10 in Kentucky, and 51 in Ohio. Our study examines the experiences of 19 Illinois zones, all 10 Indiana zones, 6 in Kentucky, and 12 in Ohio.

4. In 1987 the Ohio Legislature—in a move that runs counter to the logic of enterprise zones—eliminated eligibility criteria related to community economic distress. We examine Ohio's experience with the 1982 version of the program.

5. This chapter is primarily based on data collected as part of the Michigan Enterprise Zone Evaluation Project. Funding for the project was provided by the Michigan Department of Commerce and the Wayne State University College of Urban, Labor and Metropolitan Affairs. The conclusions are our own and do not represent the views of either funding source. For an extended discussion of the project's methodology and its findings both for the Benton Harbor, Michigan, and the Illinois, Indiana, Kentucky, and Ohio zones, see Sheldon, A. W., & Elling, R. C. (1988). *Michigan's enterprise zone program: Progress, prospects, problems and recommendations.* Detroit: Wayne State University Center for Urban Studies; Sheldon, A. W., & Elling, R. C. (1990). *Enterprise zones in four states: Panacea or placebo?* Detroit: Wayne State University Center for Urban Studies.

6. Green, R. B., & Brintnall, M. A. (1987). Reconnoitering state-administered enterprise zones: What's in a name? *Journal of Urban Affairs, 9,* pp. 159-170.

7. Green & Brintnall, Comparing state enterprise zone programs.

8. Green & Brintnall, Comparing state enterprise zone programs, p. 53.

9. An obvious cause of variation in economic activity is the fact that the 47 zones have been in operation for different periods. To correct for this, we use annualized measures of activity.

10. See U.S. Department of Housing and Urban Development. (1986). *State designated enterprise zones: Ten case studies.* Washington, DC: U.S. Government Printing Office; and U.S. General Accounting Office. (1988). *Enterprise zones: Lessons from the Maryland experience.* Washington, DC: U.S. General Accounting Office, Program Evaluation and Methodology Division, Report 89-2.

11. Jones, E. (1983). Enterprise zones: Preliminary observations. *Journal of Voluntary Action, 12.*

12. It is difficult to weigh this because what constitutes a "normal" relocation rate is unknown.

13. Birch, D. (1979). *The job generation process.* Cambridge: MIT Press; and Birch, D. (1987). *Job creation in America.* New York: Free Press. The number of investing firms is positively correlated with the number of new jobs generated (.43), but is unrelated to either jobs retained (.08) or dollar amount of investment (.01). The number of qualifying firms investing annually in a zone is positively correlated with the number of new jobs created in each of the states although the correlations range from .29 in Indiana to .87 in Ohio. The number of firms is strongly positively correlated with amount of investment in Indiana (.62) and Kentucky (.89) but is unrelated to investment in Illinois (.01) or Ohio

(.09). Differences in the objectives of state programs may be at work here. In Illinois any kind of investment, however small, is encouraged. Number of investing firms is most strongly, positively correlated with "retained" jobs in Ohio (.66) and Illinois (.52)—the two states in which number of firms is least strongly correlated with amount of investment. At least in Ohio, the link between number of firms receiving EZ benefits and the number of retained jobs may reflect that state's emphasis on EZs as a vehicle for retaining existing businesses.

14. Green & Brintnall, Comparing state enterprise zones programs.

15. Our operationalization of provisions that provide direct tax savings is least satisfactory because it simply sums the number of benefits offered. A better measure of tax incentives would be their dollar value to firms. Because tax benefits are highly idiosyncratic due to differences in firm characteristics, however, they cannot be determined without detailed information from investing firms.

16. HUD, *State designated enterprise zones.*

17. Wilder, M. G., & Rubin, B. M. (1988). Targeted redevelopment through urban enterprise zones. *Journal of Urban Affairs, 10,* (1), pp. 1-17.

18. Rubin & Zorn, Sensible state and local economic development.

19. Peirce, N., & Steinbach, C. (1981, February 14). Enterprise zones—Would they mean the loss of other federal help? *National Journal, 7,* pp. 265-268; Pryde, P. (1981). Urban enterprise zones: A preliminary analysis. In R. Friedman & W. Schweke (Eds.), *Expanding the opportunity to produce.* Washington, DC: Corporation for Enterprise Development; Wilder & Rubin, Targeted redevelopment, pp. 296-300.

10

Comparative Dimensions of
State Enterprise Zone Policies

RODNEY A. ERICKSON
SUSAN W. FRIEDMAN

Since it was introduced more than a dozen years ago, the Enterprise Zone (EZ) concept has generated much excitement as a policy tool for targeting economic development efforts to relatively small geographic areas suffering from economic distress. Although legislative measures were introduced in the early 1980s to establish a federal EZ program in the United States, the first legislation was not enacted until the passage of Title VII (Enterprise Zone Development) of the Housing and Community Development Act of 1987 [Public Law 100-242]. Title VII authorizes the Secretary of Housing and Urban Development (HUD) to designate 100 severely distressed EZs across the nation. The absence, however, of tax or other financial incentives in the law left the EZ program based only upon interagency coordination and expedited handling of existing HUD or Department of Agriculture programs within the zones. In 1989, HUD Secretary Kemp suspended implementation of the legislation, choosing instead to await the

AUTHORS' NOTE: The authors received the cooperation of many individuals in the completion of this research. Michael Savage, Janice Knutson, and Robert Brever of the U.S. Department of Housing and Urban Development provided data and other information for our use. John Fieser of the Economic Development Administration provided considerable advice on research design. We also wish to thank the many state and local enterprise zone coordinators who gave of their time to provide us with information. The conclusions and policy implications of this research are, however, the sole responsibility of the authors.

outcome of Bush Administration initiatives to put some "teeth" into the zone program.

While Congress fiddled in the early 1980s, state governments across the nation began to enact their own versions of EZ legislation. Although model state legislation was publicized by the American Legislative Exchange Council (ALEC),[1] state legislatures put their own particular twists on the EZ idea and a variety of different programs began to emerge. At present, there are 36 different EZ programs in 35 states with three additional states having enacted geographically-targeted economic development programs. Thus, considerable experimentation with the EZ concept has occurred over the past decade in the United States, despite the absence of any federal program.

The purpose of the research presented here is to explore the comparative aspects of the structure of state EZ programs and to discuss the findings of our recently completed research relating program structure to the effectiveness of state-sponsored EZs as job and investment generating policy tools.[2] This is clearly only one of the ways the programs could be evaluated, because most do not limit their goals to economic development. The chapter begins with an analysis of the results of survey information on contemporary state EZ programs, working toward the identification of similarities and differences in program structure and the development of a typology of programs. Program dimensions are then related statistically to zones' economic development performance.

Structural Variations
in State EZ Programs

Given the nebulous nature of the EZ concept, it is not surprising that the structure of state EZ programs varies enormously. The package of incentives offered by states may be slanted toward either capital or labor subsidies and the programs themselves may be highly complex or relatively simple in their structure and administration. These variations become even greater if one considers the respective state tax structures and the extent to which the incentives duplicate other general incentives offered by the states. The zones may be selected according to a wide range of criteria, and may cover a large portion of the state or be limited to one city.

The structures of these diverse state EZ programs were examined and compared to determine the extent to which programs could be classified into several dimensions of a typology of EZ programs.[3] After finding that the existing summary sources on the characteristics of the programs were both out-of-date and not always reliable, we contacted the state program managers to verify and update existing information on the state zone programs. An initial round of telephone interviews took place in early 1988 and a second round of contacts was completed for newer programs in mid-1989. In late 1989, a final set of interviews was undertaken to update the information on all the state programs at that time.

Administrators from 38 states representing 39 programs were contacted and information packages were received from all but one.[4] Three of the states contacted—Maine, Mississippi, and South Carolina—have geographically targeted programs that cannot, strictly speaking, be considered EZ programs. They are included in our tables as a separate category, but were not included in any statistical analyses because they are not sufficiently comparable. The program in South Carolina and the new Mississippi program are essentially state-wide initiatives with increasingly higher incentives for "moderately developed" and "least developed" areas. The Maine program uses a system of "job opportunity grants" contingent on the creation of new "quality jobs" rather than the traditional tax or financial incentives used in EZ programs. In addition, there are "flexible grants" allocated to the zones for use in staff support and special projects.[5]

Based upon the three rounds of telephone contacts and the materials provided by state EZ program coordinators, we assigned the various EZ designation criteria and employer/employee incentives to a common set of categories. Seven zone-designation criteria were selected for verification:

(1) unemployment,
(2) minimum and/or maximum population size limits for the zones,
(3) population decline,
(4) poverty level,
(5) median income,
(6) the number of welfare recipients or related public assistance indicators, and
(7) the extent of property tax arrearages or property abandonment.

A total of 12 program incentives were included in the categorization. One set of incentives includes five investment incentives (property tax credits, franchise tax credits, sales tax credits, investment tax credits, and other significant employer tax credits); another set includes four labor incentives (a credit per job created; a selective hiring credit requiring either zone residence or some measure of poverty, unemployment or disadvantage; a job training tax credit; and a tax credit for employees); and a final set includes three finance incentives (an investment fund associated with the program, preferential treatment for Industrial Development Bond allocation, and any refundable credits). When job creation or selective hiring were conditions of another credit or business eligibility this was also recorded (see Table 10.1).

Capital gains exemptions, depreciation allowances, and free ports were not included as separate categories in our analysis. We found little or no use of these incentives in state EZ programs. A capital gains exemption was reported by the summary sources only for the Kentucky program. The category of other employer tax credits was taken to include such credits as Kentucky's capital gains incentive, a credit for unemployment payments, and a large tax deduction that was not directly linked to investment. We also did not include incentives targeted to lending institutions because those incentives are very limited. Rather than include the oft-cited distinction between limited and unlimited designations, we decided simply to verify the number of active zones, finding this latter indicator to be an easier measure to interpret. A limited program, such as that in Illinois, may well have more zones than an unlimited one such as that in Pennsylvania, depending upon the nature and timing of program implementation and requests for zone designation from constituent units of government.

We chose not to include the numerous local incentives in our analysis because obtaining accurate data would have been very difficult and time-consuming. Therefore, the property tax incentive was only included if officially part of the state program, that is mandated or encouraged at the state level. Where state program coordinators indicated that property tax was a local option, this was noted but not counted in the analyses (see Table 10.1, pp. 160-161). Tax increment financing (TIF)[6] is locally administered and, again, difficult to verify; thus, it is not included in the analysis presented here. It does seem likely, however, that TIF may be an important factor in the development of some zones and some investigation of its implementation, perhaps by case study, would be helpful in the future.

From a perusal of the legislative intent of the programs it is clear that the official goals are broader than economic development (Table 10.2). Indeed, none of the states cite economic development as the sole intent of the EZ programs. Further examination of the EZ legislation reveals that the promotion of health, safety, and public welfare are also important goals in a majority of the states. Job creation is cited as a goal in almost half of the programs (17 out of 36), and is often linked either explicitly or implicitly to the provision of jobs for zone residents. Eight of the programs cite neighborhood revitalization or a concern with deteriorating buildings, and three claim that their programs will promote community development. Another aim occasionally expressed is that of promoting a broadly based collaboration among government, business, labor, and community organizations (see, in particular, Florida and Illinois). The Florida legislation, which was in large part a response to the Miami riots of 1980, mentions crime as a major concern, and the Georgia constitutional amendment includes a phrase alluding to the "inordinate demand for public services" in certain sections of Atlanta.

In certain cases the promotional literature of the EZ programs provides some indication of the goals for those programs that lack clear legislative statements of intent. For example, Indiana's Enterprise Zone Fact Sheet states that the first goal of its program is to "revitalize specific distressed geographic areas" and the second is "to create jobs for zone residents." The Minnesota Status Reports stress economic development for the competitive zones and the retention of firms in border cities (see Table 10.2, pp. 162-163). In brief, all of the programs contacted indicated economic development as a primary goal, but most included references to other objectives.[7]

A number of EZ programs have been designed to favor particular kinds of development, particularly manufacturing activities rather than retail businesses. For example, Connecticut's program gives higher benefits to manufacturing enterprises, Oklahoma's is limited to manufacturing and processing activities, and New Jersey's excludes retailing and warehousing from jobs credit eligibility. Recent changes to some other state EZ programs have also included such provisions. Pennsylvania's program now favors small industrial activities and export

Table 10.1 Criteria and Incentives for the State EZ Programs, November 1989

	Designation Criteria								Investment Credits						Labor Credits					Finance			
	unemployment	min-max pop.	pop. decline	poverty level	median income	welfare assi.	buildings	TOTAL	property	franchise	sales	investment	other employer	TOTAL	job	selective hire	training	employee	TOTAL	investment fund	IDB preference	refunds	TOTAL
AL	L	–	L	L	–	L	–	10	–	×	×	×	–	3	Cn	Cn	×	–	2	–	–	–	0
AZ	C	mi	–	C	–	–	C	4.5	–	–	×	–	–	0	–	×	–	–	1	–	×	–	0
AR	L	–	–	R	R	L	C	6	–	–	×	×	–	1	–	Cn	–	–	1.5	×	×	–	1
CA(N)[a]	R	mi	–	R	R	–	C	11.5	L	–	×	×	×	2	–	×	–	×	2	×	×	–	2
CA(W)[a]	R	mi	–	R	R	–	C	11.5	×	–	×	×	×	2	×	×	–	–	1	×	×	×	2
CO	C	ma	–	–	C	C	–	3.5	L	–	×	×	×	3	×	–	×	–	2.5	–	–	×	1
CT	C	–	C	C	–	C	C[d]	3	×	–	×	×	×	2	×	–	×	–	1	×	×	–	0
DE[b]	C	–	–	–	–	–	L	–	×	–	–	×	×	3	–	×	–	–	1	×	L	–	2
DC[c]	L	–	C	L	L	–	–	5	L	–	–	×	×	2	–	×	–	–	–	–	–	–	0
FL[e]	C	–	–	–	L	–	–	10	×	–	×	×	×	3	–	×	–	–	–	–	–	–	0
GA	C	–	–	C	C	–	–	2	L	L	–	–	–	1	–	Cn	–	–	0	–	–	–	0
HI	C	×	C	R	C	–	–	2	L	–	×	×	×	3	Cn	×	–	–	0.5	×	×	–	0
IL	C	ma	–	–	C	–	C	4	×	–	×	×	×	3	–	×	–	×	1.5	–	–	–	1
IN	R	–	C	C	C	–	C	9	×	–	×	×	×	2	–	×	–	–	2	×	–	–	0
KS	C	–	–	–	C	–	–	5.5	–	–	×	×	–	2	×	Cn	–	–	2	×	–	–	0
KY	R	–	C	C	C	C	C	6	–	–	–	–	×	1	–	Cn	–	–	0.5	–	–	–	0
LA	R	–	C	R	C	–	–	3	–	–	×	×	×	3	×	×	–	–	1.5	×	–	–	1
MD	C	–	C	–	R	–	C	–	×	–	×	×	×	2	×	×	–	–	2	–	–	–	0
MI	C	–	–	C	C	C	C	6	×	–	–	×	×	3	–	–	–	–	0	×	–	×	1
MN	R	mi	–	C	C	–	–	5.5	–	–	×	×	–	2	–	Cn	–	–	1	–	×	×	0
MO	C	×	C	R	C	R	C	10	–	–	–	×	×	3	×	×	×	–	3	×	×	×	1
NV	R	–	–	–	R	R	–	3	L	L	–	×	×	0	×	×	–	–	0.5	–	–	–	0
NJ	R	–	C	R	C	–	R	9	L	–	–	×	×	3	×	×	–	–	2	×	×	–	2
NY[e]	R	mi	C	R	–	–	C	10.5	L	–	×	×	×	3	×	×	×	–	2	×	×	–	2
OH	C	×	–	–	C	C	–	8	–	×	×	×	×	2	×	–	–	–	2	×	–	–	0
OK	C	–	–	–	C	–	–	2	–	×	–	×	–	1	–	–	×	–	0	–	–	–	0

State				
OR[f]	–	–	0.5	0
PA	4	1	0	2
RI	2	0	2	0
TN	5.5	2	1.5	0
TX	6	1	0.5	0
UT	4	1	2	2
VT	5.5	0	2	0
VA	2	2	1	2
WV	3	2	1	1
WI	6	3	1	0
Other Geographically Targeted Programs:				
ME[h]	7	0	(1)	(1)
MS	4	1	1	1
SC	4	0	1	0

KEY

Criteria		Incentives		Values for Totals
C	considered	Cn	a condition of	*For Criteria:*
I	part of an index		another credit	C = 1
R	required		or of business	full pop. (x) = 3
mi	just minimum pop.		eligibility	mi or ma = 1.5
ma	just pop. maximum	L	local option	*For Incentives:*
				x = 1, Cn = 0.5, L = 0

SOURCE: Legislation, program statements, and state EZ coordinators, 1989.

NOTES: a. $CA_{(N)}$ and $CA_{(W)}$ are California's Nolan and Waters EZ programs.

b. Specific "target areas" are identified in the legislation.

c. The initial three zones for DC were specified in the legislation.

d. Specified as the lack of owner-occupied housing.

e. Zones can also qualify on the basis of the Community Conservation index and if they are eligible for an Urban Development Action Grant or a Community Development Block Grant, or if they are a Neighborhood Strategy Area.

f. Legislation in 1989 left designation requirements open.

g. Some franchise tax reduction is effective in 1991 for certain projects.

h. The Maine program has no tax credits. It uses job opportunity grants contingent upon the creation of new "quality jobs." There are also "flexible grants" allocated to zones for use in staff support, special projects, and so on.

Table 10.2 Statements of Intent for State EZ Programs

	received legislation	statement of intent	health safety & welfare	job creation	neighborhood revitalizing	community development	pub-private collaboration	economic development only
Alabama	x	x	x	—	—	—	—	—
Arizona	x	—	x	—	—	—	—	—
Arkansas	x	x	x	—	—	—	—	—
California (N)	x	x	x	—	—	—	—	—
California (W)	x	x	—	—	—	—	—	—
Colorado	x	x	x	x	x	—	—	—
Connecticut	x	—	—	(x)	(x)	—	—	—
Delaware	x	—	—	—	—	—	—	—
Dist. Columbia	x	[x]	—	x	(x)	(x)	—	—
Florida	x	x	x	x	x	x	x	—
Georgia	x	x	x	x	—	—	—	—
Hawaii	x	x	x	—	—	—	—	—
Illinois	x	x	x	(x)	x	x	x	—
Indiana	x	—	—	x	(x)	—	(x)	—
Kansas	x	x	x	x	—	—	—	—
Kentucky	x	x	x	x	—	—	—	—
Louisiana	x	x	x	—	—	—	—	—
Maryland	x	x	x	x	—	—	—	—
Michigan	x	x	—	x	x	—	—	—
Minnesota	x	—	x	(x)	—	(x)	—	—
Missouri	x	—	—	x**	—	—	—	—
Nevada	x	—	—	x**	—	—	—	—

New Jersey	x	x	—	—	x	—	x	—
New York	x	x	—	x	x	—	x	—
Ohio	x	—	—	—	—	—	—	—
Oklahoma	x	—	—	—	—	—	—	—
Oregon	x	x	x	x	—	—	—	—
Pennsylvania	x*	x	x	x	—	x	x	—
Rhode Island	x	x	—	x	—	—	—	—
Tennessee	x	—	—	—	—	—	—	—
Texas	x	x	x	x	—	—	—	—
Utah	x	—	—	—	—	—	—	—
Vermont	x	x	—	x	—	—	—	—
Virginia	x	x	x	—	x	—	—	—
West Virginia	x	x	x	x	—	—	—	—
Wisconsin	x	—	—	(x)	—	—	—	—

Other Geographically-Targeted Programs:

Maine	x	x	—	x	—	—	—	—
Mississippi	x	—	—	—	—	—	—	—
South Carolina	—	—	—	—	—	—	—	—

KEY

(N)   California's Nolan EZ program.
(W) California's Waters EZ Program.
(x)   Denotes promotional literature or
[x]   Short statement
*   Derived from administrative rules rather than legislation.
**   Found in discussion of business qualifications

SOURCE: Survey data, 1989.

163

services, a policy changed informally in 1987 and formally in 1988. As of 1989, Oregon's program also excludes retail businesses; Arkansas' program favors manufacturing, computer-related business services, and warehouse operations employing 100 or more workers (and having no retail sales); in Tennessee, the job credit is also limited to industrial and selected manufacturing categories.

In our contacts with state EZ coordinators, we also discussed issues of regulatory relief, marketing, and coordination with other programs, but did not include these in the statistical analysis of program structure. Regulatory relief appears to be used rarely, and the second and third more closely characterize program implementation than program structure. Nevertheless, we felt that it was important that these issues be explored in order to better understand program effectiveness.

Despite the EZ concept having been initially based upon "unfettered capitalism" and the enthusiasm of some EZ proponents for a minimization of governmental controls, we found that very little regulatory relief was being granted by the states. In fact, in those states that offer some regulatory relief (for example, Kansas), businesses seldom, if ever, requested it. The regulatory relief that has been offered tends to be procedural rather than substantive, and is usually in the form of one-stop permits, fast-tracking, and fee reductions. When there has been substantive relief, it has usually been limited to assistance with zoning changes, variances that may well have been granted without an official policy of regulatory relief.

Although the majority of states reported some efforts to market the zones, most marketing is done at the local level, occasionally with some state assistance. Many coordinators noted that the state office would like to play a more active role, but had been unable to assist because of a shortage of funds and personnel.

Most state EZ coordinators indicated that an effort was being made to coordinate the program with other policy initiatives, particularly federal programs such as UDAG (Urban Development Action Grants), CDBG (Community Development Block Grants), and EDA (Economic Development Administration). In several cases, the same office administers the zone program and some of the others, so coordination is not difficult to achieve. In a few cases, however, the zone administrators felt that the federal programs were not designed to meet the state's particular needs, and that federal program administrators tended to be unresponsive. Several states reported that efforts to coordinate with federal programs were being undertaken at the local level.

Dimensions of Program Structure

A number of statistical techniques including principal components analysis, Pearson correlations, and multidimensional scaling were used to explore the structure and characteristics of state EZ programs. Given the enormous variation among programs, it did not seem appropriate, for the most part, to classify them into mutually exclusive categories. Instead, we sought to identify dimensions that might help account for the variation and that also could prove useful in our analyses of economic impact.

The principal components analysis failed to describe program variation in terms of a few common factors. The first factor accounted for only 17% of the variance. No variable or set of variables was clearly represented by any of the factors, further evidence of the significant diversity that exists among state EZ programs.

One positive outcome from the statistical analyses was a distinction between those programs that include many designation criteria and program incentives and those that have few. The Pearson correlation coefficient (0.80) between the number of criteria and the number of incentives is positive and statistically significant, and early experiments with multidimensional scaling provided further evidence that state EZ programs could be arrayed along a small-scale versus large-scale dimension. This relationship can be illustrated by plotting the number of designation criteria (weighted according to their strength) against the number of incentives (Figure 10.1). It seems that states offering many incentives tend to pay more attention to the designation process, perhaps to limit public expenditures and/or to target program areas better. There is also evidence of a regional breakdown; most states from Appalachia and the Deep South (West Virginia, Kentucky, Tennessee, Arkansas, Louisiana, and Georgia, with the notable exception of the recent Alabama program), some western states (Arizona, Utah, Nevada, and Oregon), as well as Virginia, Oklahoma, and Hawaii fall into the *small-scale* category. Industrial states from the northeastern seaboard (New Jersey and New York), some midwestern states (Missouri, Indiana, and Ohio) along with California and Florida are characteristic of the *large-scale* category. Programs grouping toward the middle are Michigan, Wisconsin, Minnesota, Maryland, Vermont, and Texas. Further study might demonstrate that these regional patterns are related to the size and influence of state government, population and labor force characteristics, employment needs, and other such

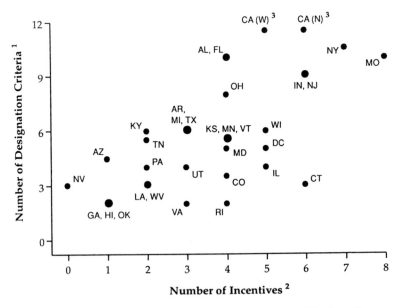

Figure 10.1. Plot of Number of Designation Criteria versus Number of
Incentives, by State

1. Totals for designation criteria calculated as in Table 1
2. Totals for number of incentives equals actual number of incentives (i.e. values for conditions
and business eligibility not included)

factors. In any case, a classificatory dimension based on the number of
criteria and incentives used appears to be a useful one to describe some
fundamental program differences.

Other classification dimensions come from the literature on EZs
and an attempt to predict what the possible outcomes of the various
programs might be.[8] The distinction between investment, labor, and
finance incentives was used to classify the EZ programs in terms of
economic slant (see Table 10.3).

To develop this measure, each particular incentive was weighted
according to its size, the respective state tax burdens, and duplication
with other, existing state economic development incentives. For example, job tax credits, as opposed to selective hiring credits, can amount
to a few thousand dollars per job (for example, Minnesota) or just a few
hundred dollars (for example, Kansas). Although California and Connecticut both have corporate income tax rates greater than 9.0%, states

Table 10.3 Economic Orientation of State EZ Incentives, November 1989 (arranged in descending order of number of incentives)

	I / F / L		I / F / L		I / F / L		I / F / L
MO	IIIIII / FFFF / LLLLL	DC	IIII / FFFF / LL	VT	— / FF / LLLL	LA	II / — / LLL
NY	IIIIII / FFFF / LLLL	WI	IIIIII / FF / LL	VA	IIII / FF / LL	TN	II / — / LLL
CT	IIIIII / FF / LLLLL	CO	IIII / FF / LL	AR	II / FF / LLL	PA	— / FFFF / —
CA(N)[a]	IIII / FFFF / LLLL	FL	IIIIII / — / LL	TX	II / FFFF / L	HI	II / — / L
IN	IIIIII / FF / LLLL	KS	IIII / — / LLLL	DE	II / — / LL	OR	IIII / — / L
NJ	IIIIII / FF / LLLL	MD	II / FF / LLLL	MI	IIIIII / — / —	AZ	— / — / LL
IL	IIIIII / FF / LLL	MN	IIII / FF / LL	UT	II / — / LLLL	GA	II / — / —
AL	IIIIII / — / LLLL	OH	IIII / — / LLLL	WV	IIII / — / LL	OK	II / — / —
CA(W)[a]	IIII / FFFF / LL	RI	IIII / — / LLLL	KY	IIII / — / L	NV	— / — / L

SOURCE: Legislation, program information, and state EZ coordinators, 1989.
NOTE: a. CA(N) and CA(W) represent California's Nolan and Waters programs, respectively.
TYPE OF INCENTIVE: I = Investment; F = Finance; L = Labor.
Totals from Table 10.1 doubled to make whole numbers, i.e., each letter represents 1/2 incentive.

such as Missouri, Mississippi, and Illinois have rates of 5.0% or less. Connecticut is also an example of a state where there is considerable duplication of incentives; many of the EZ incentives parallel those of the state's Urban Jobs Program, with somewhat higher credits allocated for development in the zones. Initial analyses with figures weighted according to these three factors proved no more effective in predicting economic impact, and so we chose simply to use the number of incentives in each of the three categories for our analysis. The only adjustment that was made was to add 0.5 to the labor category when jobs or selective hiring were conditions of another credit or of business eligibility.

Over half of the states have more verified investment incentives than either the labor or finance types; only three relatively new programs had no investment incentives recorded (Vermont, Arizona, and Nevada). Clear labor or finance orientations are much less common. Only Texas (a relatively new program) and Pennsylvania (an administrative program) had more verified finance incentives than any other kind. Labor orientations were detected for Maryland, Louisiana, Arkansas, Arizona, Utah, and Nevada, none of which were large-scale programs having more than four verified incentives. The incentive structures of Pennsylvania, Michigan, and Nevada stand out in that they each have only one kind of incentive—finance for Pennsylvania, investment for Michigan, and labor for Nevada[9] (see Table 10.3).

Another dimension included in our classification of EZ programs is a ranking of programs on the basis of the number of active zones, which provides a rough measure of targeting. Programs that include a large portion of the state (such as in Louisiana, Kansas, and Arkansas) may be very different and have much different economic outcomes than those that have few zones (for example, Michigan, Georgia, and Nevada). Our data indicate that more than half of the state EZ programs had less than 20 zones. Of the 32 active programs, 14 had between 5 and 19 zones, and 5 programs had 1 to 4 (see Table 10.4).

We also considered a distinction based on the size of the zones, using either area or population figures. Again, the idea was to examine the importance of targeting. From our contacts with the state managers, however, it is clear that reliable figures for zone size would be very difficult to obtain for some states. This appears to be a measure that ought to be considered in the assessment of particular programs, but one that is difficult to include in any overall typology.

One final category separates one of the programs from all of the others implemented to date. That is a distinction between Pennsylvania's administrative program and the other programs, all of which have been created by act of the state legislature. Pennsylvania's

Table 10.4 Number of Active Enterprise Zones (November 1989)

No Zones	1–4	Number of Zones 5–19	20–74	>75
Arizona	Maine	California(N)[a]	Alabama	Arkansas
Hawaii	Michigan	California(W)[a]	Delaware	Kansas
Rhode Island	Nevada	Colorado	Florida	Louisiana
West Virginia	Tennessee	Connecticut	Illinois	Ohio
	Vermont	Georgia	Missouri	
		Indiana	Oklahoma	
		Kentucky	Oregon	
		Maryland	Pennsylvania	
		Minnesota	Texas	
		New Jersey		
		New York		
		Utah		
		Virginia		
		Wisconsin		

SOURCE: State EZ coordinators, 1989.
NOTE: a. $CA_{(N)}$ and $CA_{(W)}$ represent California's Nolan and Waters enterprise zone programs, respectively.

program was created by executive order of then-Governor Richard Thornburgh and has been basically a targeting and realignment of existing state government programs to EZs. Because of its uniqueness, the Pennsylvania program might serve as a model for other states or even the federal government, and it seems important to examine its effectiveness. Indeed, existing federal EZ legislation enacted in the Housing and Community Development Act of 1987 [Public Law 100-242] relies primarily upon the coordination among governmental agencies and the targeting of existing programs, that is, it adopts a basically administrative approach.

Toward a Typology of State Enterprise Zone Programs

No simple set of EZ types emerges from the statistical analysis of variations in program structure that can easily be put into "boxes." Instead, what emerges from our analysis is an identification of dimensions that can either help account for some of the variation or that appear to be useful in predicting program impact.

The first dimension is based on the number of criteria and incentives, and suggests that the programs could be aligned according to a large-scale versus small-scale dimension. A regional pattern is apparent with the smaller and simpler programs found predominantly in Appalachia, the Deep South, and the West, while large-scale ones predominate in the Northeast and Midwest, with the notable exceptions of California and Florida.

The second dimension is intended as a measure of economic orientation. Although some programs have fairly balanced structures with similar numbers of investment, finance, and labor incentives, others are marked by a dominance of one or two types of incentives. This classification scheme makes a useful addition to the typology since even small-scale programs can be shown to be oriented to a particular kind of incentive.

As a measure of targeting, we included a third classification scheme based on the number of zones per program, which vary from one to several hundred. Since some programs could give us only approximate figures, we grouped the states into four size categories. Following the initial rationale for these programs, most do, in fact, have relatively few zones. Those that include four or fewer zones are relatively new programs or experimental ones. With the exception of Ohio's program, which operates primarily through local incentives, the programs that include large proportions of the state are generally found in the less-industrialized states. There is relatively little overlap between this category and the others.

The final category of administrative, as opposed to legislative, creation includes only Pennsylvania. There is some overlap here as well, because the Pennsylvania program is the only one limited to finance incentives. Because of its interesting structure, this program is one that would certainly warrant further examination by states with zone programs still in the planning phase.

Program Structure and EZ Effectiveness

Our empirical analysis of the effectiveness of state-sponsored EZs in fostering economic development is based upon survey data of zone characteristics and performance gathered by HUD.[10] Local zone coordinators were asked to provide information on baseline demographic, socioeconomic, and land-use conditions of the host communities. This same information was also requested for the state-designated EZs, as well as employment, number of business establishments, and zone size at the time of designation. Zone coordinators were asked to report the number of establishments investing in the zone, the jobs created or saved since designation, and specific characteristics of the establishments involved. The survey consisted of two rounds, the first of which gathered performance data through 1985 and the second of which provided information through 1986. There are 357 zones in 186 communities across 17 states within the HUD data set, representing all states with EZ programs by 1984 except Delaware.

Empirical analysis of these data indicated that state-sponsored EZs provided some significant increases in both jobs and business investments in many zone areas that were characterized by severe socioeconomic distress and population decline. Although EZs are no panacea for ailing areas, growth rates of gross job increases were higher than the national rate in nearly a third of the zones included in the study. In the average zone, over 460 jobs were created or saved in the period between designation and survey response, typically a period of about two years. Zones usually were more successful in generating jobs through business expansion, new ventures, or relocations than in staving off closures, although rather large numbers of jobs were often involved where closures were prevented. More than 80% of the investment decisions made in the zones were attributable to expansions of existing establishments or to new business ventures, and investing businesses were typically relatively small employers. Manufacturing activities overwhelmingly dominated the tally of jobs created or saved in the zones.

In order to examine the potential effects of state policy variables on EZ performance, we regressed jobs created or saved per year (JPY) and establishments investing in the zone per year (EPY) on a set of independent variables reflecting both control and policy variables. The control variables included ZPOP (the residential population of the zone at the time of designation); ZAREA (zone area); SUNDUM (dummy variable [1] if EZ is in a Sunbelt state); MSADUM (dummy variable [1] if zone is in a metropolitan statistical area [MSA]); ZUNEMP (zone unemployment rate); ZPOV (zone families in poverty); ZMIN (minority share of zone population); ZINDDUM (dummy variable [1] if more than 25% of zone land use is industrial); and EMPCHG (MSA or county [if nonmetropolitan zone location] employment change over same period of time since zone designation). The state EZ policy variables included MKTG (dummy variable [1] if state plays a part in marketing the zones); INCENT (number of verified incentives in the state's zone program); WELFARE (a social welfare index based on socioeconomic distress criteria for designation and labor-oriented incentives);[11] NZONES (an index of the number of zones designated by a state); DESIG (the number of verified criteria used in zone designation); PENN (dummy variable [1] for the Pennsylvania program); and TIME (the length of time the zone had been operational). A full set of data was available for 91 and 94 zones, for establishments investing in the zones and jobs created or saved, respectively.

The relationships between zone performance and the control and state EZ policy variables are presented in Table 10.5. Pearson correlation coefficients indicate that larger (population) zones, and those with more of an industrial land use character, are consistently associated with higher zone performance. MSA location is significantly and positively associated with the number of establishments investing in the zones, and zone area is positively and significantly related to job generation. Interestingly, the Sunbelt dummy is negatively related to zone performance, an indication that the Frostbelt states may have more aggressive and, as noted previously, larger-scale programs than many of the Sunbelt states. The positive relationship of zone performance and minority population share suggests that high minority concentrations are not an impediment to zone performance, at least in the ranges represented in our analysis. Any individual control variable accounts for relatively little of the total variation in zone performance, however.

Correlation coefficients between zone performance and policy variables (Table 10.5) indicate that two variables have consistently strong relationships to performance in both the establishments and jobs measures. The number of incentives unique to the zone program is positively related to performance and the number of zones is negative; both account for a substantial share of variation in performance. In addition, the welfare index is negatively associated with establishments investing in the zone, while both the Pennsylvania program dummy and the length of time the zone was operational are positively related to performance. It is clear that no single variable—control or policy—dominates zone performance, an indication of a complex development process involving both indigenous characteristics and the nature of the policy prescriptions.

Groups of control variables reflecting zone location and scale (ZPOP, ZAREA, SUNDUM, and MSADUM), zone environment (ZUNEMP,

Table 10.5 Pearson Correlation Coefficients Between Zone Performance Measures and Control and State EZ Program Variables (logarithmic form)

| | *Correlation Coefficients* | |
| | *Establishments* | *Jobs* |
Variable[a]	*(1nEPY)*	*(1nJPY)*
Control Variables:		
1nZPOP	0.41***	0.42***
1nZAREA	0.15	0.18*
SUNDUM	−0.37***	−0.30**
MSADUM	0.37***	0.15
1nZUNEMP	0.13	0.13
1nZPOV	0.01	0.03
1nZMIN	0.31***	0.36***
ZINDDUM	0.30***	0.28***
1nEMPCHG	0.05	0.07
State Policy Variables:		
MKTG	0.13	0.06
1nINCENT	0.45***	0.35***
1nWELFARE	−0.26***	−0.12
1nNZONES	−0.53***	−0.27***
1nDESIG	−0.06	0.01
PENN	0.25***	0.16
1nTIME	0.24**	0.10
	n = 94	n = 91

SOURCE: Adapted from Erickson and Friedman, in press.
NOTE: a. See Table 10.1 for definitions of variables.

ZPOV, and ZMIN), zone land use (ZINDDUM), and the condition of the regional economy (EMPCHG) were each regressed separately on zone performance for both the establishments and jobs forms of the dependent variable.[12] As suggested in Table 10.5, the growth pattern in the larger regional economy was in no way related to zone performance and zone land use accounted for a relatively small amount of the variation in zone performance. The zone environment variables also accounted for a relatively small share of variation. Of the control variables, the strongest set was the location and scale group, which explained statistically 29% of the variation in the establishments equation and 20% in the jobs equation. Overall, the policy variables group performed significantly better than any of the other sets, accounting for 49% and 24% of the variation in the establishments and jobs equations.

The better performance of the explanatory variables in the establish-ments equation is probably a reflection of the volatility of employment that is associated with any given number of investment decisions.

When all independent variables were included in the regression analysis, the models achieved relatively high degrees of explanation of zone performance, especially in the case of the establishments equation, which accounted for 58% of the total variation. Standardized regression coefficients indicated that the number of incentives in the EZ package, the number of zones designated by the state, and the Pennsylvania program variable were generally the most important factors in zone performance when all variables were included in the analysis. In the Pennsylvania program, the financial and administrative resources of various state agencies are directly targeted into the zones, so that its character is clearly not one of restricted governmental involvement as some early EZ advocates proposed.

Subsequently, 21 zone coordinators from the 20 highest residual zones (that is, higher than expected performance) for each equation[13] were interviewed by telephone to ascertain their views regarding the factors responsible for the zone's high performance. There was near unanimity among the coordinators that the successes of their zones were a result of four recurring factors. These include:

(1) a zone selection process that focuses on areas with good development potential;[14]
(2) the marginal but catalytic effect produced by EZ designation in combi-nation with other development policy tools;
(3) an array of development incentives sufficient to appeal to a wide variety of businesses, but focused on one or two really critical incentives; and
(4) strong local marketing and public-private cooperation in promoting the zone.

Conclusions and Policy Implications

The analysis of survey data provided by state program coordinators in late 1989 provides considerable evidence of the tremendous diversity of state-sponsored EZ policies across the nation. Some EZ programs are characterized as large-scale—those having many designation cri-teria and incentives—although others are far more modest. States in the

Frostbelt have generally embraced more comprehensive programs than those in the Sunbelt. There are also substantial differences among programs in the particular slant of their EZ incentives toward labor, investment, and financial inducements. While most states have used the EZ policy tool rather sparingly by identifying 20 or fewer zones, a few states have designated very large numbers of zones. All of the EZ programs have resulted from state legislation except the Pennsylvania program, which was created by executive order of the governor and relies primarily upon coordinating and targeting the resources of existing line agencies into the zones.

Using data from an extensive HUD survey covering 357 zones in 17 states, our analysis indicates that state-sponsored EZs have provided significant job and business investment increases in many zones. Like many programs, however, there are a relatively few very successful zones that stand in sharp contrast to a multitude in which little growth has occurred since designation. One of the major objectives of the research reported here has been to identify what, if any, dimensions of the state EZ policies have been related to the positive changes that have taken place in the zones.

Based on the analysis of data for a subset of more than 90 zones located in 14 states and subsequent interviews for high performing EZs, we believe that states should concentrate their efforts on a relatively small and select set of zones that are characterized by genuine development potential. Such areas are characterized as having basic labor skills, public infrastructure, and transportation access that can make the areas attractive for investment with the marginal but catalytic contributions that EZ designation, incentives, and visibility can provide. To accomplish this objective without creating a self-aggrandizing program that overlooks distressed areas is a critical task. Alternative programs may be more appropriate in the most distressed areas. An attractive package of incentives focused around a very selective set of inducements targeted to the needs of existing or potential EZ businesses makes an important contribution to higher zone jobs and investment performance. Direct involvement of state line agencies to target financial and other resources as in the Pennsylvania case may increase chances for success. Finally, state-local and zone area public-private working partnerships seem to be an important ingredient in stimulating redevelopment within enterprise zones.

Notes

1. ALEC is an organization of members of Congress and state assemblies; it included a pro forma version of an EZ bill in its handbook of suggested state legislation in 1980.

2. Erickson, R. A., Friedman, S. W., & McCluskey, R. E. (1989). *Enterprise zones: An evaluation of state government policies.* Final Report to U.S. Department of Commerce, Economic Development Administration, Technical Assistance and Research Division, Washington, DC.

3. See also, Brintnall, M., & Green, R. E. (1988). Comparing state enterprise zone programs: Variations in structure and coverage. *Economic Development Quarterly, 2,* 50-68. Our basis for classification differs from that of Brintnall and Green in that our aim is to assess economic effectiveness rather than to characterize management styles and implementation.

4. The State of California has two slightly different EZ programs—the Nolan program and the Waters program—both administered from the same office in the State's Department of Commerce.

5. For a preliminary discussion of the problems encountered by the Maine program, see the following report : Market Decisions, Inc., and The Irland Group (1989). *Evaluation of Maine Job Opportunity Zone Program.* Final report prepared for the Job Opportunity Zone Commission and the Maine Department of Economic and Community Development, Augusta, ME.

6. Tax increment financing is a technique whereby a local government can raise funds for investments in infrastructure, rehabilitation, and so on, on the basis of anticipated increases in tax revenue following the redevelopment of a specific area in its political jurisdiction.

7. For a 1985 survey of the administrative interpretation of state EZ program goals, see the following article: Green, R. E., & Brintnall, M. (1987). Reconnoitering state-administered enterprise zones: What's in a name? *Journal of Urban Affairs, 9,* 159-170.

8. For a discussion of this literature, see Erickson, Friedman, & McCluskey, *Enterprise zones,* footnote 2, pp. 10-18.

9. Nevada's program, which is basically a local one, is credited with a one half labor incentive due to a business eligibility requirement.

10. Details concerning the survey procedures can be found in Erickson, Friedman, & McCluskey, *Enterprise zones,* footnote 2, pp. 42-44.

11. See Erickson, Friedman, & McCluskey, *Enterprise zones,* footnote 2, pp. 33-36 for additional information on the construction of this index.

12. Complete results of the regression analysis can be found in Erickson, Friedman, & McCluskey, op. cit., footnote 2, pp. 65-92, or in Erickson, R. A., & Friedman, S. W. (in press). Enterprise zones II: A comparative analysis of zone performance and state government policies. *Environment and Planning C: Government and Policy.*

13. There was considerable duplication between the two sets of high performance zones.

14. Some other authors have also argued that development potential is critically important to zone success in job and investment generation: Stimpson, J. (ca. 1983). Observations on the Connecticut enterprise zone program. HUD Memorandum to Benjamin Bobo; Sheldon, A. W., Elling, R. C. (1988). *Michigan's enterprise zone program: Progress, prospects, problems and recommendations.* Detroit, MI: Wayne State University, Center for Urban Studies.

PART THREE

Placing the American Enterprise Zone Experience Within the Context of Its International Antecedents

11

The British Enterprise Zones

PETER HALL

The Theoretical Origins

The precise origins of the Enterprise Zone are a rich subject for historical, even metaphysical, inquiry. Stuart Butler, in a book that introduced the notion to the American public, stated:

> In the formal sense, the term "Enterprise Zone" was publicly unveiled in a speech by Sir Geoffrey Howe, M.P., in June 1978, when he was economics spokesman for the then opposition British Conservative Party. But as Sir Geoffrey freely admitted in his speech, the germ of the concept came chiefly from Peter Hall, an urban planning expert at Reading University and a former chairman of the Fabian Society, the intellectual centre of democratic socialism in Britain.[1]

Specifically, Butler referred to a paper given by the present author to the annual conference of the Royal Town Planning Institute in Chester, England, in June 1977.[2] But this harks indirectly back to an earlier statement: the highly iconoclastic "Nonplan: An Experiment in Freedom," published by four authors in the magazine *New Society* as early as 1969.[3] The authors of that manifesto, which included Hall himself, *New Society*'s editor Paul Barker, architectural historian Reyner Banham, and architect Cedric Price, argued that "The whole concept of planning (the town-and-country kind at least) has gone cockeyed":

> Somehow, everything must be watched; nothing must be allowed simply to "happen." No house can be allowed to be commonplace in the way that

things just *are* commonplace: each project must be weighed, and planned, and approved, and only then built, and only after that discovered to be commonplace after all.[4]

The authors therefore proposed

a precise and carefully controlled experiment in non-planning . . . to seize on a few appropriate zones of the country, which are subject to a characteristic range of pressures, and use them as launchpads for Non-Plan. At the least, one would find out what people want; at the most, one might discover the hidden style of mid-20th century Britain.[5]

The article proposed three such experimental zones in southern and midland England. It was received in embarrassed silence, and was undoubtedly premature. The context, it should be noted, was growth: Britain at that point was at the end of a long period of economic expansion, and the emphasis—as again in 1990—was on the way in which planning controls inhibited and distorted the physical manifestations of that growth.

By 1977, the background was quite changed: The Chester Conference focused on what was then seen as the crucial issue of the day, the dramatic decline of the economies of the inner cities, which had been a major theme of three major consultants' reports published a few months earlier. Hall addressed this problem: "The biggest urban areas have seen their growth slow down, stop and then reverse. They are losing people and jobs." Reviewing the conventional strategies to rebuild their economies, he concluded that for some, none might work. Here, he suggested,

the best may be the enemy of the good. If we really want to help inner cities, and cities generally, we may have to use a final possible remedy, which I would call the Freeport solution. Small, selected areas of inner cities would be simply thrown open to all kinds of initiative, with minimal control. In other words, we would aim to recreate the Hong Kong of the 1950s and 1960s inside inner Liverpool or inner Glasgow.[6]

This radical solution would include three elements. First, each area would be completely open to immigration of entrepreneurs and capital—meaning no immigration controls. Second, it "would be based on fairly shameless free enterprise"; "Bureaucracy would be kept to the absolute minimum." Third, residence would be based on choice, because the area would effectively be outside the United Kingdom's normal legislation and controls. Hall concluded:

> Such an area would not conform at all to modern British conventions of the welfare state. But it could be economically vigorous on the Hong Kong model. Since it would represent an extremely drastic last-ditch solution to urban problems, it could be tried only on a very small scale.

He ended with a disclaimer, that in the event proved ironic:

> I do not expect the British government to act on this solution immediately, and I want to emphasize that I am not recommending it as a solution for our urban ills. I am saying that it is a model, and an extreme one, of a possible solution.[7]

As Hall later admitted, his appeal to Hong Kong was in part based on a misapprehension: He had then visited the colony only once, and had not studied it in depth. He had failed, in particular, to appreciate the huge scale of its subsidized public housing program, which—as commentators were later to emphasize—played a vital role in allowing employers to resist demands for higher wages. But Hall could defend his basic point: However subsidized, Hong Kong had proved an outstanding example of successful transfer into new products in response to world market demands.

Hall later produced a reformulation and a defense of his original argument for a debate with academic critics in the *International Journal of Urban and Regional Research*.[8] Here, he asked:

> Authorship of the idea has been widely ascribed to me—and this seems to have puzzled a large number of people who have heard me described as a socialist or (perhaps more accurately) as a social democrat. How, it is asked, does a person of that persuasion defend an idea based on a return to the principles of *laissez-faire*. . . . Has he abandoned his principles, or his mental balance, or both?[9]

He went on to argue that the global restructuring of the economy demands that advanced industrial nations keep one step ahead, through constant innovation; but that

a short-run—and even medium-run—anomaly will remain . . . a large pool
of structurally unemployed people, consisting of two elements: first, older
workers, especially male, displaced from contracting industries in which
they formerly had special skills, and now forced to choose between unemployment and low-skill occupations; secondly, young workers, both male
and female (but especially male), lacking educational and industrial qualifications. The latter group, in particular, tend to form a marginal group in
declining inner cities.[10]

Enterprise zones might provide some jobs for this group: "They
might do so in two ways, one not so good (but better than nothing), one
much better (in fact positively good)."[11] The first way would be through
in-migration of large corporations seeking cheap labor, the second
would be through indigenous innovation and trading up the skill curve.
Both Singapore and Hong Kong have proved that this is possible, Hall
argues:[12]

Unlike Liverpool and Glasgow, these economies never seem to have had
the problem of mismatch between the supply of labour and the demand for
it. The argument is that by switching on to their development path, we can
emulate it—and take the workers up.[13]

Hall ended his plea:

It would be foolish to claim too much for the enterprise zone idea. It was
conceived as a rather rare kind of social scientific laboratory experiment,
on a small scale, with participants who would be willing because they
would be self-selecting.[14]

His critics attacked the idea because they said it ignored economic
realities. Doreen Massey found her "credulity strained" by the notion:
"The gradual evolution from sweatshop (employing unskilled labour)
to software consultancy (employing skilled) is not—so far as I am
aware—a widely recognized model of company growth."[15] William
Goldsmith recognized that "Enterprise zones would surely work in the
short run" because firms would shift operations to them; but in the
longer run, "the workers threaten to organize along Easy Street, and
there is a new round of lay-offs and shut downs, so that firms can move
all the way to Hong Kong or Honduras or Haiti, from Easy Street to
Ecstasy."[16]

The Zones in Reality

Hall's disclaimer, that his plan was without practical significance, soon acquired an ironic ring. Sir Keith Joseph, a leading Conservative politician close to Margaret Thatcher, took up his idea in a conference arranged by the Adam Smith Institute, announcing that the next Conservative government would establish a number of *demonstration zones* in which "the Queen's writ shall not run." This idea was endorsed and elaborated in an even more significant speech by a colleague, Sir Geoffrey Howe, in the Isle of Dogs in London Docklands on June 26, 1978, when he "unravelled three different concepts to be found in Professor Hall's proposals": the *Crown Colony,* exempt from most legislation and taxes and denied all state benefits; the *Freeport* where goods could be imported, processed, and reexported free of tariffs; and the *Enterprise Zone,* where substantial areas of land would be "given as much freedom as possible to make profits and create jobs"; he rejected the first but accepted the second and third, which could be combined.[17]

Firms would be freed of all planning control save "very basic anti-pollution, health and safety standards," plus some legal obligations including some Employment Protection legislation. The zones would be managed through a "new model of authority . . . with *some* of the qualities of a New Town Corporation."[18] He warned that "of course the grey men whose job it is to consider the 'administrative difficulties' of any new idea would be ready enough to start manufacturing the small print that could stop the initiative in its tracks."

"This," one commentator remarks, "according to many commentators, is precisely what the grey men did to it."[19] The official scheme, which came out of the Local Government Planning and Land Act 1980 and the Finance Act 1980, allowed Local Authorities, New Towns, or Urban Development Corporations to prepare an Enterprise Zone scheme for a site in their area, within which there would be a mixture of fiscal benefits and administrative simplifications for ten years from designation.[20] Specifically, these zones would enjoy a simplified land-use planning regime with minimal conditions like health and safety; new and existing commercial and industrial enterprises would be exempt from rates (property tax) and from a tax (later rescinded everywhere) on development of land; they could also offset expenditure on buildings against Corporation Tax. There would be greatly reduced requirements for industrial training and for statistical reporting.[21]

Clearly, many of the more radical elements of the original proposal—the free migration of labor, the encouragement of immigrant entrepreneurs, the general freedom from mainstream legislation including removal of protection under the Employment Protection Acts—had disappeared, while others had been transformed almost beyond recognition.[22] The author of the notion was subsequently to comment that this was "a particularly poignant example of the way that, especially in Britain, radical ideas are taken on board by the establishment, only to be sanitized into something completely harmless."[23] There were, admittedly, good reasons: EEC membership, Inward Processing Relief, and customs warehousing greatly reduced the attraction of the Freeport status; tax havens were ruled out because they might be abused.[24] The legislation did contain two fundamental elements of the original proposal: a reduction in planning and bureaucracy, and a big reduction in fiscal burdens. But the first of these, ironically, was further diluted in the course of implementation.[25]

In this first round during 1980-1981, 11 zones were eventually designated: Clydebank, Belfast, Swansea, Corby, Dudley, Speke, Salford/Trafford, Wakefield, Hartlepool, Tyneside, and the Isle of Dogs.[26] A further 13 were designated in 1983-1984: Allerdale, Glanford, Middlesbrough, North East Lancashire, North West Kent, Rotherham, Scunthorpe, Telford, Wellingborough, Delyn, Milford Haven, Invergordon, and Tayside.[27]

The original 11 varied in character, from inner cities (Isle of Dogs, Belfast, Salford), through peripheral conurbation areas (Speke, Clydebank) and areas of industrial dereliction (Dudley, Salford, Swansea), to planned industrial areas with services in place (Team Valley in Gateshead).[28] But most, it is important to realize, were blighted urban areas with substantial areas of derelict or abandoned land; and few had any substantial residential populations. They therefore represented a kind of carte blanche for the experiment. Yet, ironically, as one commentator put it:

> Development planning in the zones is as elaborate as planning elsewhere, if not more so. Instead of the most basic anti-pollution, health, and safety standards we have those applied nationally. Particular types of activity are reserved entirely or restricted to particular parts of the zones.[29]

The most striking instance is retailing: Because of the sensitivity of existing retail interests in each municipality, many imposed restrictions of their own. Corby excluded casinos, fun fairs, bingo halls, and betting shops; Clydebank banned "Space Invader" parlors.[30] And this underlies the fact that there was no "new model of authority"; rather, there was a variety of arrangements, generally based on local authorities or other public sector bodies (the Scottish Development Authority at Clydebank, the London Docklands Development Corporation at the Isle of Dogs).[31]

The zone authorities, however, did behave in a new and uncharacteristic way: Even Labour-controlled authorities, hostile to the entire idea, competed vigorously for the few available places; having got them, they enthusiastically followed the precepts. True, there had been major changes of attitude at just the time that the legislation was introduced: Public authorities were beginning to market themselves, and compete with each other to attract industry, dismantling bureaucratic obstacles in the process, and it could be said that the legislation simply catalyzed this process. Most importantly, because the speed of development proved to depend crucially on public ownership of land, public authorities were not required to dispose of their land to the private sector; and in practice, those zones with a high proportion of publicly owned lands were the ones with most development and employment creation in the first year of operation of the scheme.[32]

Monitoring the Zones

One element survived from the original notion of the zones as experimental laboratories: There was vigorous independent year-by-year monitoring.[33] This was conducted by two successive teams of consultants, whose detailed conclusions are substantially in agreement. A fairly definitive verdict can therefore be given on the performance of the zones in practice.

The first set of monitoring was conducted by Roger Tym and Partners over the first two years of the scheme. At the end of that period, the consultants found that 295 firms and 2,884 jobs had been attracted to the zones in 1981-1982, 474 firms and 5,035 jobs in 1982-1983: a total for the two years of 725 firms and 8,065 jobs.[34] Clydebank (1,637), Swansea (1,046) and Corby (1,591) had all attracted more than 1,000 jobs, thus accounting for over half the total.[35] Just under half the firms and jobs were in manufacturing, nearly one third in transport and distribution.[36] Wholly new firms accounted for some 60% of incoming firms and half the jobs by 1982-1983;[37] 86% of relocating firms came from the same county, 92% from the same region. Thus, "the pattern of net effects attributable to the location of activity is similar to that in Year Two: probably three-quarters of the incoming firms would be operating in the same county and at least 85 percent in the same region if there were no EZ."[38]

The most important incentive by far, as quoted by the firms in the zones, was relief from property taxes:[39] 71% of firms listed this, while relaxed planning controls were mentioned by a mere 1%.[40]

The generation of jobs had not been done without cost. The consultants concluded:

> The physical and economic circumstances of the EZs are such that heavy "up-front" expenditure has been required to enable them to generate employment. The investment has had to precede the jobs. The total public cost of the EZs amounts to £132.9 million in the period 1981-83. This total comprises £16.8 million for the rates relief, £38.0 million for the IBAs [Initial Business Allowances], £39.8 million for public sector development and £38.3 million for other public investment. Much of the latter two items would have been spent in the areas concerned anyway. The major additional cost is the £54.8 million attributable to the rates relief and the IBAs.[41]

This suggested that each additional job had cost £54.8 million divided by 8,065, or £6,800 per job generated. The results were thus modest: at a total public cost of £132.9 million, the creation of about 8,000 new jobs, of which about three quarters would have located in the same area anyway, zone or no zone. More than one third of the new jobs had been generated in only three of the zones, among which, interestingly, the Isle of Dogs was not one.

In 1987 came another—and possibly definitive—official monitoring exercise, commissioned by the Department of the Environment (the British government department primarily responsible for urban policies) from PA Cambridge Economic Consultants.[42] It evaluates the experiment against two criteria: first, "The extent to which zones have maintained and/or generated additional economic activity and employment, both on zone [sic] and in their local areas"; second, "The extent to which the zones have contributed to the physical regeneration of their local areas through the provision of infrastructure, environmental improvement and the stimulation of local property markets."[43] The evaluation was based on a survey of 760 firms face-to-face and over 1,100 by postal questionnaire, with half of all EZ firms responding.[44]

The public costs of the experiment, the consultants pointed out, consist both of direct Exchequer costs in the form of rate relief and capital allowances for property development; and of public expenditures usually associated with infrastructure, which would not otherwise have occurred.[45] Over the period 1981/1982 to 1985/1986, only partway through the life of the experiment, the public cost was estimated at £396 million in 1985/1986 prices, or £297 million net of infrastructure costs that would probably have been incurred anyway; 51% represented capital allowances, 28% rate relief, and 21% infrastructure and land acquisition.[46]

In return for this expenditure, by 1986 there were just over 2,800 firms in the 23 British Enterprise Zones, about 70% of them in the 10 original first-round zones (Belfast in Northern Ireland was excluded from the analysis). Total employment was about 63,300.[47] Just over 48% of firms and 56% of employees were in manufacturing, but there were wide differences between zones.[48] The firms tended to be small: 88% had 50 employees or less.[49] About 23% of them were previously on site; 37% were transfers; 14% were branches; and just over 25% were new start-ups.[50] Eighteen percent of the branches and 58% of the transfers originated in the local area immediately surrounding the zone, 31% and 80% from the local region.[51] Only 18% of all firms were more than six years old and the majority, 66%, were in the medium technology group.[52]

Of the 63,300 jobs the consultants found, only about 35,000 were a direct result of EZ policy; most of these additional jobs were local transfers, but some were new, and there were linkages. Subtracting the losses that had occurred to local areas immediately outside the zone, and adding indirect benefits to these areas (such as linkages and construction jobs), the consultants concluded that the net job creation in the zone and in the local economy immediately around it totaled just under 13,000.[53] The consultants found that the cost to the public purse of each additional job created in the zones themselves was some £8,500; the cost of each additional job in the wider local area (including the Enterprise Zones) was between £23,000 and £30,000, depending on whether construction jobs were included or not[54]; the lower estimate includes construction jobs, the higher excludes them but includes multiplier effects.[55]

Over three quarters of the companies in the zones thought that the effect of EZ status had been favorable, and the results indicate that they had performed relatively better than firms elsewhere in their local areas.[56] As in the earlier exercises, firms judged exemption from rates as the most important incentive; it was quoted by 94%,[57] although this may be in part illusory because there was evidence that part was appropriated by landlords.[58] Capital allowances and the relaxed planning regime were also cited as important by a significant number,[59] and between one quarter and one third of all firms regarded the public infrastructure on zones as critical or significant.[60] The effect of relaxing planning controls was difficult to judge because in reality many zone authorities were principal landowners and had greater control powers than available under legislation. Most authorities had sought to maintain some broad pattern of land use while liberalizing where possible conventional planning barriers to development.[61]

The survey of developers showed that capital allowances in the zones had begun to attract private finance capital from the south of England into EZs in northern and northwestern Development Areas.[62] In the south, these allowances could be regarded as deadweight because they were not necessary to stimulate development.[63]

That is perhaps significant, because the most dramatic single development in the Enterprise Zones occurred in July 1987, almost simultaneously with that report: an agreement by the Canadian developers Olympia and York to proceed with a huge office complex at Canary Wharf in the middle of the London Docklands area, taking advantage of the Enterprise Zone status and providing an estimated 43,000 office jobs. What was not clear was how far large-scale development on this valuable site might not have happened anyway. In the event, Canary Wharf soon proved to have exhausted the capacities of the relatively modest light rail scheme that was at that point under construction; late in 1989, agreement seemed to have been reached between the developers and London Regional Transport for a £900 million extension of the Jubilee underground line, but as late as March 1990 final details were still being hammered out.

Conclusion

Two firm conclusions, at least, can be drawn from the British experiment. The first is that there was a huge gap between the grand sweep of the original concept and the reality of what was actually achieved. Some commentators clearly found conspiracy in all this. Professor Denman of Cambridge University said that "the bureaucrats have succeeded in frustrating the government's original plan," Stan Taylor spoke of "policy drift"; but Morrison's impartial study concludes that these critics may have overemphasized the differences.[64] Whether the saga provides material for an episode of *Yes Minister,* as many undoubtedly believe, or whether the original notion was in various ways not capable of implementation, remains for debate.

The second conclusion is that the experiment in practice produced relatively small numbers of really new jobs, and at appreciable—but perhaps not excessive—cost. This, doubtless, lay behind the decision of the Thatcher government not to extend the experiment. Since 1987, it has placed far greater weight on the Urban Development Corporation as a mechanism for rapid assembly, development, and disposal of urban land; and on the simplified planning regime as a general tool of development throughout the country. It has also revived the Freeport notion from the original proposal, causing one commentator to conclude that "Whitehall perhaps stole the Emperor's clothes, but the Empire struck vigorously back."[65]

And, additionally, in parallel with the highly controversial Community Charge to replace household property taxes—introduced in Scotland in April 1989, in England and Wales a year later—the government has established a uniform business rate throughout the country, so that vagaries in local business property tax have been removed. In this respect, the British government appears to have demonstrated that it has learned from experience: the Enterprise Zone experiment is over, but the lessons are embodied into new policies that may yet achieve the same objectives.

Notes

1. Butler, S. M. (1981). *Enterprise zones: Greenlining the inner cities.* New York: Universe Books, p. 95.

2. Hall, P. (1977). Green fields and grey areas. *Papers of the RTPI Annual Conference, Chester.* London: Royal Town Planning Institute. Reprinted in: Hall, P. (1981). *The enterprise zones concept: British origins, American adaptations.* Berkeley: University of California, Institute of Urban and Regional Development, Working Paper 350.

3. Banham, R., Barker, P., Hall, P., & Price, C. (1968). Non-plan: An experiment in freedom. *New Society, 26,* pp. 435-443.

4. Ibid., p. 435.

5. Ibid., p. 436.

6. Hall, Green fields and grey areas, p. 5.

7. Ibid., p. 5.

8. Hall, P. (1982). Enterprise zones: A justification. *International Journal of Urban and Regional Research, 6*, pp. 416-421.

9. Ibid., p. 416.

10. Ibid., p. 418.

11. Ibid., p. 418.

12. Ibid., pp. 418-419.

13. Ibid., p. 419.

14. Ibid., p. 420.

15. Massey, D. (1982). Enterprise zones: A political issue. *International Journal of Urban and Regional Research, 6*, p. 430.

16. Goldsmith, W. W. (1982). Enterprise zones: If they work we're in trouble. *International Journal of Urban and Regional Research, 6*, p. 439.

17. Morison, H. (1987). *The regeneration of local economies*. Oxford: Oxford University Press, p. 84.

18. Ibid., p. 84.

19. Ibid., pp. 84-85.

20. Ibid., p. 85.

21. Ibid., p. 85.

22. Ibid., p. 85; Hall, P. (1989). *Cities of tomorrow: An intellectual history of urban planning and design in the twentieth century.* Oxford: Blackwell, p. 357.

23. Hall, Cities of tomorrow, p. 357.

24. Morison, Regeneration of local economies, pp. 85-86.

25. Ibid., p. 86.

26. Ibid., p. 85.

27. Great Britain Department of the Environment. (1987). *An evaluation of the enterprise zone experiment.* PA Cambridge Economic Consultants. London: Her Majesty's Stationery Office, p. 13.

28. Morison, Regeneration of local economies, p. 90.

29. Ibid., p. 86.

30. Ibid., p. 87.

31. Ibid., p. 88.

32. Ibid., pp. 88-89.

33. Ibid., p. 90.

34. Tym, R. & Partners, & Weeks, L.-D. (1984). *Monitoring enterprise zones: Year three report.* London: Roger Tym Associates, p. 144.

35. Ibid., p. 56.

36. Ibid., p. 144.

37. Ibid., p. 144.

38. Ibid., p. 144.

39. Ibid., p. 144.

40. Ibid., p. 80.

41. Ibid., p. 148.

42. Great Britain Department of the Environment, An evaluation.

43. Ibid., p. 1.

44. Ibid., p. 1.
45. Ibid., p. 1.
46. Ibid., pp. 10-12.
47. Ibid., p. 18.
48. Ibid., p. 21.
49. Ibid., p. 21.
50. Ibid., p. 25.
51. Ibid., p. 30.
52. Ibid., pp. 26, 28.
53. Ibid., pp. 52-53.
54. Ibid., p. 2.
55. Ibid., p. 2.
56. Ibid., p. 85.
57. Ibid., p. 57.
58. Ibid., p. 75.
59. Ibid., p. 57.
60. Ibid., p. 62.
61. Ibid., p. 70.
62. Ibid., p. 70.
63. Ibid., p. 68.
64. Morison, Regeneration of local economies, p. 83.
65. Ibid., p. 83.

12

Assembly Industries, Technology Transfer, and Enterprise Zones

JOSEPH GRUNWALD

Latin America and East Asia

Compared to East Asian *newly industrializing countries* (NICs), the economic development of Latin American NICs has been disappointing. Not only has the economic growth of the East Asian NICs far outpaced the growth of Latin American countries, but also the income distribution in East Asia has become considerably more equal than in Latin America.

The first reaction to this picture is that the Latin American NICs should follow the East Asian development model. The growing literature on this subject, however, has made it clear that this conclusion is superficial.[1] First, there are significant cultural and historical differences between the two regions that make recommendations for one area to copy the other highly questionable. Then there is the fact that the East Asian NICs have not followed a single growth model. Their diversity may be even greater than Latin America's.

The disparities among the *four tigers* in East Asia—South Korea, Taiwan, Hong Kong, and Singapore—have resulted in various styles of development that have led all four of them to become formidable industrial exporters. South Korea and Taiwan are lands of substantial size and population; the other two are small city-states that in the past had been significant entrepôt economies. Industrialization in South Korea has progressed on the basis of huge, privately owned, national conglomerates—called *chaebol*—that have spanned a variety of activities.[2] In Taiwan and Hong Kong, the main economic agents have been medium or small—often family-owned—private enterprises. Foreign firms have played a major part in Singapore.

The role of the state in economic development has varied considerably among the four tigers. Although diminishing, the size of the public sector has been large in South Korea and Taiwan, comparable to the proportions existing in many of the larger Latin American economies of which government enterprises have been a major part. Hong Kong is usually considered an exception, because it appears that the authorities have stayed out of the economy. The government role, however, has not been trivial there. By providing inexpensive housing and, through special arrangements, cheap food from mainland China, the Hong Kong authorities have been able to restrain wage demands, thus preventing a slowdown in the industrial export expansion.

If one adds geopolitical disparities and differences in priorities and economic specialization, it becomes apparent that the four tigers could not have pursued a single development model—just as the major Latin American NICs, Argentina, Brazil, and Mexico, have not followed a unique growth pattern.

Nevertheless, there are lessons to be learned. Although in most aspects there are sharp contrasts, the two regions have certain features in common. One is that the state has played an important role in economic development. Another is that both regions have gone through periods of import-substituting industrialization.

Although governments are major actors, there are key differences in their roles in Latin America and East Asia. In the East Asian NICs, government-business relations have usually been cooperative, if not collaborative. Somehow, state interventions there have managed to conform to the market and so have promoted the enormously successful export orientation of the four tigers. In Latin America, government-business relations frequently have been adversarial rather than cooperative. Latin American NIC regimes, responding to elite pressure groups and their own self-interest, have built up a huge and unwieldy public sector while ignoring efficiency. The myriad public enterprises, combined with continuing import substitution policies that have protected inefficient domestic industries, have smothered market signals and absorbed precious public resources, thus eroding opportunities for national economic dynamism.

The greater equality in the distribution of income in East Asian countries compared to Latin America can be attributed in part to education and in part to the substantial land reforms there.[3] In Latin America, land tenure arrangements have been slow to change. There are still huge estates, owned by absentee landlords, that are under-utilized and/or misused, existing side by side with a vast number of microfarms, too small for efficient cultivation and for providing adequate subsistence to their owners, forcing many of these small owners to labor under pre-capitalist, serflike conditions for large landholders.

A central distinction of the East Asian NICs has been the emphasis on education. The four tigers, as Japan before them, have recognized very early that low wages alone do not make a sound base on which to build healthy economic development. They have known that international competition demands a substantial level of technology, that technology is transferred through human beings, and that, because technology is ever rising, human capital must be continually upgraded.

In Latin America, education has not enjoyed as high a priority. Compared to the Far East, a smaller proportion of national resources was spent on education even before the debt crisis. Just to cite one type of data: In 1965 the proportion of the relevant age group enrolled in secondary education was more than double in the Republic of Korea than that of either Brazil or Mexico. Although for all countries the proportions have increased sharply since then, by the mid-1980s the gap had widened for Brazil (95% for Korea versus 36% for Brazil) and had not improved much for Mexico (55%). Even literate Argentina had only three quarters of Korea's proportion of school-age persons in secondary school in 1986. For Brazil and Mexico the lag is even worse for higher education. In 1986, South Korea had 33% of the corresponding age group enrolled in higher education, compared to 11% (1984) for Brazil and 16% for Mexico.[4]

Table 12.1, about foreigners studying in U.S. universities, also indicates a Latin American educational lag. Allowing for differences in population size, more than 10 times as many Koreans and Taiwanese as Latin Americans received U.S. Ph.Ds. during the past three decades. Most significantly, the difference was 22 times for engineering doctorates and even in the social sciences the East Asians exceed the Latin Americans by 6 times. Specifically, 8 times as many far-away Koreans and 23 times as many Taiwanese received U.S. Ph.D. degrees than did the next-door Mexicans between 1960 and 1988. In the engineering fields the gap is enormous: relative to their populations—45 times more U.S. Ph.D. degrees for Taiwanese than for Mexicans!

Table 12.1 Doctorates per Million Population Received by Foreigners at U.S. Universities, 1960–1988

	Social Sciences	Natural Sciences	Engineering	All Ph.D.s
Latin America	7	18	7	41
Korea and Taiwan	43	169	156	423

SOURCE: Calculated from *Science and Engineering Doctorates: 1960-1988, NSF 89-320*, (Washington, DC, 1989), Table 6, pp. 136-146. The data are based on the average population for the period.

Obviously these data must not be interpreted as reflecting the true discrepancies in educational levels between Latin American and East Asian countries. For one thing, it has been generally recognized that, on average, Latin American universities have been superior to those in the East Asian countries and therefore the felt need to study abroad may have been less in Latin America. For another, a greater proportion of Latin Americans may have studied in non-U.S. universities than has been the case with East Asians. Nevertheless, the above differences are so striking that they must reflect a significant difference in emphasis given to education between the two regions.[5]

On the historical side, compared to the Latin American NICs the four tigers have been newcomers to industrialization, implying important but subtle differences between the two regions. In Argentina, Brazil, and Mexico, small but significant manufacturing had begun in the last century. When the four tigers embarked on their industrialization shortly after the middle of the current century, the Latin American NICs already had about one fifth of their labor force in manufacturing and an even larger proportion of their gross national products originated in that sector.[6] It should not be surprising, therefore, that attitudes toward different economic activities would vary between the two regions. In the beginning, the four tigers welcomed any manufacturing activity— no matter how lowly—as an opportunity for economic growth. By that time, Latin American NICs had given high priority to more advanced industrial activities.

For example, when assembly work was introduced by U.S. companies into Mexico in the 1960s, it was seen there as a means of absorbing border unemployment, but not as a contribution to national industry. The four tigers have treated assembly operations as a stepping-stone toward industrial development. In both regions assembly operations are export industries and both have used special enterprise zones for them. In Taiwan and South Korea, some, but not all, assembly production has taken place in *Export-Processing Zones* (EPZs); in Mexico all such exports have been produced in *maquiladoras,* a type of EPZ system, as discussed below.[7]

The operation of assembly plants can serve as a significant vehicle for technology transfer, as the East Asian experience has demonstrated. Because the Mexican experience with this economic activity has been unique, it will be used as a case study. As an example of how distinct approaches to the introduction of a new economic activity can lead to divergent results in the diffusion of technology, the first part of the following discussion compares the operation of assembly industries in the two regions. The second part examines the policy implications for a viable future of assembly operations in Mexico.

The Maquiladora in Mexico Today[8]

When in 1964 the United States discontinued the *bracero* program that had permitted Mexicans to work in U.S. agriculture on a seasonal basis, the Mexican government introduced a border industrialization program to absorb the labor force left unemployed at the border. This program—in effect a huge enterprise zone—permitted duty-free (in-bond) imports of machinery, equipment, and components for processing or assembly within a 20-kilometer strip along the border, provided that the imported products were reexported. Subsequent legislation has exempted the maquiladoras, as these assembly plants are called in Mexico, from the requirement of Mexican majority ownership. Further official changes have allowed (with a few exceptions) the establishment of maquiladoras in the interior of the country, and decrees in 1983 and 1989 permitted the sale of up to 20% and 50%, respectively, of maquiladora output within Mexico, subject to certain restrictions and approval by the authorities.

Starting with less than half a dozen U.S. assembly factories in the mid-1960s, there are, as of early 1990, about 1,800 plants with almost half a million employees, nearly all close to the U.S. border. Japanese maquiladoras and, most recently, Korean plants, although still less than 10% of the total, have become increasingly prominent.[9] The phenomenal explosion of maquiladoras during this decade coincided with the massive devaluation of the Mexican peso. When the peso dropped from about 4 U.S. cents in the early 1980s to less than 0.04 U.S. cents in the second half of the decade, Mexican wages in dollar terms fell from the highest in the Third World to among the lowest.

Japanese, U.S., and other countries' firms have benefitted from establishing assembly plants in Mexico, now saving about three quarters of assembly wage costs by operating there. Additional benefits are derived from the lower cost of packing materials, utilities, and other infrastructure expenditures.

For Mexico, also, the maquiladora has been a blessing, particularly during this decade. After petroleum, it is now the largest foreign exchange earner for the country and a significant employer, accounting for about 12% of export earnings and creating almost 10% of industrial employment.[10] Since 1982, the onset of the current economic recession, the maquiladora industry has been practically "the only game in town"—Mexico's most dynamic sector.

Assembly in East Asia

When the United States faced international competition after many years as the uncontested economic power in the early postwar world, U.S. enterprises explored the globe for low-wage partner countries with which to share production. U.S. firms divided production into the capital- and knowledge-intensive processes where they still held a comparative advantage, and labor intensive processes—primarily assembly operations—where high wages made them uncompetitive. U.S. companies shifted labor-intensive production processes to South Korea, Taiwan, Hong Kong, and Singapore where wages were among the lowest in the newly developing world and only a fraction of those in Mexico at that time.

Maquiladora-like assembly plants in the four countries have rapidly become integrated into those nations' domestic economies. Some U.S. companies established subsidiaries, others entered joint ventures with local businesses, and many more subcontracted with local firms. Local entrepreneurs quickly abosrbed technologies from "maquiladoras" and adapted the new know-how to domestic and export production. Soon, local firms supplied assembly plants with most components previously imported from the United States.[11] It did not take long for four tiger firms to produce these products from beginning to end.[12]

The key to this development has been that assembly industries have been part of domestic industry from the start. The EPZs have been an adjunct to the country's general export production. Their importance in the Taiwanese and Korean economies, never massive, has declined significantly.[13] Neither official regulations nor public attitudes isolated assembly operations from other economic activities. There has never been a special designation for assembly industries (such as *maquiladora* in Mexico) to set them apart legally. Outside of the EPZs, assembly and production for the home or export markets have taken place in the same plant; no restrictions have limited selling output of assembly operations within the country. Plants, whether in the EPZs or outside, have imported inputs for export production duty free.[14]

From the beginning, local firms in the East Asian NICs have been involved in assembly industries as subcontractors, in joint ventures, or as suppliers. Entrepreneurs, managers, and workers learned production technologies, including managerial know-how, from U.S. parent companies and applied them to production for the home market and to other rapidly emerging export production.

Assembly industries thus became an important springboard for industrialization of the four tigers. Not being confined to the EPZs, they have contributed to transfer of high technology and managerial skills. Even the EPZs have helped to upgrade the labor force.

The combination of low wage cost plus advanced technology has become unbeatable and has helped make the four tigers the formidable international competitors they now are.

The Mexican Situation

In Mexico, the situation has been dramatically different. The maquiladora has remained essentially a foreign enclave, isolated from the rest of the economy. There is still little involvement of Mexican capital in assembly production and in supplying maquiladoras.[15]

Despite legislation allowing the establishment of maquiladoras in the interior, more than 90% of the plants cluster in Mexican towns near the U.S. border. This is understandable because it minimizes transportation costs for U.S. companies, facilitates trouble-shooting by managers and engineers based at U.S. headquarters, and permits factory managers to live in the United States and work across the border in Mexican plants.

The situation is similar for Japanese maquiladoras because most of them are subsidiaries of Japanese subsidiaries in the United States.

Therefore, unlike the situation in East Asia, linkages of assembly operations to domestic production have been weak. Isolation of the maquiladora has been largely self-imposed by Mexico through laws, regulations, and attitudes. The maquiladora has been separated officially from other production through an EPZ-like arrangement that has made it difficult to establish linkages to Mexican economic development. Assembly production and production for the domestic market or for regular exports rarely have occurred under the same roof, giving Mexican managers and technicians little opportunity to apply to other economic activities what they learn from the technologically advanced foreign plants in which they work. Despite the 1983 decree allowing up to 20% of maquiladora output to be sold within Mexico, fear of "unfair" competition has resulted in only a negligible amount of licensed domestic sales so far. Mexican firms have thus been deprived of direct access to sophisticated subassemblies produced by the maquiladoras, sometimes forcing them to import high-tech Mexican-made items from the United States.

As a legacy of the high trade barriers that, until recently, have protected Mexican industry, Mexican firms have not been internationally competitive; they have been unable to meet international prices, quality standards, and delivery schedules. Therefore, only a trivial proportion of materials used in assembly plants have been of Mexican origin. Less than 1% of all materials has consisted of Mexican components for assembly and, if one adds janitorial supplies and packing materials, the proportion of total inputs of Mexican origin has rarely exceeded 3%.

Contributing to the isolation of the maquiladora within the Mexican economy is the belief that assembly is an inferior economic activity, like taking in someone else's dirty laundry, not worthy of significant Mexican resources and effort. The maquiladora has never been considered a bona fide manufacturing industry in Mexico. Even in official Mexican foreign trade statistics, sales of the maquiladoras to the United States and other countries have been recorded as services rendered to foreigners and not as exports of manufactured goods.

In this view, national capital and entrepreneurship would be better served in indigenous industrialization efforts than in assembly plants or in efforts to supply them. As long as national industries have been protected through high trade barriers, this view has reflected the reality that Mexican firms could make more money producing for the home market than for exports, including the maquiladora.[16] The prevailing attitude toward the maquiladora has been: Let the foreigner do it!

Moreover, the maquiladora has been subject to severe criticism by some Mexican academics and others, ranging from accusations of sweatshop exploitation to complaints about health hazards and pollution. Furthermore, observers have pointed to leakage of foreign exchange earnings when Mexican workers in the border plants spend their wages in the United States and to the fact that employment has been given primarily to young, low-wage (and nonmilitant) women who previously were not in the labor force, and not to men who form the bulk of the under- and unemployed.

In sum, the EPZ system and regulations designed to protect local industry, as well as Mexican attitudes, have helped prevent the emergence of significant linkages to the rest of the Mexican economy. Often the same people who hold assembly work in low esteem and therefore wish to keep Mexican resources away from it have criticized it as not contributing to Mexican industrialization. If these activities are judged ill suited for national capital and a controlled foreign enclave is deliberately created, then they cannot be condemned for not being integrated into the national economy and not doing more for national economic development. It makes no sense to hold both views and to pursue self-defeating policies.

Because of its contribution to foreign exchange earnings and employment, Mexico has tolerated—but not promoted—the maquiladora.[17] Since the debt crisis and the ensuing economic depression, criticism has been muted in realization that the maquiladora is currently the best thing the Mexican economy has going for it.

Policy Implications

As long as the country suffers under crushing external debt and the long-lasting economic slow down and declining real wages, the maquiladora will remain the most dynamic sector and critics will be silent. In a recovering Mexico, however, the maquiladora will need to be integrated into the Mexican economy if assembly industries are to remain dynamic and viable in the long run.

Integration necessitates the pursuit of the following policy objectives:

- Greater participation of Mexican capital and Mexican entrepreneurs in assembly production as owners and suppliers.
- Relaxation of Mexican government limitations on sale of maquiladora output in the domestic market.
- Increased education and training of Mexican workers, supervisors, and managers in new technologies, know-how, and skills.
- Expansion of maquiladoras into the Mexican interior.

The first objective requires the continued lowering of trade barriers and elimination of unreasonable protection of Mexican industry. This will force Mexican firms to become more cost and quality conscious, and thus more internationally competitive, providing the basis for them to venture into production for exports and for the maquiladora.

In addition, an important incentive for export production is the drawback of duties on imported inputs. This would make inputs accessible at world prices to Mexican producers who need to compete internationally.

Over $10 billion in components and materials are currently being used in the maquiladoras, almost two thirds from the United States and most of the rest from Japan, other East Asian countries, and Europe.[18] This provides an enormous opportunity for Mexican production.

Greater international competitiveness would also make Mexican producers desirable partners in joint ventures with foreign companies or attractive subcontractors for firms in the United States, Japan, or elsewhere. The objective is not to reserve the maquiladora for Mexican capital. After all, foreign ownership alone does not make a foreign enclave. It is deliberately isolating assembly operations that results in the enclave and weakens the maquiladora's contribution to the country's industrialization. Involving Mexican firms facilitates the transfer of technology from maquiladora operations to other productive activities. If the Mexican firm as a partner or subcontractor is also engaged in non-maquiladora activities, such as producing home-market goods, the diffusion of technology can occur almost automatically. This has been the principal way through which assembly technology has been transferred in the East Asian NICs.[19]

In regard to the second objective, the Mexican government has recently taken an important step that might help the integration of maquiladoras into the economy. In official regulations, promulgated in mid-May of 1989, up to 100% foreign ownership of manufacturing enterprises is permitted.[20] Presumably, this will allow the conversion of a 100% foreign-owned maquiladora—the only manufacturing activity previously exempt from the 49% limitation—to a regular manufacturing enterprise. In this case, assembly production can exist side-by-side with other production and, presumably, can be sold without restriction in the country. Therefore, one may further assume that not only foreign majority-owned plants but also Mexican majority-owned maquiladoras would be permitted unlimited domestic sales of assembly output.[21]

The third objective is based on the fact that the vehicle for technology transfer is people and it is their knowledge that must be upgraded to make technology increases possible. Several major U.S. firms have already gone quite far in upgrading the skills of their Mexican employees. Some provide further training for Mexican technical and supervisory personnel in the parent companies in the United States. More needs to be done by foreign firms, but education, the enrichment of Mexico's human capital, is primarily a Mexican responsibility as an essential part of the economic development effort.

In regard to the last objective listed above, experience has shown that maquiladoras in the interior of Mexico have greater linkages to the local economy than those at the border: A larger share of materials used in plants is of national origin and there is no leakage of wages into the United States. Moreover, assembly plants, although taking advantage of lower labor costs, can aid in reducing underemployment and raising incomes by locating in the large pockets of poverty in Mexico's interior. This is a classic objective of enterprise zones.[22]

Hopefully, new Mexican regulations will remove the existing sharp separation of assembly production from other manufacturing, a separation that stands in the way of technology transfer and other linkages. The absence of such a differentiation in the East Asian countries helped make assembly operations a stimulus for economic growth.

The Obstacles

There may be resistance in Mexico against government policies effecting these changes. The pejorative image of assembly production will not easily change. Furthermore, despite increasing liberalization of the Mexican economy, local businesses continue to fear foreign competition and may oppose the unrestricted sale of maquiladora products on the domestic market, unless a major share of materials used is of Mexican origin. As potential maquiladora suppliers, Mexican firms will have to expose themselves to the rigors of the exacting requirements of high-tech assembly production, a difficult shift for many of them.

The other side of the coin is that foreign firms might resist these trends. For one thing, U.S., Japanese, and other foreign management of maquiladoras might hesitate to share ownership of plants and vital technology with Mexican firms. Unless such sharing could bring them significant cost advantages, foreign enterprises would prefer to assemble in their own subsidiaries where they control production schedules and quality, and safeguard their technology.[23] For another thing, U.S. labor would not wish to see a larger share of maquiladora inputs produced abroad. The principal argument to convince U.S. labor to tolerate production sharing has been that it permits U.S. firms to remain competitive and stay in business by transferring only assembly work abroad but maintaining employment at home for production of machinery, equipment, and, especially, components for the maquiladoras. What happens to this argument if most components were produced in Mexico? The fact that the U.S. economy will benefit from a strengthened Mexican trading partner in the long run may not be persuasive to U.S. workers who, due to these changes, lose their jobs today.[24]

Foreign firms are also reluctant to move maquiladoras deep into the interior of Mexico. Although increased transportation costs might be offset by lower wage costs, foreign firms would miss amenities of the faraway U.S. border and might also find the backcountry infrastructure—housing, roads, and utilities, especially communications—wanting. Because the border infrastructure has become increasingly strained due to overcrowding resulting from the recent maquiladora explosion,[25] a few of the new maquiladoras have been established further inland, but almost always less than 200 miles from the U.S. border.

Conclusions

This chapter has given an example of how a Latin American country has missed an opportunity for indigenous production and absorption of technology that East Asian countries have grasped profitably, and has outlined the necessary changes for assembly industries to become a building block in the construction of competitive industry in Mexico. Reform of the maquiladora, erasing its legal and psychological separation from other manufacturing, will merge assembly industries into the Mexican economy.

The maquiladora as an enterprise zone—an EPZ system—could thus serve Mexico as a stepping-stone toward accelerated industrialization as it has in East Asian countries. There is no ground for any fear that wages need to be kept artificially low for Mexico to become a major international competitor. The four tigers have allowed wages to increase as technology has risen through continuing education, training, and improvement in labor skills.[26]

It is not necessary to follow the development models of the four tigers. It is only necessary to recognize that the East Asian NICs have shown one of the ways through which technology can be absorbed from the industrial countries and through which national industrialization can be advanced. The four tigers squeezed every drop of benefit out of assembly industries and moved up the ladder of technology as they upgraded their labor force. If there is any lesson to be learned from East Asia, it is that there are no prejudices against any form of technology transfer and that education holds the highest priority in economic development.

Notes

1. In the current literature dealing with Latin American–East Asian comparisons, see, for example, Gereffi, G. (1989). Development strategies and the global factory: Latin America and East Asia. *The Annals; American Academy of Political and Social Science*, September; and G. Gereffi, & D. Wyman, Determinants of development strategies in Latin America and East Asia. In S. Haggard, & C. Moon (eds.), *Pacific dynamics: The international politics of industrial change*. Boulder, CO: Westview; and the references cited in the articles.

2. Among the major chaebol groups are Samsung, Goldstar, Hyundai, and Daewoo—each one of them a multiple of the largest enterprises in Latin America. See, Gereffi, G. (1988, May). Industrial structure and development strategies in Latin America and East Asia, Duke University, Working Paper, No. 39, May 1988.

3. The United States played a major role in promoting, if not implementing, land reforms in several East Asian countries soon after World War II.

4. *World Bank Development Report 1988, 1989*. Oxford University Press, World Development Indicators, Tables 30 and 29 respectively. World Bank statistics do not include Taiwan, but other information points to an even greater educational advantage of that island over Brazil and Mexico.

5. It is important to recognize that education alone does not insure technology transfer. The Soviet Union has spent a larger share of national resources on education and has

graduated more engineers than the United States, but is still technologically far behind. Management know-how is needed for high yields from human capital.

6. Grunwald, J. (1970, July/August). Some reflections on Latin American industrialization policy. *The Journal of Political Economy, 78*(4), Part 2.

7. The first developing country EPZ was established in Kaohsiung, Taiwan in 1966, about the same time that Mexico's maquiladora program got under way. See Grunwald, J., & Flamm, K. (1985). *The global factory.* The Brookings Institution, p. 71.

8. See also Grunwald & Flamm, *The global factory,* particularly chapter 4, pp. 137-179.

9. There are also several European maquiladoras in Mexico and after considerable difficulties, Taiwanese plants were about to be established in 1990. An important motivation for the establishment of East Asian maquiladoras in Mexico has been access to the U.S. market unhampered by quotas or "voluntary restraint agreements."

10. Projected from data in Gonzáles-Aréchiga, B., & Barajas Escamilla, R. (Eds.). (1989). *Las maquiladoras.* Töns H. Hilker, coordinator, El Colegio de la Frontera Norte—Fundación Friedrich Ebert.

11. Even in the EPZs—by definition, enclaves that are apart from the rest of the economy—the use of local materials has risen to more than one third of the total in South Korea and to almost one half in Taiwan.

12. U.S. firms that had supplied components for assembly in East Asia seemed content to let the Koreans and Taiwanese produce them, so saving transportation costs and importing the assembled product into the United States more cheaply.

13. See also Warr, P. G. (1989, June). Export processing zones and trade policy. *Finance & Development,* International Monetary Fund and World Bank.

14. EPZ plants have been directly exempted from duties; plants outside the EPZs have paid the duties when importing but have been reimbursed (through drawbacks) when exporting the products containing the imported inputs.

15. Aside from a few small and medium-sized plants, there is a significant participation of Mexican capital only in industrial parks for maquiladoras, in consulting firms, and in the supply of packing and cleaning materials for assembly plants.

16. Social returns from assembly production, however, would be higher than private returns, if investment in maquiladoras would lead to greater absorption of technology and upgrading of labor skills.

17. The Mexican government has frequently solicited foreign investments in Mexican economic sectors through advertisements in foreign media, such as U.S. newspapers and magazines, but maquiladoras have been excluded until the mid-1980s; even after then their appearance in Mexican government advertisements has been rare.

18. Estimated from data in *Estadística de la industria maquiladora de exportación,* Insituto Nacional de Estadística, Geografía e Información, 1988, and in United States International Trade Commission (1988, December), *Imports under items 806.30 and 807.00 of the tariff schedules of the United States, 1984-87,* USITC Publication 2144. Washington, DC: International Trade Commission.

19. See note 23 below.

20. Certain restrictions remain. See: Reglamento de la Ley para Promover la Inversión Mexicana y Regular la Inversión Extranjera. Secretaría de Comercio y Fomento Industrial, *Diario oficial,* Martes 16 de mayo de 1989.

21. However, the most recent Mexican government decree on maquiladoras limits the sale of maquiladora output on the domestic market to 50% of the previous year's net export earnings for each firm. (Article 20 of Decreto para el fomento y operación de la Industria Maquiladora de Exportación. Secretaría de Comercio y Fomento Industrial, as published in *Diario Oficial,* December 22, 1989, p. 16.)

22. Some observers believe that an EPZ should be used only as an instrument in a "nation-wide export-oriented development strategy" and not for other purposes such as developing backward regions. Healy, D. T. (1990, March). The underlying conditions for the successful generation of EPZ-local linkages: The experience of the Republic of Korea. *Journal of the Flagstaff Institute, 14*(1), p. 65.

23. Mexican regulations require that new technologies be licensed. Once they are licensed, they can be used in Mexico, after a limited period of protection, without restriction, so that the foreign firm will lose control over its technology property. This may have been a deterrent for foreign companies to transfer technology in Mexico. The reason that this has not been an issue for the four tigers is not that East Asian laws are more protective of foreign interests, but that, to the contrary, the absence of relevant formal licensing rules has facilitated the copying of technology. Reverse engineering, imitation, and outright piracy have made it impossible for foreign firms to safeguard much of their technology in East Asia. There may not be a great difference in scruples between Mexican and East Asian producers, but the fact that there are laws on the books in Mexico that may discourage foreign firm from entering into joint venture arrangements permitting the easy flow of know-how to Mexican counterparts, has handicapped Mexico vis-à-vis the freewheeling four tigers. In early 1990, Mexico agreed to modify its patent laws to conform more closely to U.S. intellectual property rights legislation, so limiting certain technology transfer.

24. Unlike in the East Asian situation, U.S. firms may resist giving up component production because there would be little savings in transportation costs buying from Mexico assembled Mexican-made components (see also note 12 above).

25. Many areas along the border, where the growth of assembly industries has been particularly high, have experienced shortages of water, sewage facilities, schools, housing, hospitals, transportation, and other public services, and a few also suffer from pollution caused by some maquiladoras (especially in furniture assembly).

26. For example, at the end of the 1970s Singapore experimented with a policy of deliberate and substantial wage hikes in an attempt to reduce low-skilled jobs and move "toward high-wage, high-productivity, high-technology products" (Grunwald & Flamm, *The global factory,* p. 232).

13

Puerto Rico as
an Enterprise Zone

RAMÓN E. DAUBÓN
JOSÉ J. VILLAMIL

Historical Background

Puerto Rico became a possession of the United States as a result of the Spanish American War in 1898. Subsequently, in 1917, it became a non-incorporated territory and, since 1952, a Commonwealth. The meaning of this last—still the political status of Puerto Rico—is little understood and has lent itself to much confusion. Rather than trying to untangle what has been an ongoing source of debate in the Island and in Washington for decades, for purposes of this chapter it is sufficient to state that Puerto Ricans residing in the Island pay no federal income taxes, are American citizens, can travel freely to the United States, hold U.S. passports, are recipients of many federal welfare programs—some with ceilings imposed on them—and benefit from a number of special federal provisions. Among the latter are Section 936 of the Internal Revenue Code, discussed below, and the fact that the Government of Puerto Rico receives from the federal government all excise duties collected on Island rum exported to the mainland.

On the other hand, U.S. citizens residing in the Island—Puerto Rican or not—do not vote in presidential elections, have a representative in Congress with voice but no vote and, of course, pay local income taxes and contribute toward social security and other entitlements.

The Island's population in 1980 was 3.2 million and by 1990 it is projected to be 3.4 million, in an area of 3,500 square miles. It is

primarily an urban population concentrated in the San Juan Metropolitan Area, with 1.4 million in population, and other urban areas. In fact,
the small size of the island and its very high population density makes
it resemble a large urban conglomerate rather than a geographic unit
with clearly defined rural and urban areas.

The early decades of this century were characterized by some political turmoil but a great deal of economic change brought on by the
imposition of the occupying power's economic needs and preferences.
Thus, from an economy and its related social organization, based on
small plantations of coffee, tobacco, and spices for export and a diversified small scale agriculture for local consumption, Puerto Rico became a one crop economy, due primarily to the expressed needs in the
U.S. market for that product and the actions of the sugar interests.

As a result, Puerto Rico's farmland was rapidly transferred to sugar
and its agricultural labor transferred into a rural proletariat in large
corporate plantations. Exports to the mainland grew under the protective umbrella of a preferential price arrangement which, in return for
establishing a quota on exports, provided the growers and refiners with
a fixed price well above market levels. The effects of that dependence
on sugar still haunt Puerto Rico, and defined its economic structure
until quite recently.[1]

The Forties

In the late thirties, the Popular Democratic Party, under the leadership of Luis Muñoz Marín, was created with a progressive platform of
land reform and modernization. In 1940 the Party became a majority in
the Legislature and the process of change that was to transform Puerto
Rico was set in motion. The governor of Puerto Rico, a presidential
appointee, was Rexford G. Tugwell, a former member of the New Deal
brain trust and a well known planner with a clear social conscience. It
was Tugwell, in partnership with Muñoz and a group of young tech-
nocrats in the Popular Party, who stimulated the legislation in the early
forties that provided support for the development efforts to come.
Among these were the establishment of a central planning agency, a
budget bureau, an industrial development company, land reform legislation, and the centralization of many utilities, previously either privately or municipally held.

In the early forties Puerto Rico was in desperate economic and social
conditions, with an income per capita just above $240 and social

welfare indicators similar to those of the poorest countries in the region. It was, in fact, called "the poorhouse of the Caribbean" in a much publicized book in the late thirties.[2]

The Objectives

The initial policies and strategies in the period 1942 to 1946 were oriented to achieving social welfare objectives. Thus, land reform and redistribution were major items in the government's program. Legislation was approved that made it illegal for any corporation to own over 500 acres, public agencies were created to operate large farms, and a massive program of land distribution was initiated.

Nevertheless, the World War II meant that Puerto Rico had a unique opportunity to begin manufacturing some items for its own needs, because imports from the mainland were severely restricted. It was thus that the government used resources derived from the export of rum to establish and operate five state owned factories to produce glass bottles, paper, cardboard (to supply the well established rum industry) and cinder blocks and cement (to supply the anticipated needs for industrial infrastructure).

It is interesting to read the Congressional reactions to Tugwell's efforts to develop Puerto Rico, for they invariably took the position that this was socialism or worse. In fact, in hearings held in Puerto Rico in 1943, the House Insular Affairs Committee went as far as calling these efforts communist and accusing local officials and Governor Tugwell of leaning in that direction.[3]

There was no unanimity, however, within the Popular Party with respect to the manner in which Puerto Rico should develop its economy. A sector within the leadership of the Party had never been totally pleased with state ownership; operational problems in four of the five plants brought about by inexperience, mismanagement, and the potential for labor problems eventually gave this sector the upper hand.

By the end of the war steps were taken to change the orientation from state ownership to private ownership. By 1948 the plants were liquidated or sold to private interests. The process was partly a result of the onset of the Cold War mentality, which made state ownership an unacceptable option for a U.S. possession, but also of the conviction of a number of leading government officials that state ownership would not generate the necessary jobs quickly enough.

The Instruments

Legislation approved in 1948 created the agency and the tax incentives that made rapid industrialization possible in the following decades. The Economic Development Administration was created to promote U.S. private investments and a tax incentives program was put in place which made it possible to offer 100% income tax exemption to industrial operations in Puerto Rico. A number of steps were taken to provide the roads, ports, and electric energy infrastructure and accelerate Puerto Rico's modernization, financed with the surplus revenues generated by excise taxes on rum.

During the fifties and sixties, Puerto Rico's economy grew at average annual rates in excess of 7% in real terms and it was generally held up as an example to the developing world. Puerto Rico became an obligatory place for development economists to visit and the Point Four Program initiated by the Truman Administration brought thousands of developing-country officials and technicians to the island. In 1961, the creation of the Alliance for Progress in many ways represented the peak year in terms of influence for Puerto Rico.

The Alliance for Progress was in fact a transfer of Puerto Rico's experience to all of Latin America. Its first director was Teodoro Moscoso, the architect of Puerto Rico's industrialization efforts since the forties, and the Alliance itself was drafted by technicians whom Moscoso had brought to Puerto Rico during the period. Puerto Rico provided the model for a development strategy based on modernization and industrialization, and by assigning a role to government of promoter, major catalyst, and provider of infrastructure.

The Approaching Limits

The early years of the sixties found Puerto Rico with significant achievements in improving social and economic conditions. In part, improvement was due to the massive out-migration of the population in the previous decade, which had a noticeable impact. Puerto Rico had by the early sixties a well established industrial sector, its government sector operated efficiently, and it seemed well on its way to permanent and rapid economic growth.

By the mid sixties, however, conditions had changed in the world economy and the model adopted by Puerto Rico began to confront serious problems. One was the application of federal minimum wage legislation to Puerto Rico, although with some modifications in terms of areas subject to it. Of greater importance, however, was the fact that a number of other countries had begun to compete with Puerto Rico for industrial investment, becoming in fact export platforms. In most instances, these countries offered significantly lower wage costs than Puerto Rico.

In general terms, the increasing competition meant that Puerto Rico had an increasingly hard time in securing labor-intensive industries. The emergence of the four tigers in Asia (Taiwan, South Korea, Hong Kong, and Singapore) was a major element in this situation and a new strategy became mandatory.[4]

New Objectives

Objectives began to change in the mid sixties, and the major emphasis was placed on devising a development strategy aimed at securing more local links among industry groups. Although never expressed formally, in fact, the mid sixties saw the abandonment of an industrialization policy aimed at securing unconnected labor-intensive industries.

The Shift to Heavy Industry

The new strategy sought to attract heavy industry to Puerto Rico, particularly in the petrochemicals sector, with the idea that the availability of cheap petroleum and petroleum-based products would stimulate the development of "downstream" activities which would generate the needed employment. It was assumed, although again never explicitly stated, that the refineries and basic petrochemicals operations themselves would not generate significant employment.

Between 1965 and 1972, Puerto Rico in fact experienced a significant boom in petrochemicals investment. The reasons were complex, but this was a time in which construction of refining capacity in the coastal states of the mainland was being severely restricted, and operations in Puerto Rico were exempted from import quotas then in effect.

The results, though, were less than hoped for. Total employment in the industry was never more than 7,000 and the hoped for downstream activities did not materialize. A major conceptual error in the scheme seems to have been the assumption that the availability of petroleum or petroleum derivatives would be incentive enough to promote *forward linkages,* the establishment of other industrial processes using them as raw materials. The fact was that in many cases, location was more market than input oriented and these downstream activities located instead on the mainland near the major markets. The multiplier and forward linkage effects were achieved, but they did not benefit Puerto Rico.[5]

The strategy persisted until the mid seventies when the Arab embargo, changes in federal legislation and regulation, and the energy crisis made the petrochemicals industry in Puerto Rico nonviable. The result was that most of the petrochemicals complexes—including the biggest of them, Commonwealth Oil Refining—were closed. The sites are still maintained and persist to this day as monuments to a failed strategy.

The results of the mid seventies crisis persisted for a decade. Construction fell to minimal levels, the economy grew at rates hovering around 1% in real terms between 1975 and 1983 and in three of those years the rate of growth was negative, 1975, 1981 and 1982. It was the period in which the economy's character changed. In what many have considered a threshold, in 1976 federal transfer payments surpassed investment, a condition that still prevails.

The Seventies

The seventies then marked the end of a stage in Puerto Rico's development strategies, that of the heavy petrochemicals complexes, and the beginning of a phase that still persists: development based on Section 936 of the U.S. Internal Revenue Code and on transfer payments.

Section 936

Puerto Rico had had the benefit of Section 931 of the U.S. Internal Revenue Code since the twenties. This measure, approved by Congress to assist the Philippines, permitted U.S. corporations established in the island possessions to repatriate their accumulated earnings without payment of federal income taxes once they had liquidated operations.

Section 936, approved in 1976 at the urging of the Government of Puerto Rico, changed Section 931 in that it permitted U.S. corporations to repatriate annual earnings without the payment of federal taxes.

Together with Section 482, which permitted firms to transfer to subsidiaries the intangible assets associated with the development of new products and processes, it provided Puerto Rico with a potent new instrument to deal with industrialization in an increasingly competitive world. In fact, Section 936 has been defended as being an instrument available to Puerto Rico to compensate for the myriad federal laws and regulations that have made it less competitive with other industrializing countries.

The impacts of 936 have been important in defining Puerto Rico's economic growth over the past 15 years and in determining the Island's present economic structure. In general terms, the operation of 936 has had a beneficial impact in two ways: one, by permitting the banking system to improve its liquidity, thus generating the capacity to make more loans and at a cheaper interest rate and two, by generating a large, sophisticated, technology intensive manufacturing sector, particularly in the pharmaceuticals and electronics fields.[6]

Throughout the years since its adoption, Section 936 has been under attack by the Treasury and sectors of Congress who believe that corporations have benefited beyond what they have generated in jobs in Puerto Rico. In 1982, Congress made a dent in the benefits by limiting profits from passive income and in 1985, further restrictions were legislated, limiting the approved uses of 936 credits. The Commonwealth, which collects a *tollgate tax* on profits repatriated to the United States, has also been active in regulating the uses of 936 funds.

The fact is that the Puerto Rican economy of the seventies and eighties has been heavily dependent on Section 936 and the operations of corporations that benefit from the section. Altogether, about 100,000 direct—and an estimated 200,000 indirect—jobs have resulted from it and the tax payments to the Commonwealth, both from the tollgate tax and the 10% local income tax that they pay, have amounted to approximately $7 billion in the period 1976-1989.[7]

Transfer Payments

The other side of the coin, with respect to the evolution of the economy in the past two decades, has been the increasing dependence of Puerto Rico on federal transfer payments. In 1972, federal transfers were approximately 6% of personal income. By the mid eighties they were over 20%, where they have remained. The figure for transfer payments reached a total of some $5 billion in 1989, with net transfers totaling about $3.7 billion, or approximately $1,100 per capita. Per capita personal income in 1989 was estimated by the Puerto Rico Planning Board at $5,653 and total personal income was $18.7 billion.[8]

A large share of the transfer payments have been in the nutrition assistance program. Puerto Rico, in contrast to the food stamps received by states, receives a fixed amount in the form of a block grant which in the past year amounted to $925 million.

The Changing Economic Structure

The nature of economic trends in Puerto Rico in the past two decades has meant a significant change in several structural conditions. Thus, manufacturing has become responsible for 62% of total net income, because of the huge impact of nonmanufacturing income generated by Section 936 companies. This compares with 33% in 1975. Government's share has continued to increase over the years and is now responsible for close to 25% of total economic activity, with public employment hovering around 30% of total employment. The third major structural change has been the emergent preeminence of the financial sector. Due to 936 funds deposited in local banks, Puerto Rico's financial sector has become very large relative to the size of the economy. Total banking deposits averaged around $20 billion in 1989 (with a total GNP of $20 billion), of which approximately 40% were funds deposited by Section 936 companies.

Puerto Rico as an Enterprise Zone

The Nature of the Incentives

Commonwealth

As evidenced, Puerto Rico has been the archetypal Enterprise Zone. But seeing it as one requires us to focus on the instruments developed locally and at the federal level that have made possible the type of development experienced in the past four decades. At the Commonwealth level the major instrument has been the local tax exemption granted to firms locating on the Island. That incentive has changed over the years in the following manner. When first approved in the forties, the exemption was for 100% and the length of time dependent on the location of the plant and other considerations. In the 1978 revision, under a pro-statehood government hostile to the tax exemption mechanism, the exemption was based on a sliding scale beginning with 90% exemption and ending at the end of the exemption period at a much lower level. The most recent revision in 1985, under a pro-Commonwealth government, maintained the 90% tax exemption but extended it for the period for which the exemption was granted, which could be from 15 to 25 years depending on the plant's location.

Federal

At the federal level, the existence of Section 936 has been unquestionably the major element in promoting manufacturing activity in the past 15 years. It has also acted to improve access to credit for local firms by increasing the liquidity of the banking sector and by decreasing the cost of credit. The importance of 936 is that it is a federal provision which, in effect, singles out Puerto Rico for special treatment.

The rationale for this special treatment is that Puerto Rico is not only seriously disadvantaged vis-à-vis the states, but that it further faces very adverse competitive conditions as a result of the application of federal minimum wage and other federal regulations. Puerto Rico thus finds it very hard to compete with the Dominican Republic or any number of countries where wages are much lower and there are no significant environmental, health, or safety regulations.

The Ownership of Capital

Local Versus Nonlocal

The enterprise zone concept is not necessarily aimed at creating local entrepreneurs, but rather to generate jobs in disadvantaged urban areas. This means that the issue of entrepreneurship has not been a major concern. In Puerto Rico, however, there has always been a stated concern for the balance between local and nonlocal ownership of manufacturing and other economic activities, even if actual efforts and priorities (and consequently results) did not bear this out. This concern has, however, translated itself recently into a number of new initiatives taken to stimulate the development of local entrepreneurs. Among these initiatives was the creation of an economic development bank, setting up a semipublic corporation to stimulate the development of firms in high-tech areas and the up-grading of the position of director for Puerto Rican Industries in the Economic Development Administration.

These efforts have been partially successful in the five years since they were put in place; nevertheless, the government has not produced a clearly articulated policy on what it wants to achieve with respect to local entrepreneurs and how to go about doing it.

The Structure of Nonlocal Industry

Nonlocal industry is highly concentrated in the so-called 936 firms, that is, U.S. corporations operating in Puerto Rico under Section 936. These firms tend to be large, capital-intensive operations that generate relatively few jobs per million dollars of investment. They are geared to the export markets and more often than not have a captive export market primarily through sales to their parent corporations. A notable change in recent years has been the assumption of managerial responsibilities by local managers as opposed to expatriates. Although the shift from manager to entrepreneur has been slow, and there are yet only a few examples among the Island managers, the potential for developing a local entrepreneurial group has been strengthened by the fairly extensive opportunities in management of Section 936 companies now available to local professionals. A policy of promoting and facilitating the entrepreneurial capabilities of these managers might seem promising at this point.

The Fragile Competitiveness of Puerto Rico

The competitive position of Puerto Rico vis-à-vis other countries has deteriorated over the recent past due to the application of federal environmental legislation and regulations, and because of the nature of transportation costs in an island context. In addition, the fact that Puerto Rico depends exclusively on petroleum for the production of electric energy has meant that in the recent high cost years, Puerto Rico has experienced a serious disadvantage.

A major item in determining the Island's competitiveness has been the situation with respect to transportation costs. Puerto Rico is subject to U.S. coastwise shipping laws which prevent it from using foreign bottoms for shipping to and from U.S. ports. Over the years the argument has been made that this has aggravated Puerto Rico's fragile competitive position, and several attempts have been initiated to obtain a formal exemption for the Island. None have prospered and it is unlikely that coastal states and shipping interests would favor such an exemption.

The Lessons

The Model as a System

There are a number of lessons that can be learned from Puerto Rico's experience, some of which can be useful in formulating the enterprise zone program for U.S. cities. Perhaps the major one is that local tax exemption can be a powerful instrument, but that it is not sufficient by itself. If it had not been for Section 936, for example, the experience with Puerto Rico's industrialization program would have been a great deal less favorable. In effect, Puerto Rico has been able to provide a double tax exemption to firms from the United States locating in the Island.

A second lesson has been the need to deal with a surplus labor force through specific programs. It has been abundantly clear from the experience of Puerto Rico that industrialization itself will not solve the unemployment problem in a labor surplus economy such as an inner city in the United States. One explanation is that wage and capital costs make the production function of firms establishing operations in the zone be capital intensive. A second reason has to do with the fact that not all the unemployed are able to handle an industrial job unless provided with extensive job training.

In Puerto Rico's case, the massive out-migration that took place early in the process and that resulted in the emigration of close to a million persons made a significant difference. Even today, the out-migration continues, although at a much slower pace. Had it not been for migration, it is almost certain that unemployment and underemployment today would be much higher than the present level of about 15%. The out-migration from U.S. inner cities, however, works to their detriment, since those who leave are the employables.

Impacts

Employment

The nature of employment in Puerto Rico changed very quickly once the industrialization program began. One immediate transformation was the demise of the home needlework industry which up to the early fifties employed as many as 60,000 persons, and the quick decline in agricultural employment which went from over 200,000 to the present levels of around 40,000 in less than three decades. Industrial employment grew quickly, although perhaps the salient feature was not so much growth, but the transformation of its character. Much of industrial employment is now highly paid (an average $7.00 per hour) compared to the rest of the economy ($4.50 per hour average). A similar transition is to be expected in urban U.S. enterprise zones, lending weight to the preference for low-skill industries in the earlier promotion efforts.

Income Distribution

Not much information exists on income distribution in the Island, although it is fair to say that an improvement took place in the fifties and the sixties and then a deterioration occurred in the following two decades as a result of the same factors that were at work in the United States. The tax system became less progressive and a series of measures were approved that benefited the higher income groups. The emerging high-tech industrial structure in recent years also gravitates in favor of higher wage employment and a more unequal distribution within the industrial labor force. The existence of a massive welfare program that affects 60% of the population has had an impact on how one determines income distribution, for it would certainly be very different if the large welfare payments did not exist. One piece of statistical evidence, which suggests that income distribution probably deteriorated in the seventies and early eighties, is that real personal income per capita grew at an annual rate only slightly above 1.2% between 1971 and 1984.

One major issue affecting the welfare of the population has been the decay in public services aimed at the poor. This was brought on by continuing fiscal restraints, mismanagement of the bloated public sector, and excessive dependence on federal transfers. Thus, health and education services have been hard pressed to maintain acceptable standards, as a result of which the Island is rapidly consolidating a rigid classification scheme with those attending private schools having a built-in advantage over those attending public schools, and those receiving private medical services having an advantage over the rest of the population. The most recent estimates by the government indicate that roughly 60% of the population is medically indigent.

Government Finances

A major problem that has developed over the past few years is the increasingly fragile nature of government finances. The government has experienced deficits—technically unconstitutional—in its budget over the past decade which have been resolved through the use of nonrecurring income sources. The blame for the increasing weakness of government finances has been laid on the tax exemptions provided to industry and the consequent narrowing of the tax base. This criticism is not completely justified, however. The tax exempt operations have typically paid a higher amount in taxes than the non-tax exempt industries and corporations. Also, there is no assurance that had these tax exempt plants not established themselves in Puerto Rico that an equivalent tax paying operation could have been established.

The Lessons

Economic Stability

One crucial lesson to be learned from Puerto Rico's experience as an enterprise zone and promoting its development through the importation of capital is that it is a highly unstable process due to its sensitivity to changes in the external context. To the extent that Puerto Rico faced relatively little competition in the fifties and early sixties, the industrial promotion efforts were successful in bringing to the Island low wage, labor-intensive plants.

As soon as politically reliable low wage locations became more available in places such as the Far East, the Caribbean, and elsewhere, the program had to shift to more capital-intensive industries (petrochemicals in this case) which depended to a large extent on Congress maintaining preferential treatment of oil imports to Puerto Rico. When that was done away with, this and the energy crisis of the seventies meant the end of that phase.

Finally, the past and present phases of the industrialization efforts have depended on the stability of Section 936. Each time Congress has dealt with 936, a decrease in investment flow occurs and a great deal of uncertainty concerning the future of Puerto Rico's economy surfaces. The deus ex machina of external investments is dependent on the whim of either fate or distant legislators.

What this suggests is that a successful enterprise zone program would do well to stimulate local entrepreneurs, even if the pay-offs take longer to occur. An alternative is to consider the linking of these locally based activities with nonlocal economic activities in such a way that the latter generate demands for the former. This has been done in Puerto Rico in the past five years and a consequence has been that rapid growth of local industry in the period has been due to a large extent to the local acquisitions by Section 936 companies of various inputs.

Social Consequences

The social consequences of development have been debated over the past few decades in Puerto Rico. One major item has been that much of the success of the development effort has been due to the emigration of a large percentage of the population and that in fact the government pursued such an emigration policy as part of its modernization strategies. It may very well be, but the industrial development program did not depend on that massive emigration process for its success.

The nature of social problems in the Island spring from a variety of sources, and it is difficult to produce any empirical evidence linking the enterprise zone model to the manifestations of social pathology. It is fair to say, however, that Puerto Rico's is a low income society with consumption patterned on that of the United States. This may be responsible for generating social stresses as aspirations prove to be increasingly out of the grasp of most of the population. This problem is, by the way, one that could increasingly affect other poor countries in the periphery as the globalization of information progresses.

Conclusions

Puerto Rico's experience has been described in many articles and books over the past decades. At one time it provided a preferred model for development in poor countries. It was the site for a large Point Four Program in the forties, to which technicians and development economists came from all over the world to examine Puerto Rico's experience. The Island's economy grew rapidly, the political system was democratic, government institutions seemed to work efficiently, and there was a great deal of social innovation.

The model has become tarnished in the past two decades and it is no longer the path to follow for most developing countries. The reasons are many, one being the special relationship with the United States which has been a prerequisite for success. Another has been the growing recognition that with the increasing number of available sites for industrial operations, the type of industrialization efforts based on attracting industries from the industrialized nations does not offer the payoffs that it did in Puerto Rico's case. Finally, the availability of Section 936 in Puerto Rico's case has presented an advantage not easily transferable elsewhere.

Although not the model for developing countries that it once might have been, Puerto Rico's experience as a federal enterprise zone contains a number of lessons for depressed areas in the United States with which it shares several characteristics, aside from poverty; a population of U.S. citizens, with access to U.S. welfare programs, and subject to the same regulations.

Notes

1. The best overall review of Puerto Rico's history in English is that of Lewis, G. (1963). *Puerto Rico: Freedom and power in the Caribbean.* New York: Monthly Review Press.

2. Perloff, H. (1950). *Puerto Rico's economic future.* Chicago: University of Chicago Press.

3. Committee on Insular Affairs, House of Representatives. (1943). *Investigation of political, economic, and social conditions in Puerto Rico.* Washington, DC: U.S. Government Printing Office.

4. Villamil, J. J. (1983). Puerto Rico 1948-1979: The limits of dependent growth. In J. Heine (Ed.), *Time for decision: The United States and Puerto Rico,* pp. 95-116. Lanham, MD: North South Publishing. A very thorough analysis of the Puerto Rican economy was carried out by the U.S. Department of Commerce in 1979. See U.S. Department of Commerce (1979). *Economic study of Puerto Rico* (2 vols.). Washington, DC: U.S. Government Printing Office.

5. Villamil, Puerto Rico.

6. A number of studies have been carried out on the impacts of Section 936 by the Commonwealth Government, the U.S. Treasury Department, and by private entities. Treasury has prepared six reports charting the progress of Section 936 since its approval. The most recent and extensive study on 936 was sponsored by the Puerto Rico Bankers Association in 1989 and it provides clear evidence that in fact the cost of credit in Puerto Rico is substantially below that in the United States, and that the presence of Section 936

funds in the banking system has been a determining factor in increasing access to credit by small, local commercial and industrial entities.

7. Figures on tax payments have been provided by the Commonwealth Treasury Department.

8. All macroeconomic information utilized in this paper is from the Puerto Rico Planning Board, the agency charged with the responsibility of producing the Island's social accounts.

PART FOUR

The Future of Enterprise Zones in The United States

14

The Evaluation of
Enterprise Zone Programs

FRANKLIN J. JAMES

Introduction

As yet, there has been no thoroughly acceptable evaluation of the impacts and cost-effectiveness of an enterprise zone program. This might seem surprising. Techniques of program evaluation are well developed and widely understood.[1] In addition, enterprise zone programs have been in operation for almost a decade in Great Britain, and state programs in the United States have been going on for almost as long.[2] Since Ronald Reagan first proposed a national program in 1980, 37 states have adopted enterprise zone programs, some ambitious in scope.

This chapter reviews methodological issues raised in evaluating enterprise zone programs. Evaluations of enterprise zone programs have not been decisive or convincing one way or another, in part because none of the programs were designed from the beginning for effective evaluation, and in part because few high quality efforts have been made to evaluate the programs.

Tough methodological problems impede quality evaluations of most economic development programs. Most federal and state economic development programs have provided discretionary assistance to individual projects or firms, and have spread their aid widely among communities. Aid under these programs has been too geographically dispersed to enable researchers to seek out evidence of success or failure in trends in the health of community economies. Thus, determining program effects has involved making difficult judgments of how individual projects or firms were affected by government aid. Few researchers have had the stomach or the resources to overcome this hurdle.

As other chapters in this volume have discussed, enterprise zone programs are highly unusual in that they generally (though by no means always) concentrate their resources in comparatively few, small geographic areas. Tax and other zone incentives (such as regulatory streamlining) are available to all eligible establishments within a zone as a matter of right. The fact that aid is available to all firms in zones irrespective of need mutes interest in the question of how the programs affect individual establishments. The fact that aid is frequently concentrated geographically enables a focus on program impacts on zone economies. The geographic concentration of aid could generate community economic impacts measurable without the subjectivity inherent in evaluations of other programs.

Thus, this chapter concludes that efforts to evaluate enterprise zone programs may be more feasible and successful than have been efforts to evaluate earlier economic development programs. The chapter identifies the principal weaknesses of existing evaluations of zone programs. An outline of a promising strategy for evaluating the zone programs is developed.

Issues for Enterprise Zone Programs

Tax incentives appear to have some unique advantages for economic development efforts, because they are attractive to businesses that cannot be reached by direct government financing or subsidy programs. The tax system can deliver subsidy or other incentives to virtually every private sector enterprise, without government bureaucrats as middlemen. By contrast, direct government subsidy can carry red tape, delay, and stigma.

There are persistent doubts, however, about the effectiveness of tax incentives in stimulating business investment or altering business location or employment choices. Econometric research has yet to demonstrate that either state and local development incentives or state and local taxes have a significant impact on business location, although evidence is growing that taxes may have an effect.[3]

It is currently fashionable to focus economic development activities on fostering or strengthening small business enterprise. It is widely believed that small business generates a disproportionate number of new jobs.[4] However, the research supporting this view has been challenged by subsequent, more careful analysis of the data.[5] There is special doubt that tax incentives will have much impact on the investment or location decisions of small business. Small businesses are frequently relatively unsophisticated in dealing with government, and so pressed for survival that it would be an expensive luxury for them to devote much managerial energy to cumbersome economic development or tax avoidance schemes. Because small businesses frequently fail to earn taxable profits in their early years, tax credits or deductions against profit taxes may be particularly ineffective for small business.

At the same time, there is some apprehension among experts that a zone program might, if "successful", distort intra-regional patterns of business locations and investment in wasteful or inefficient ways. Erickson, Friedman, and McCluskey conclude that

> an appropriate enterprise zone policy . . . will necessitate a rather delicate balancing strategy. Enough incentives are needed in any zone to encourage private investment; yet, too strong a package is likely to result in unproductive reshuffling of economic activities and needless and costly subsidies.[6]

Thus far, most evaluations of enterprise zone programs have not been highly flattering to the concept. Indeed, as more has been learned it has become more difficult to espouse zone programs as a cost-effective economic development tool.[7] Evaluations of enterprise zones in the United Kingdom have reported that the British program is a useful but not decisive economic development program for distressed communities.[8] An evaluation of a zone in Swansea reports that businesses locating in the zone were attracted primarily by the availability of attractive sites for development, sites that had been prepared under earlier regional economic development programs that had been cut back by the Thatcher government.[9]

One recent evaluation of state enterprise zone programs in the United States analyzed zones in the 17 states with the longest established programs. It concluded rather blandly that "enterprise zones are no 'miracle cure' or panacea for economic distress, but that notable improvements have occurred in very many zones."[10] The authors of this evaluation made follow-up contacts with coordinators of 21 zones with outstanding performance. They found that all of the zones had "high development potential", like the Swansea zone in the United Kingdom. Zone coordinators regarded zone designation as the "marginal factor that put the place 'over the top,' thereby performing a catalytic role."[11] Marketing of zones to the business community was regarded as critical for zone success.[12]

Evaluation evidence raises particular doubt that tax incentives will be cost-effective, compared with earlier economic development and community development programs. Peter Hall, the originator of the concept of enterprise zones, has estimated relatively high costs per job generated in zones: $30,000 to $60,000 per job.[13] This makes British zones about as expensive per job as was the U.S. Local Public Works program or the EDA Title I program, two of the least efficient U.S. economic development programs.[14]

A recent evaluation of New Jersey's enterprise zone program estimates program costs per job of between $8,000 and $13,000.[15] If accurate, this would make the program competitive in terms of costs per job with the UDAG program, generally regarded as highly efficient.[16] The UDAG program, however, provided a once and for all capital investment in projects. By contrast, firms in New Jersey's enterprise zones will continue to receive tax advantages for many years. If program costs per job *per year* remain at levels that prevailed during 1987 and 1988, then the costs per job would be $40,000 to $60,000 over a decade, and would continue to mount as time went by. It thus appears that the long-run costs per job in the New Jersey program may also be high.[17]

High costs per job in enterprise zones are plausible because, as has been pointed out, tax incentives in zones are generally nondiscretionary. This means that all firms in the zones which qualify for tax breaks get them, whether or not the breaks are needed to attract the business to the zone. This is an unfortunate but inevitable side effect of eliminating the bureaucratic middleman, and the simplicity which results.

Overview of the Problem of
Evaluating Enterprise Zones

Unfortunately, the evaluation evidence quickly summarized in the previous section offers relatively little insight into the effectiveness or desirability of individual enterprise zone programs. Enterprise zone programs differ greatly in their political origins, objectives, management methods and philosophy, incentives, patterns of zone designation, and so forth.[18] As a result of these differences, evidence from one program may not be generalizable to another. In addition, the greatly different tax and business environment in the United Kingdom raises questions concerning the generalizability of evidence from that program to the United States.

More relevant, there are serious doubts about the quality of information provided by most extant evaluation studies. This is particularly true for survey-based evaluation such as that by Erickson, Friedman, and McCluskey. Their study is based on surveys by HUD of zone operators. Such operators can be assumed to be advocates of their programs. Even if the evidence and opinions they provide were unbiased, it would differ greatly in quality and reliability. Such evidence is likely to be misleading and less than useful. There are serious problems even in those studies that use more substantive methodologies.

The main tasks required to evaluate an enterprise zone program are to:

- identify central goals of the zone program, and quantitative and qualitative indicators of the degree to which goals are accomplished;
- specify the components of the program, especially its incentives, which are likely to affect business behavior, and examine their aptness for producing desired effects;
- select and implement appropriate research methods to provide quantitative and qualitative indicators of program effects.

These tasks or responsibilities provide a convenient structure for the discussion.

Identifying Goals
of Enterprise Zone Programs

Few evaluations have more than scratched the surface in their efforts to measure program impacts. They have frequently focused on job trends and ignored equally valid and relevant indicators of program impacts. As a result, evaluations have failed to provide measures of program effects that are adequately comprehensive to assess the programs. This is a particular concern for a program as controversial as enterprise zones.

Although not the only standard, the goals of a program typically provide the most appropriate and valid basis for assessing program success.[19] Enterprise zone programs differ considerably in their goals.

The initial British program, for example, emphasized physical redevelopment goals for abandoned or unoccupied industrial or port areas of cities. The best measures of success would then be the extent of new development, construction, rehabilitation, and infrastructure investment in the zone. Most state programs in the United States have emphasized job creation as their primary goal.[20] For programs with this goal, net new jobs attracted to a community by an enterprise zone program would be the best indicator of the success.

Some state programs have also emphasized job targeting goals. Job targeting means getting jobs to the unemployed, impoverished, minorities, and others.[21] Job targeting is fostered in enterprise zone programs through zone designation criteria emphasizing community distress, through incentives for job targeting, or through coordinated employment and training efforts for the disadvantaged. Thorough evaluations of programs with job targeting objectives would seek to identify who gets jobs, and the effects of the enterprise zone program on indicators of the economic well-being of the disadvantaged.

Other state programs have emphasized community development goals, such as fostering housing development as well as investment in neighborhood improvements and infrastructure.[22] States with prior experience in targeted economic development or community development efforts are most likely to use enterprise zone programs to accomplish these auxiliary goals. Evaluations of programs with these goals might seek to track the effects of zone programs on housing investment, property values, neighborhood satisfaction of residents, displacement of residents and businesses, and more.

Thorough evaluations of programs with multiple goals requires the examination of a variety of impacts in order to provide comprehensive indicators of program success. The same can be true even of those programs with straightforward job creation or physical development objectives. If successful, any zone program will affect many dimensions of state and community welfare. It would thus be prudent for evaluators to examine the most comprehensive range of potential program impacts that their resources, time, and information base permit.

Analysis of Program Incentives

Enterprise zone programs differ greatly in the incentives they have chosen to offer. Making matters more complex, the programs generally offer packages of incentives, rather than a single, potent one. A broad range of incentives is argued to be more attractive to a broad range of businesses, and to be more attractive to a single business as its circumstances and needs change.[23]

So far, evaluations have not provided systematic efforts to determine the value of various incentives to various types of investors or businesses. Although evidence from evaluation studies suggests that some types of incentives may be more attractive to businesses than are others, such conclusions are typically backed up more by surveys of businesses than by hard economic analysis. Given the high level of ignorance concerning which incentives are effective and which are not, it is impossible to generalize the findings of the evaluation of one program to another. It is not yet possible to use evaluation research in policy analysis regarding program design.

HUD's survey of zone programs in 17 states disclosed a dozen different types of incentives in use in the programs:

- Investment Incentives
- Property tax credits
- Franchise tax credits
- Sales tax credits
- Investment tax credits

Other employer investment credits

- Employment Incentives
- Job creation tax credits
- Selective hiring credits (zone residents, poverty, etc.)
- Job training tax credit
- Employee tax credits
- Finance Incentives
- Preferential Industrial Development Bond Financing
- Tax increment financing
- Investment fund associated with the program
  Source: Erickson, Friedman, and McCluskey, 1989

Some of the tax incentives listed above were refundable, that is, payable in cash to taxpayers with inadequate tax liability to claim credits fully. Other states permitted some tax credits against the unemployment tax payments. In addition, one state offered a capital gains tax exemption.[24]

In order to stimulate business investment, some early proponents called for relaxation of fair employment laws, worker safety rules, civil rights, and environmental protection regulations. Local land use regulation might also be abrogated or relaxed.

Today, the concept of extensive deregulation as a development incentive is defunct and indefensible. Nevertheless, some state programs have called for streamlined regulatory processes as an incentive for business investment. Such process changes have included one-stop shopping, fast tracking, and reduced fees.[25]

The likely effects of a zone program clearly depend upon which incentives are offered, the magnitude of the incentive, and the ease with which taxpayers can claim the incentive. On the most general level, "investment" tax incentives will tend to be more effective in stimulating capital investment, and less effective in stimulating job creation or extra economic opportunities for workers or zone residents. Indeed, evidence from the national investment tax credit has suggested that the credit fostered the substitution by employers of physical capital for production workers, and may actually have reduced the supply of low-skilled blue collar work. Similarly, employment incentives will tend to be more effective in producing or attracting new jobs. Selective hiring tax credits (such as the national Targeted Jobs Tax Credit) will be more effective in targeting jobs to the disadvantaged and to zone residents.

The likely effects of incentives also depend on the size of the incentive and the degree to which strings are attached. Incentives can be too small to generate a response by investors. Evidence from earlier evaluations suggests that tax incentives that are clear, simple, certain, and direct are likely to be more effective for stimulating business investment and job creation in enterprise zones. Refundable tax breaks are more certain for businesses, and thus are likely to be more effective in leveraging a business response than are either deductions or non-refundable credits. Tax incentives that are contingent on circumstances outside the business's control, such as business profitability and overall tax liability, are less effective in changing business plans and policies.

In the United Kingdom, for example, exemption from the property tax is generally reported to be the most important inducement from the business point of view. The property tax is not contingent on business profitability or hiring, but only on location and facility ownership. (Evaluation studies report this incentive to be particularly valuable to larger establishments who own their own facilities.) One high quality evaluation of tax incentives in the United Kingdom concluded that 60% of the overall value of zone tax incentives were appropriated by landlords of rental space through higher rent charges.[26]

In the evaluation of the New Jersey enterprise zone program, sales tax exemptions are reported by businesses to have had the greatest impacts on their location decisions, relative to other incentives imbedded in the corporate profits tax.[27] This is not surprising, because profits tax breaks are contingent on business profitability, while the sales tax exemption is available to all business, even non-profits.

Measurement of the Economic Impacts of the Program

Measuring the economic impacts of the zone program requires a quantitative estimation of how the economy of the zone is different as a result of the program. This is a difficult judgment under the best of conditions, and no extant evaluation provides conclusive evidence, even on the narrow range of job impacts most have chosen to focus on.

Before and After Studies

Perhaps the most basic approach is to compare economic conditions and trends in the zone before the enterprise zone program with those prevailing after the program. Discontinuities in trends provide crude indicators of program impacts.[28]

This approach is not entirely persuasive, because discontinuities in trends may be produced by many factors in addition to the influences of zone programs. For example, a healthier regional or national economy could have such an effect, as could special factors operating in the zone other than the enterprise zone program. It is also a difficult method to apply in many instances, because few economic statistics are maintained on a neighborhood or small area basis, aside from population and housing data from the decennial census. A special survey is generally needed to document business activity in a zone.[29] Thus, the development of high quality before and after trend data would generally require at least three surveys of business activity in a zone, one well before the zone program becomes operative, one at the time of its initiation, and one following implementation of the program by enough time to permit it to have significant impacts. This is clearly impossible, except by happenstance, or in the event of careful program planning to permit subsequent evaluation.

Evaluations have sought shortcuts in using the before and after methods. In the General Accounting Office's evaluation of the Maryland enterprise zone program, employment trends before and after zone designation were measured in three Maryland zones. The GAO used a single survey of employers participating in the zone program following the implementation of the program. Employment histories were compiled for these participants, both for the period prior to zone designation and the period following designation. In those cases where discontinuities in zone employment suggested positive zone effects, the GAO examined potential causes through contacts with establishments with discontinuous employment histories. It was concluded that zone incentives were not a factor boosting employment growth in the zones.[30]

The single-survey procedure used by GAO and by other evaluators is inherently questionable, because it overstates economic growth in an area. Formerly active businesses which have moved from the zone or failed are not available for surveys and are not included in historical measures of zone activity.

Attitudinal Studies of Zone Businesses

A second commonly used method also entails surveys of zone businesses following zone designation. The surveys are designed to identify businesses or other investors who would not be in the zone in the absence of the zone program, and the economic impacts of their zone activities. In this approach, businesses that report that zone incentives were significant factors in their location in the zone, or their investment in the zone, are assumed to be net additional economic activity produced in the zone by the program.

This approach is also not entirely persuasive. Business respondents can frequently be assumed to exaggerate the effects of zone incentives, in order to preserve special tax breaks or other benefits of zone location which the businesses enjoy. In addition, survey respondents are often ignorant of the factors shaping the policies of the business, because many surveys of businesses fail to reach knowledgeable decision makers. In cases where lower level people answer questions, their answers may be more in the nature of public relations than public information. Perhaps most importantly, such surveys fail to measure business activity lost to the zone as a result of zone designation, and thus overestimate zone benefits. New employers and new business facilities attracted by zone incentives can be assumed sometimes to displace earlier businesses.

The survey approach was used in a recent evaluation of New Jersey's enterprise zone program.[31] Businesses that reported that zone incentives were the primary or the only reason for their zone activity were assumed to be net new business activity in the zone. This survey was made in all 10 of the state's enterprise zones. The survey approach has also been used in a number of the evaluations of zones in the United Kingdom.

Comparison Areas

In effect, an enterprise zone program amounts to a natural experiment. In many cases, the results of the experiment can best be interpreted if economic conditions and trends are monitored in a generally similar geographic area in the same region as the enterprise zone.[32] Selecting and monitoring such comparison areas—similar areas in which enterprise zone incentives are not available—provides a standard for assessing what might have happened in the enterprise zone in the absence of the program.

To be meaningful, comparison areas should be selected that meet designation criteria as an enterprise zone, and that are as similar as possible to actually designated areas in economic, social, geographic, and public service terms. Such similarities bolster confidence in the expectation that economic trends would be similar in the zone and the comparison area in the absence of the enterprise zone program.

Unfortunately, it is far more common to compare economic trends within enterprise zones to trends in the overall region within which the zone is located, or even relative to the nation as a whole. This approach is not generally appropriate. Metropolitan areas are too heterogeneous and the economic forces shaping metropolitan economies are too different from those shaping particular zones to make the comparison highly useful.

Rubin and Wilder used such an approach in their evaluation of the Evansville enterprise zone. Their evidence for the effectiveness of the zone program is that the *competitiveness* of the zone for economic activity was above average for the entire Evansville metro area in the period following the designation of the zone.[33] Strikingly, they fail to provide evidence on the period prior to zone designation so their finding does not warrant any inference regarding the effectiveness of the zone. Shift share analysis was used to measure zone competitiveness. Reliance on shift share analysis is itself highly questionable. Measures of competitiveness provided by shift share analysis are unstable over time.[34] Worse, Rubin and Wilder make inferences concerning a state enterprise zone program on the basis of experience in only a single, possibly idiosyncratic zone.

Indirect Economic Effects
of Enterprise Zones

As has been pointed out, enterprise zone programs can have effects outside zones which are important to consider. Zone incentives, if significant, could so enhance the competitiveness of zone establishment as to hurt business competitors outside zones. To the extent that zone incentives generate the reshuffling of business locations discussed above, or that they distort the location choices of new establishments, they will also weaken the economies of surrounding communities. If so, then gains in employment and investment within zones could be matched by employment and investment declines outside the zone.

No evaluation of U.S. zone programs has taken such *displacement* effects into account. In his evaluation of the Tyneside zone, Talbot used a sample of *out-zone* establishments as a comparison group for his analysis of firms within the Tyneside enterprise zone in Great Britain, in order to determine whether the competitiveness of these establishment had been reduced by the zone.[35] Erickson and Syms provide indirect evidence, through their surveys of property rents and values on the periphery of a zone in the Manchester area of Great Britain.[36] Clearly, more of this type of analysis should be done in the United States.

Incautious evaluations also run the risk of overstating program impacts through the misuse of regional economic multipliers. If a zone program merely shifts the geographic patterns of business investment and job creation within a metro area or region, then it will have no impact on aggregate regional economic activity. Such a program need not be a zero-sum game, because it can reduce the economic dependence of disadvantaged persons and distressed communities. It would be inappropriate, however, to use regional economic multipliers to explore the overall economic impacts of the program.

Only if a zone program generates new business activity which would not otherwise exist in the state or region is the use of multipliers appropriate.[37] By failing to distinguish between new economic activity in the state, and new activity in enterprise zones, the New Jersey evaluation uses multipliers in a way that greatly overstates program benefits.[38]

Effective Evaluation Strategies

Despite the complex issues raised by efforts to measure impacts, the fact is that empirical evaluation of enterprise zone programs may be more feasible than has been true in the past for economic development programs. The preceding discussion justifies several conclusions. Future evaluations of enterprise zone programs should

- examine a much more comprehensive array of potential program impacts; and
- provide much more analytic and thoughtful consideration of the effectiveness of alternative incentives;
- select and implement with greater care research methods for measuring program impacts;
- be more sparing in the use of regional economic multipliers, and more aggressive in measuring displacement effects of programs.

By and large, most existing evaluations have been so-called *impact evaluations,* that is, they have aimed at measuring net economic effects of the programs, and the relationships between goals and effects.[39] A concern with *process* evaluation has been noticeably absent. Process evaluation focuses on the degree to which a program is implemented appropriately, or as intended.[40]

The failure of research to provide high quality process evaluation is understandable, because the ideological context of enterprise zone programs is one arguing for more circumscribed roles for government and its bureaucrats. Tax and regulatory incentives are argued to have virtually automatic effects, and thus to require little implementation.

Evaluation evidence, however, is reasonably clear that zone marketing is a critical determinant of success. Decades of government experience with economic development efforts also makes it clear that governments have a major role in providing supportive investments and regulatory policies if zones are to be effective.[41] The same is true if job targeting efforts are to work in enterprise zone programs.[42] Thus, much more effort should be placed on providing quality process evaluations, needed if the implementation of zone programs is to be optimized.

It also seems clear that there is a need for greater federal involvement in the evaluation of state enterprise zone programs. Thus far, evaluation efforts in the United States have been fragmented and uncoordinated. As a result, it is very difficult at present when faced with evaluation results to determine if the results are an accurate depiction of the effectiveness of the program, and, if they are, whether the results have implications for other enterprise zone programs. A strong federal role could improve matters by

- developing and applying first rate, convincing methodologies in evaluations of programs in several states;
- facilitating comparative analyses of the success or failure of various types of zone programs, and the factors that contribute to success.

Preliminary analyses of state programs suggest that a meaningful typology of state programs could be developed to structure a federal evaluation of zone programs.[43]

Despite 10 years of presidential advocacy for a national zone program, the political support has been inadequate to create a new national program. President Bush's recent call for an "experimental" enterprise zone program appears to be stalled in Congress, just as previous proposals have been. The administration proposed a demonstration program of 50 or fewer nationally designated enterprise zones, backed up by federal tax incentives.

Support for a high quality national evaluation of state enterprise zone programs could be argued to be an inexpensive alternative to a new national demonstration program. Such an evaluation might preserve some political impetus behind the zone concept. If the results were favorable regarding the cost-effectiveness of enterprise zone programs, it might also help create a political environment in which a new national effort might be possible.

Notes

1. Nachmias, D. (1979). *Public policy evaluation: Approaches and methods.* New York: St. Martin's Press; Weiss, C. H. (1972). *Evaluation research: Methods of assessing program effectiveness.* Englewood Cliffs, NJ: Prentice-Hall.

2. Riposa, G. (1989). State urban enterprise zones: Origin, policy context, and administrative constraints. *International Journal of Public Administration, 12*(1), pp. 19-44.

3. Howland, M. (1985). Property taxes and the birth and intraregional location of new firms. *Journal of Planning Education and Research,* pp. 148-156; Newman, R. J., & Sullivan, D. H. (1988). Econometric analysis of business tax impacts on industrial location: What do we know, and how do we know it? *Journal of Urban Economics,* pp. 215-234.

4. Birch, D. L. (1978). The processes causing economic change in cities. Paper prepared for a Department of Commerce Roundtable.

5. Armington, C., & Odle, M. (1982, Winter). Small business—How many jobs? *The Brookings Review,* pp. 14-17.

6. Erickson, R. A., Friedman, S. W., & McCluskey, R. E. (1989). *Enterprise zones: An evaluation of state government policies.* Washington, DC: U.S. Economic Development Administration, p. iv.

7. Birdsong, B. C. (1989). Federal enterprise zones: A poverty program for the 1990s. Washington, DC: The Urban Institute.

8. Bromley, R.D.F., & Morgan, R. H. (1985). The effects of enterprise zone policy: Evidence from Swansea. *Regional Studies,* no. 5, pp. 403-413; Talbot, J. (1988). Have enterprise zones encouraged enterprise?: Some empirical evidence from Tyneside. *Regional Studies,* no. 6, pp. 507-514.

9. Bromley, R.D.F., & Morgan, R. H. Effects of enterprise zone policy.

10. Erickson, R. A., Friedman, S. W., & McCluskey, R. E. *Enterprise zones,* p. ii.

11. Ibid., p. iii.

12. Ibid., p. iii.

13. Hall, P. (1984, February 22). *Financial Times.*

14. Bendick, M., Jr., & Rasmussen, D. W. (1986). Enterprise zones and inner-city economic revitalization. In G. Peterson & C. Lewis (Eds.), *Reagan and the cities.* Washington, DC: Urban Institute Press.

15. Rubin, M. M., & Armstrong, R. B. (1989). *The New Jersey Urban Enterprise Zone Program: An evaluation.* Wayne, NJ: Urbanomics, Table IA.

16. U.S. General Accounting Office. (1989). *Urban action grants: An analysis of eligibility and selection criteria, and program results.* Washington, DC: U.S. General Accounting Office.

17. The New Jersey program offers some incentives that may be in the nature of once and for all subsidies. An example would be exemption from Sales and Use Tax on materials and services for construction-related activities on real property. As a result, it may be somewhat unrealistic to assume that tax losses per year continue at a constant rate.

18. Erickson, Friedman, & McCluskey, *Enterprise zones;* Brintnall, M., & Green, R. E. (1988). Comparing state enterprise zone programs: Variation in structure and coverage. *Economic Development Quarterly,* no. 1, pp. 50-68.

240   Evaluation of Enterprise Zones

19. Weiss, *Evaluation research.*

20. Brintnall & Green, Comparing state enterprise zone programs.

21. Ibid.

22. Ibid.

23. However, multiple incentives increase the difficulty of clearly communicating program structure and benefits to potential business owners or managers. "Marketing" of a zone program might be facilitated by a focus of one or a few powerful incentives.

24. Erickson, Friedman, & McCluskey, *Enterprise zones.*

25. Ibid.

26. Erickson, R. A., & Syms, P. M. (1986). The effects of enterprise zones on local property markets. *Regional Studies,* No. 1, pp. 1-14.

27. Rubin & Armstrong, *New Jersey.*

28. Weiss, *Evaluation research.*

29. The Dun and Bradstreet DMI computer files offer highly comprehensive data on U.S. business establishments which could be used in documenting economic trends in zones, or for sample frames for special surveys. The DMI files include establishment address, employment, sales, industry SIC, zip code, and so on. Dun and Bradstreet maintains historical files so that longitudinal analyses may be done. Individual establishments are assigned a unique identification number that can be used to track the business over time. These data have been used in economic research beginning in 1965. See Struyk, R. J., & James, F. J. *Intra-metropolitan industry location: The pattern and process of change.* Lexington, MA: Lexington Books.

30. U.S. General Accounting Office. (1988). *Enterprise zones: Lessons from the Maryland experience.* Washington, DC: U.S. General Accounting Office, Program Evaluation and Methodology Division, Report 89-2.

31. Rubin & Armstrong, *New Jersey.*

32. Weiss, *Evaluation Research.*

33. Rubin, B. M., & Wilder, M. G. (1989, Autumn). Urban enterprise zones: Employment impacts and fiscal incentives. *Journal of the American Planning Association,* pp. 418-432.

34. James, F. J., (1973, August). A test of shift and share analysis as a predictive device. *Journal of Regional Science,*

35. Talbot, Have enterprise zones encouraged enterprise?

36. Erickson & Syms, Effects of enterprise zones.

37. It should also be recognized that the resources invested in an enterprise zone program have opportunity costs. If, in the absence of the zone program, the resources would be invested in other equally effective or superior economic development efforts, then it is not clear that applying regional economic multipliers is appropriate.

38. Rubin & Armstrong, *New Jersey.*

39. Nachmias, *Public Policy Evaluation.*

40. Ibid.

41. Bendick & Rasmussen, Enterprise Zones and Inner-City Economic Revitalization.

42. Van Horn, C. E., Beauregard, R. A., & Ford, D. S. (1986). Local economic development and job targeting. In E. M. Bergman (Ed.), *Local economies in transition: Policy realities and development potentials.* Durham, NC: Duke University Press.

43. Brintnall & Green, Comparing state enterprise zone programs.

15

Conclusions and Lessons Learned

ROY E. GREEN
MICHAEL BRINTNALL

Introduction

Nearly three fourths of the United States has chosen to identify selected areas within their borders as enterprise zones, based on the presumption that these regions are not prospects for the normal process of economic growth or rejuvenation. Further, they all, in the view of Susan Hansen, represent a "repudiation of the notion that growth elsewhere will redound to the advantage of [these] depressed regions" (Hansen, Chapter 1). Drawing these boundaries and naming this process has attracted worldwide attention.

The analysis and essays commissioned for this collection were selected to help us consider what we have come to know about enterprise zones as unique policy mechanisms, and as approaches for rehabilitative action in distressed areas of American communities. As a meta-evaluation, this volume collectively asks: What are enterprise zones in practice, and how do they work? Have we learned anything from 10 years of domestic experience that might warrant reconsideration of how government should approach economic development generally? What are the lessons from what some would calculate to be a half century of experience in the industrialized nations on the Pacific Rim? Is there much to be gained or learned from further examination and experimentation—especially from adding a national enterprise zone program overlay on the existing American state programs? Systematic description is prerequisite to evaluation, both of which are necessary for enlightened decision making and policy development.

What Do We Know about Zones?

Economic development is at the heart of the enterprise zone concept, but the pathways taken to it by states have differed from paths taken elsewhere in the world, and have even among themselves been quite varied. This is not exceptional. The British, Mexican, Puerto Rican, and Far Eastern initiators of zones have also diverged from a standard model. Some drift has occurred in the implementation process. Peter Hall confirms from the British experience that "there was a huge gap between the grand sweep of the original concept and the reality of what was actually achieved. Some commentators clearly found conspiracy in all this" (Hall, Chapter 11).

Other diversity has emerged from the inherent differences of the sites where the concept has been tried. As Joseph Grunwald's analysis makes explicit, "If one adds geopolitical disparities and differences in priorities and economic specialization, it becomes apparent that the four tigers [of South Korea, Taiwan, Hong Kong, and Singapore] could not have pursued a single development model—just as the major Latin American NICs, Argentina, Brazil, and Mexico, have not followed a unique growth pattern" (Grunwald, Chapter 12). And the Puerto Rican case study clearly shows the impacts that longer time frames, changing economic climates, and commonweal arrangements can have on policy initiatives. The entire Puerto Rican community has been defined as a zone, to give it an economic advantage vis-à-vis the outside economy rather than to single out one geographic area of its own economy for improvement.

Stuart Butler's chapter pinpoints how the American experience has diverged from other sites by focusing on the economic improvement of poor neighborhoods. He points out that

> the British program is based on the notion that vacant sites make the best enterprise zones, with the zones acting as the focal point for the economic improvement of a wide area. . . . In the United States, by contrast, most supporters of the enterprise zone idea have seen it as a tool to resuscitate specific poor neighborhoods, creating jobs primarily for local people. (Butler, Chapter 2)

As our own work, and the case studies and other comparative analyses in this volume show, states' programs have differed in the emphasis put on various development goals in their program design, especially regarding ancillary objectives such as community development, infrastructure improvement, or social conditions.[1]

Underneath this variation, however, are two fundamental commonalities in enterprise zone programs. One is the attempt at geographic targeting of development aid—isolating development assistance within preset service area boundaries. The other is the partnership of public and private enterprise to engineer growth. This latter theme has raised a world of confusion in analysis of enterprise zones, because some "pure" models have presumed the program would operate with no public intervention at all, and because some proponents have asserted that the "government-free" nature of zones is one of its greatest virtues.

Lester Salamon has tackled this confusion with the observation that

> What has so far been overlooked in the resulting debate over the proper role of government in modern America is the extent to which existing government programs already embody many of the key features of "privatization" and decentralization that conservative critics of government have recently been advocating.[2]

He further contends that

> the central reality of many of the newer tools of government action . . . [is] that they vest a major share—perhaps even the lion's share—of the discretionary authority involved in the operation of public programs into the hand of one or another nonfederal, often non-public, third-party implementor.[3]

This type of public-private development is

> what makes the use of different [public policy instruments such as enterprise zones] so significant [because] each instrument has its own distinctive procedures, its own network of organizational relationships, its own skill requirements—in short, its own political economy.[4]

Operationally, then, we might conclude that enterprise zones are high profile, areal targeting mechanisms, whose essential features include third-party, government sponsored, multiple organizational arrangements, to be used to redress economic distress (and in their American incarnation, neighborhood dysfunctions) found within subcommunity boundaries. This program mechanism, incidentally, is being explored for wider application. The newest Bush administration housing initiative, the Hope Initiative, proposes to identify housing zones in which federal housing incentives, including FHA insurance and rental rehabilitation credits, and other steps to reduce tax and regulatory barriers to affordable housing, would be removed.[5]

Property: Public and Private Rights

One of the less well examined aspects of enterprise zones is the relationship of public and private property within a zone. Several important themes arise here. Enterprise zones seek increased economic efficiency and growth: one objective of enterprise zones, of course, is to reduce public penetration into economic transactions to enhance the prospects for this. The extent to which this actually can occur, however, is questionable. As noted above, the political economy of any site is an amalgam of public and private ownership and involvement. Many important resources for people in distressed areas derive from public sources—police protection, education, infrastructure, transfer payments, and so forth.

In a recent monograph Barry Bozeman points out that an important distinction between private and government organizations

> lies in the inability to transfer the rights of ownership in government organizations from one individual or group to another. Since there are no shares of government stock, the individual cannot alter his or her "portfolio" of investments in government programs or exchange ownership rights.[6]

Unless there is a remarkably flexible community control of public services, the allocation of public goods may not be adaptable the way private ownership is to achieve requisite efficiency within a zone. Bozeman notes two corollaries as well, which are that public organizations may not be motivated to assume risk, and may not be motivated to allocate management resources efficiently, in contrast to private ownership.

Wolf also points out difficulties that may arise from the public-private partnership from the private sector point of view.

As with a purely private partnership, the participants in the enterprise zone ventures look for assurances that each side will remain committed to the original goals and promises. Unfortunately two legal principles stand in the way of a lasting and effective partnership, a relationship in which each party is truly accountable. First, several legal principles—such as the rule that governments may not bargain away the police power—may operate in such a way as to remove the public partner's obligation to live up to the arrangement. Recently, however, particularly in the area of conditional zoning and land-use development agreements, courts have become more accepting of formal contracts between governmental units and their private partners. The second potential legal trouble spot is the protection of the private partner's interest in financial and investment information. . . . Those eager to learn from the enterprise zone experience will find it hard to come by solid, empirical data indicating success or failure. (Wolf, Chapter 4)

Logan and Barron, incidentally, describe how this latter problem arose in Florida, and how the program was redesigned to improve access to needed data.

The question of property rights has taken an intriguing dimension from an international perspective with regard to intellectual property, and the receptivity of zones to technology transfer. Grunwald observes that East Asian enterprise zones have been far more successful in importing new technology than those in Latin America. The reasons are complex. Some arise from state strategies, such as an emphasis in East Asia on educational programs and worker training, which have facilitated integration of new technologies (Grunwald, Chapter 12).

But a major difference suggested by Grunwald is the state treatment of intellectual property rights.

Mexican regulations require that new technologies be licensed. Once they are licensed, they can be used in Mexico, after a limited period of protection, without restriction, so that the foreign firm will lose control over its technology property. (Grunwald, Chapter 12)

Grunwald suggests this may have deterred technology transfer to Mexico. East Asian countries, he adds, have not necessarily been more favorable to foreign interests to attract their technology, but that rather,

the absence of relevant formal licensing rules has facilitated the copying of technology. Reverse engineering, imitation, and outright piracy have made it impossible for foreign firms to safeguard much of their technology in East Asia. (Grunwald, Chapter 12).

Government Engagement and Participation

Within various enterprise zone models there has usually been more attention to what the government managing the program was supposed to accomplish than how it was supposed to do it. From some perspectives, it seems the government was expected to operate with a completely invisible hand, and to defer entirely to the self-interested actions of private groups. We know, however, that there is substance to how participating governments are involved in the management of the program. The degree and style of this government engagement with the program appears to make a difference in the performance of zones.

Bozeman proposes that all organizations are public. He argues that

> public and private organizations are generally viewed as being essentially dissimilar. Yet private organizations often have significant public aspects—they are regulated by the public sector, many receive funding from the government, and all are subject to public scrutiny. At the same time, government organizations, like private ones, are increasingly subject to market forces and may actively seek profits. Because clear distinctions between the sectors are disappearing, managers can no longer assume that their organizations are strictly private or public and therefore affected only by economic or only by political factors.[7]

Bozeman develops a picture of hybrid organizations—such as government sponsored enterprises (GSEs) in which government and business attributes converge, and multi-organization enterprises (MOEs), in which numerous public and private agencies blend their roles—which blur the distinction between public and private.

Susan Hansen's historical overview identifies how organizational trends such as these in public management have emerged in economic development. She notes that governmental action in this arena is increasingly insulated from traditional political factors such as lobbies, parties, and legislators, and more allied with nonpartisan, nonideological public-private forums (Hansen, Chapter 1).

Indeed, one important state enterprise zone program has occurred without legislative action at all. The Pennsylvania program was created by executive order of the governor, involving a special administrative integration of existing state programs targeted to distressed zones. Erickson and Friedman find, in fact, that direct involvement of state line agencies in this way may "increase chances for zone success," and put this approach forward as a model for consideration in national policy development (Erickson & Friedman, Chapter 10).

Realities of Implementation

We also know that enterprise zone programs differ—within the states, and between the United States and other national experiences—for reasons other than program design and public management approach. The realities of implementation have led to distinguishing features in many programs, such as the divergent administrative path taken by Pennsylvania, the evolutionary process in Florida condensing from blighted areas to superzones described by Logan and Barron, and the disparities among the four tigers in East Asia described by Grunwald. Varied economic conditions and local circumstances also contribute to significantly different performance, as noted by Grunwald in his contrast of Latin American and East Asian initiatives. Daubón and Villamil in their historical analysis, compared Puerto Rico from the 1940s through the 1960s to the Latin American experience with economic development, and to the American experience with enterprise zones in the 1970s and 1980s.

In general, a range of exogenous factors have led to extensive variation in applied enterprise zone operation. These factors include the degree of prior experience with economic development initiatives, the extent of community receptivity, the capacity for diffusion of ideas—including whether the program is "early" or "late" in the policy process and what other operating models are around to copy from, the extent of state administrative capacity, and fundamental economic conditions and development potential of the community.

Incentives certainly need to work in conjunction with basic market factors. In Puerto Rico, for example, development of the petroleum industry failed to create other industrial processes using petroleum as raw materials (so-called forward linkages) as it was hoped it would because location of these derivative industries was market dominated, not input dominated (Daubón & Villamil, Chapter 13).

Program diversity then falls into three broad categories—characteristics of the initial concept as perceived by the implementing government, the form and extent of governmental engagement in operating the program, and the peculiarities of local experiences with implementation. This has led to substantial differences among enterprise zone programs. Description of what has been learned from state programs is largely flavored by this fact.

Patterns of State Performance

Based on data from an extensive HUD survey covering 357 zones in 17 states, Erickson and Friedman found great diversity of state-sponsored enterprise zone policies nationally, with "substantial differences among programs in the particular slant of their enterprise zone incentives toward labor, investment, and financial inducements (Chapter 10). They concluded from an examination of 90 high performing zones in 14 states that

> states should concentrate their efforts on a relatively small and select set of zones that are characterized as having basic labor skills, public infrastructure, and transportation access that can make the areas attractive for investment with the marginal but catalytic contributions that enterprise zone designation, incentives, and visibility can provide. *To accomplish this objective without creating a self-aggrandizing program that overlooks distressed areas is a critical task.* (Emphasis added; Erickson & Friedman, Chapter 10)

Complementing this comparative analysis is the study by Elling and Sheldon on state programs in Illinois, Indiana, Kentucky, and Ohio. They concluded from their multi-variate analysis that

> variation in investment activity is often due to factors that enterprise zone programs do little to affect, such as broader market conditions or labor costs. . . . The more successful enterprise zone programs are hybrids that combine interventionist components with one or two elements of the classic enterprise zone approach. Administrative resources matter more than any other factor in our . . . analysis. . . . Elements of the classic enterprise zone model were most powerful in accounting for variation in levels of investment by firms already located within the zone, although administrative staffing again was the most important predictor of investment. (Elling & Sheldon, Chapter 9)

And similar to the conclusions drawn by Erickson and Friedman, Elling and Sheldon offer some guidance for state and local policy-makers seeking to enhance the usefulness of enterprise zones as an economic development tool:

> First, zone programs should include those elements best suited to the circumstances of the particular type of firms they wish to attract. . . . Second, what matters most for new and expanding firms is clearly the quantity and quality of administrative resources that support the program. . . . Finally, because property tax relief is so generally available in enterprise zones, and abatements are frequently available from local governments for most firms anyway, it makes the most sense to expand other opportunities for direct savings for firms. (Elling & Sheldon, Chapter 9)

The objective most common to American state enterprise zone programs is job creation. The U.S. General Accounting Office study spoke most directly to this issue. The GAO selected Maryland for study because analysts considered it to be most similar to the Kemp/Garcia legislation then before Congress. GAO's analysis found "no evidence that the Maryland enterprise zone program increases employment in the areas GAO studied." (Grasso & Crosse, Chapter 8). Analyzing employment growth patterns among participating firms before and after implementation of the enterprise zone program, GAO was able to identify some increases in employment in the zones, but could not attribute them to zone economic incentives.

Using a different method from the time series used by GAO, Marilyn Rubin employed a cost-benefit model to analyze the New Jersey program and to determine the costs of the program on a per-job generated basis. The mix of program features and incentives were substantially different from Maryland. Rubin concluded that

> the UEZ program is a cost-effective economic development tool, leveraging almost $2.00 in state and local taxes for every $1.00 forgone in state tax revenues. The study also showed that the Program is an efficient way to generate jobs, even when the multiplier effects of UEZ business activity are not considered. (Rubin, Chapter 7)

One of the basic lessons from Puerto Rico, incidentally, is that job creation requires very different strategies and incentives than other goals, such as promotion of entrepreneurship. The latter goal has required specifically focused new initiatives, such as an economic development bank, to stimulate local entrepreneurship to balance the outside ownership of business stimulated by the tax incentives (Daubón & Villamil, Chapter 13).

Surplus labor problems may also require attention outside the realm of zone incentives. Again Puerto Rico found that industrialization alone would not resolve problems of a surplus labor pool. The resolution there involved large scale export of labor and heavy reliance on social welfare transfer programs (Daubón & Villamil, Chapter 13).

In reviewing findings from the case studies in this volume, two significant conclusions emerge—pulling in slightly different directions. The first is that there is no simple continuum from failure to success; programs can be arrayed on many different dimensions, with different goals and different paths to achieve them, and it cannot readily be said that one approach is clearly more successful than another. The second is that, other things being equal, greater success appears to be related to greater state administrative involvement, whether through agency coordination as in Pennsylvania, "management activism" as found by Elling and Sheldon, or state development leadership as in East Asia.

Learning More—Evaluability Assessment of Enterprise Zones

There have been significant gains in understanding the character and diversity of state enterprise zone programs, as the studies in this volume illustrate. Nevertheless, for a concept as controversial as enterprise zones, and as central to the major issues of allocation of public resources, there is still much that is not known. One reason certainly is that research on economic development faces difficult obstacles, particularly, as James puts it, in making

> judgments of how individual projects or firms were affected by government aid. . . . Few evaluations have more than scratched the surface in their efforts to measure program impacts. They have frequently focused on job trends and ignored equally valid and relevant indicators of program impacts. (James, Chapter 14)

Evaluations have frequently been very narrow in scope. Scholars have been limited by resources, interest, or lack of data to single case studies, narrow output measures, or single periods of time. The concept itself has probably discouraged some inquiry: The invisible hand is hard to find.

Nevertheless, a fresh perspective and approach to evaluation is needed, broadening consideration to how enterprise zones work, as well as what they achieve, and linking this economic development tool to others. The evaluation process needs to develop in stages, beginning with assessment of evaluability itself—involving "a series of successive rounds of data collection conducted in order to gain as full an understanding as possible of the objectives, implementation, and management of a program [type], and how it relates to other program [types] in the same program domain."[8]

Beaumont's chapter here suggests that just such an evaluation analysis is needed, especially because Congress is again debating a national enterprise zone program. She notes succinctly: "It is certain that additional and more sophisticated research would be useful to assist the country in understanding how to improve conditions in distressed areas" (Beaumont, Chapter 3). Grounding enterprise zone evaluation in a context of how it relates to alternative approaches is especially important. As Hansen notes:

> Subnational governments have found it easier to encourage the mobility of capital than of labor. It remains to be seen whether enterprise zones will succeed where other state and local policies have not: by creating jobs and investment in disadvantaged or declining regions. (Hansen, Chapter 1)

Planning for evaluation is not alien to the enterprise zone concept. As Butler notes, the diverse state experience creates a laboratory for assessment that is not unhoped for. He states:

> In this sense one of Sir Geoffrey Howe's original purposes for enterprise zones is being fulfilled: Enterprise zones at the state level are indeed a set of laboratories in which a wide variety of economic development strategies are being tested, and where successes and failures will serve as a guide to better policies in the future. (Butler, Chapter 2).

States themselves have recognized this need. Logan and Barron report that the need for better evaluation in Florida was a precipitating reason for initiating extensive changes in that program. They say:

> One of the major criticisms of the "old" enterprise zone program was the lack of data for evaluation of the program. The state could not prove or disprove the effectiveness of the program due to the confidential nature of tax information . . . and the lack of reporting requirements. (Logan and Barron, Chapter 6)

Evaluation and program design can constructively go hand in hand.

A Distinctive Advantage of Enterprise Zones for Evaluation

What have in the past seemed to be formidable obstacles to evaluation of the program are beginning to appear more tractable. As James declares here:

> Tough methodological problems impede quality evaluations of most economic development programs. . . . [but] despite the complex issues raised by efforts to measure impacts, the fact is that empirical evaluation of enterprise zone programs may be more feasible than has been true in the past for economic development programs. (James, Chapter 14)

The essential characteristic of enterprise zones, that the programs have defined territorial boundaries, allows us to design some effective assessments which can improve understanding of economic development generally. Because of the distinct location-specific nature of enterprise zones, they can become valuable tools for evaluating economic development incentives in general, allowing analysts to isolate the effects of particular incentives and practices far more precisely than has been possible in other programs.

Taking advantage of this opportunity to accomplish useful evaluation requires several steps. One, of course, is the continued refinement of ways to measure and analyze program impacts. The measurement problem spreads across research design, selection of indicators, and disentangling of collinear and probably highly interactive effects.

Identifying Program Goals

But what is equally important is more clearly identifying, program by program, what the goals are. Evaluation of the concept in the abstract is not realistic when we know each site has adapted a general bundle of ideas for local conditions and local purposes. It is up to policymakers to determine what a correct enterprise zone program is for their localities. The evaluator needs to determine what it is they actually did try, and whether it worked. As James notes, the clear message from current studies of enterprise zones is that states are trying quite different things, and often are attempting a substantial range of things, within their programs. Evaluators have typically not been aggressive in ferreting out these goals and developing research designs for them.

Variation in the international approach to enterprise zones especially highlights the need to clarify program goals before evaluation designs can be implemented. Butler makes clear how British and U.S. experiences have tried to do different things. Grunwald highlights the distinctive objectives of East Asian and Latin American programs. Daubón and Villamil show how the Puerto Rican experience is unique in that it has shown zone adaptability to changing economic circumstances, and to different perceptions of needs by the planners. Until recently, however, analysts have appeared to be more concerned with whether these different approaches have conformed to a standard model of enterprise zones, rather than detailing what these approaches have been and whether performance has met the peculiar expectations of each program.

The historical evolution of economic development initiatives makes this need for goal focused evaluation especially important, since, as Susan Hansen describes in her chapter here, and Green and James illustrate elsewhere,[9] enterprise zones are part of a moving target over time, as well as varying across states. Wolf shows in his important overview of the continuity of legal issues faced in development that changing tools are being used for common problems. Greater clarity of goals will help evaluators to compare how different tools are performing. The broader evaluation question is not whether enterprise zones work per se, but what forms and combinations of economic development approaches work in general.

Evaluating Process

Limited as it is, more attention has been given to assessing enterprise zone program impacts than looking at the process by which they have been achieved. Whether this has occurred because the ideological context implied almost automatic effects from zone incentives, for which "process" was irrelevant, or because the statewide dispersion of zone programs has made field study difficult to manage is unclear. Nevertheless, as all of the studies here suggest, state enterprise zones have arisen within a complex and fascinating context, in which existing practice, state administrative capacity, national interest groups and professional associations, and state legislatures have played a role.

But we do not know the extent to which variation in zone performance follows from *how* the state implemented the program compared to *what* incentives or design features were included. We have few hands-on guides for new program administrators, drawing on evaluation findings to help guide implementation of a successful new program. And although we know that active state marketing efforts appear to be helpful, we know little about which marketing styles are more successful than others, or how states and localities go about assessing the on-going performance of zone programs to make on-going program adjustments. We know something about the costs of incentives provided in enterprise zone programs, but little about the costs of implementation and administration. Attention also needs to turn to what Rossi and Freeman call *accountability studies,* which are "directed at providing information about various aspects of programs to stakeholders and program managers."[10]

Along with attention to process, broader attention to the legal and administrative structures in which development occurs is needed. Wolf's chapter in this volume points out the complex and well-established legal structures that have made enterprise zone programs practical. Zones have not become readily established in localities simply because of the elegance or the political popularity of the idea. They are in place in part because the legal environment, shaped over the preceding decades, was receptive to them. They have spread in part because, as Beaumont points out, of the emergence of a structure of state and local organizations, such as the National Association of State Development Agencies, that exist to facilitate sharing of information across state boundaries.

Assessing Variation

The widespread variation in state enterprise zones poses difficulties for evaluation of the programs because it is so difficult to know which programs have features in common with others. Clearly, comparison of incentive packages alone does not identify significant commonalities. Our earlier work, abbreviated here, identified a number of key dimensions of variation, and arrayed states across them. The work by Erickson and Friedman has taken this a very important step further by not only seeking variation in program approaches, but relating this variation to performance measures. Although they do identify some program features that appear to relate to success more than others, they also conclude that by and large there is no simple continuum from failure to success. Enterprise zone programs can be arrayed on many different dimensions. They have different goals, and can take different paths to achieve them.

At issue, then, is what are the salient forms of variation in programs that evaluators should look for? Our initial study drew upon seven dimensions: extensiveness of management, degree of private sector cooperation, breadth of goals, tolerance of risk, innovation, extent of marketing, and level of internal consensus. Erickson and Friedman focus on four dimensions: number of criteria and incentives, economic orientation, number of zones per program, and administrative or legislative creation. Other dimensions are suggested in other studies here.

Where Do We Go from Here?

Questions of enterprise zone program development and evaluation go hand in hand. We need to learn more, and to do more, but carefully. We need more knowledge: about impacts, about goals, and about process. Some of this can come from better and more extensive evaluations, especially those designed with attention to external validity. Federal research guidance on how individual researchers can develop study designs for individual state programs which maximize the possibilities for aggregating results across studies would be very valuable.

A carefully constructed and limited federal demonstration program, coordinated with existing state programs, is also needed. The Puerto Rican case has shown the value of double levels of local and national incentives; local tax exemptions there were clearly not enough. The goal of providing two layers of incentives is central to the proposal of the Bush Administration for a federal enterprise zone program, as promoted by HUD Secretary Jack Kemp. A federal demonstration need not employ new legislation or new incentives. The Pennsylvania model may be applicable to the federal level, in which existing federal incentives are targeted administratively to zones. There are many possibilities.

A federal demonstration should include a solid evaluation, but we believe the studies in this volume support the added conclusion that such a demonstration should be designed to support state initiative and diversity, not smother it. As Enid Beaumont puts it:

> The federal government has made a marked contribution to the development of zones at the state and local government level through its information and evaluation services. One approach is simply to continue these services because the enterprise zone concept has already achieved remarkable success. . . . If federal zones are established, however, the legislation needs to take into account the state and local experience, especially in terms of designating zones only in full consultation and partnership with state and local governments. (Beaumont, Chapter 3)

Notes

1. Green, R. E., & Brintnall, M. (1987). Reconnoitering state-administered enterprise zones: What's in a name? *Journal of Urban Affairs, 9,* pp. 159-170; and Brintnall, M., & Green, R. E. (1988). Comparing state enterprise zone programs: Variations in structure and coverage. *Economic Development Quarterly, 2,* pp. 50-68.

2. Salamon, L. M. (1989). The changing tools of government action: An overview. In *In beyond privatization: The tools of government action,* Lestor M. Salamon and Michael S. Lund, eds. (Washington, DC: The Urban Institute Press, 1989), p. 3.

3. Ibid., p. 9.

4. Ibid., p. 8.

5. The White House, Office of the Press Secretary, Fact Sheet: President Bush's Hope Initiative: Homeownership and Opportunity for People Everywhere (Washington, DC: November 10, 1989).

6. Bozeman, B. (1987). *All organizations are public: Bridging public and private organizational theories.* San Francisco: Jossey-Bass, pp. 51-52.

7. Ibid., inside book jacket.

8. Rossi, P. H., & Freeman, H. E. (1985). *Evaluation: A systematic approach* (3rd ed.). Beverly Hills, CA: Sage, pp. 87-88.

5

7

ROY E. GREEN and MICHAEL BRINTNALL   257

9. Green, R. E. (1990). Is there a place in the 1990s for federally designated enterprise zones within the context of state-administered enterprise zone program experience? *Journal of Planning Literature, 5,* pp. 38-45; and James, F. J. (1990). Let's have a new federal experiment with enterprise zones. *Journal of Planning Literature, 5,* pp. 44-52.

10. Rossi & Freeman, *Evaluation,* p. 92.

Subject Index

Study Index

About the Authors

Lee Ann Barron serves as a legislative analyst for the Florida House of Representatives, Committee on Small Business and Economic Development. The Committee oversees the Florida Enterprise Zone Program and many other state economic development programs. Previously, she was employed by the Florida Department of Community Affairs where she administered the Florida Enterprise Zone Program.

Enid Beaumont is the Director of the Academy for State and Local Government in Washington, D.C. She has recently served as Vice-President of the National Academy for Public Administration. She has been the Director of the Public Administration Program at New York University. She will become President of the American Society of Public Administration in 1991.

Michael Brintnall is Staff Associate with the American Political Science Association. He was formerly Vice President for Academic Affairs and Associate Professor of Political and Social Science at Mount Vernon College in Washington, D.C., was a research analyst at the U.S. Department of Housing and Urban Development, has served as a consultant with the Interagency Council on the Homeless, the Urban Institute, and the Battelle Memorial Institute, and previously taught at

Brown University. His recent policy research includes analysis of local media coverage of state administration of federal programs, directions in urban policy, the rental rehabilitation housing grant program, and the urban development action grant program.

Stuart M. Butler, Ph.D., is Director of Economic and Domestic Policy Studies at The Heritage Foundation, a public policy research organization in Washington, D.C. Credited with introducing the enterprise zone concept from his native Britain, his books include *Enterprise Zones: Greenlining the Inner Cities* (New York: Universe, 1981).

Scott B. Crosse is a Senior Research Analyst at Westat, Inc. Prior to joining Westat, he was an evaluator in the Program Evaluation and Methodology Division of the U.S. General Accounting Office. He holds a Ph.D. in applied social psychology from the Claremont Graduate School. He has conducted policy and evaluation research in a variety of areas, including economic development, immigration, and human services programs.

Ramón E. Daubón has taught Economics and Planning at the University of Pittsburgh, the American University, and the Catholic University of Peru. He has served as researcher and advisor to several Latin American government agencies and research organizations, and was Director of the Caribbean Office for the InterAmerican Foundation. He is currently Vice-President of the National Puerto Rican Coalition in Washington, D.C. He sits in several advisory boards of community development organizations and has published a number of pieces on community revitalization and small scale entrepreneurial development.

Richard C. Elling is Associate Professor of Political Science and Director of the Graduate Program in Public Administration at Wayne State University. In addition to his research on enterprise zones, recent work includes a chapter on "Bureaucracy" in *Politics in the American States* (Harper and Row, 1990) and a co-authored chapter on "The Politics of Intergovernmental Relations in Health" in *Health Politics and Policy* (Delmar, 1990).

Rodney A. Erickson is Professor of Geography and Business Administration and Director of the Center for Regional Business Analysis in the College of Business Administration at The Pennsylvania State

University, University Park, PA 16802. Erickson earned his Ph.D. in geography from the University of Washington (1973). His research interests include regional economic growth theory, economic development policies, and the regional impacts of foreign trade.

Susan W. Friedman is Research Associate in the College of Business Administration at The Pennsylvania State University, University Park, PA 16802. She holds a Ph.D. in geography from the University of Toronto (1988). In addition to enterprise zones, her research interests include the history of thought in the social sciences and urban historical geography.

Patrick G. Grasso is an Assistant Director in the Program Evaluation and Methodology Division of the U.S. General Accounting Office. Prior to joining GAO he was an assistant professor of political science at Wayne State University in Detroit and Oklahoma State University. He holds a Ph.D. from the University of Wisconsin—Madison, and has published on economic development, public finance, and urban issues in a number of academic journals.

Roy E. Green is the President of REG Management Resource Group, and a former Associate Professor at the Graduate School of Public Affairs, University of Colorado—Denver and the Director of Research for the National Civic League. He has been a Legislative Assistant to U.S. Senator John C. Danforth for community and economic development issues, and a Senior Legislative Specialist with the U.S. Department of Housing and Urban Development on issues pertaining to housing finance. He has published work in the areas of community and economic development, and in public sector management and finance. His most recent book is *The Profession of Local Government Management: Management Expertise and the American Community* (Praeger, 1989).

Joseph Grunwald is Adjunct Professor in the Graduate School of International Relations and Pacific Studies and in the Department of Economics, University of California, San Diego. For two decades he was Senior Fellow at the Brookings Institution. He holds a Ph.D. in economics from Columbia University, and has taught and directed research at universities in the United States and abroad. Other positions included: first president of the Institute of the Americas, U.S. Deputy

Assistant Secretary of State, and economic advisor to the Governor of Puerto Rico.

Peter Hall received his master's and doctoral degrees from the University of Cambridge. He was Lecturer in Geography at Birkbeck College, University of London (1957-1965), Reader in Geography at the London School of Economics (1966-1967), Professor of Geography at the University of Reading (1968-1989), and Professor of City and Regional Planning at the University of California at Berkeley, where he has been Director of the Institute of Urban and Regional Development since 1989. His principal works include *London 2000* (1963), *World Cities* (1966), *Urban and Regional Planning* (1975), *Great Planning Disaster* (1980), *Cities of Tomorrow* (1989), and *London 2001* (1990).

Susan B. Hansen, Associate Professor, has taught at the University of Pittsburgh since 1980. Her Ph.D. is from Stanford University. She is the author of *The Politics of Taxation* (Praeger, 1983) and a forthcoming book, *The Political Economy of State Industrial Policy.* She has published numerous articles on state politics, tax policy, and economic development.

Franklin J. James is a Professor of Public Policy in the Graduate School of Public Affairs of the University of Colorado at Denver. Formerly, he directed the Legislative and Urban Policy Staff of the U.S. Department of Housing and Urban Development, and has been a member of the senior research staff of the Urban Institute and the Rutgers University Center for Urban Policy Research. He holds a Ph.D. in economics from Columbia University.

The Honorable Willie Logan, Jr., has represented the City of Opa Locka in the Florida House of Representatives since 1982. Representative Logan serves as Chairman of the House Committee on Small Business and Economic Development. Prior to his election to the House, Representative Logan served as Mayor for the City of Opa Locka, part of Florida's largest enterprise zone. He is employed as executive director of the Opa Locka Community Development Corporation.

Marilyn Marks Rubin (Ph.D., New York University) is an Associate Professor of Public Administration and Economics at John Jay College of the City University of New York (CUNY) where she is co-ordinator of the Master's Program in Public Administration. Her areas of specialization are public finance and urban economic development. She has published several articles on these topics and has also served as a consultant to numerous governmental and private organizations.

Ann Workman Sheldon, a sociologist (Ph.D., Michigan State University), specializing in organizational systems and evaluation research, is currently the Research Coordinator at the Center for Urban Studies, Wayne State University. Her recent work includes policy studies on economic development, industry-university technology transfer, human services delivery systems, and family support programs.

José J. Villamil has taught at Rutgers University and the University of Pennsylvania and was Special Assistant to the Governor of Puerto Rico. He is presently Professor of Planning at the Graduate School of Planning at the University of Puerto Rico and Chairman of Estudios Técnicos Inc., a consulting firm. He is former President of the Puerto Rico Economics Association and the Inter American Planning Society, and presently sits in Puerto Rico's Governor's Council of Economic Advisors and other advisory and civic boards. He has written extensively on Puerto Rican and Latin American development issues.

Michael Allan Wolf, Professor of Law at the University of Richmond, has written several articles on law and planning issues, and is the co-author of *Land-Use Planning* (1989). As Director of the EZ Project, Professor Wolf has monitored zone activity on the federal, state, and local levels; helped design state legislation; testified before legislative committees; and lectured extensively on the subject throughout the country.